D1503376

THE ANSWERS

THE ANSWERS

to your questions about life

Karen L. Garvey

INTENT, LLC

THE ANSWERS

Copyright © 2006, 2007 by Karen L. Garvey
All rights reserved
Printed in the United States of America

No part of this book may be used or reproduced in any manner whatsoever without written permission except in the case of brief quotations in the context of reviews. For information, contact

INTENT, LLC

373 Nesconset Highway #125
Hauppauge, New York 11788

ISBN 0-97-646631-7

This book is dedicated to "the greatest power on earth."

Acknowledgement

From the beginning, I have enjoyed a circle of supporters that have made this entire journey more fun and meaningful.
The circle grew and grew, but the two who have traveled with me from the beginning with unconditional acceptance, encouragement, and support are Striker Corbin and Jeanne Burton.
I am grateful to them both.

I thank the following supporters who tirelessly assisted me in making this book possible in more ways than they may realize: Lorraine Boss, Ken Teape, Selma Giray, as well as the Dyers, Jo Garvey, and Kelly Teape.

I would also like to acknowledge Gavin D. who unknowingly nudged me onto a course of outbound ascension.

And "heartfully," I thank GH, CE, Wyce, BD, TE, Seth, BF, HDT, EG, JG, AGB, MW, Pat, Wexel, JL, and AR.

Introduction

Receiving this book was extraordinary, but it was no accident. I have learned that effective, beneficial communications with entities requires permission. Although our guides work towards establishing communication with us, it is not until we acknowledge the assistance and become open to it that communications can grow. By opening up to the guidance, we are granting permission.

A year or so before I began communicating directly with souls who passed, a client of mine said, "You have a gift for bridging the gap between the spiritual and the intellectual." She elaborated by indicating that as a successful businessperson, I could communicate effectively with cerebral people, yet, without using the language or tools of the spiritual, I could communicate as easily with those who were engrossed in the metaphysical, be it holistic medicine, yoga, chakras, religion, etc.

I didn't think much about it until, soon after, another person said, essentially, the same thing. Then another. Not one for believing in coincidences, I tried to figure out the meaning, but it eluded me.

Around the same time, my fleeting intuitive sense began to strengthen, often in very compelling ways. I began to pick up on events immediately after they occurred, but before they were publicly known such as 9/11 and the tsunami in Southeast Asia. My sense expanded to "knowing" the circumstances behind crimes which were later reported and even "seeing" articles which appeared in the next day's paper.

Although the information I received was often regarding tragic events, I didn't feel negative emotions as I sensed the events. Instead, I was filled with an awareness about the "universal" reasons why they had occurred and an understanding of how different souls participated for the greater enlightenment of humankind. I usually experienced a sense of peace with this knowledge.

I welcomed the strengthening sense and set out to develop it further, which I did with the assistance of my once-very-grounded husband. He sought methods for me to accelerate this skill. Progress was so rapid, it was startling. I look back and realize that events and people I had been attracting in over the prior five-to-seven years had been preparing me

1

for this leap. Further, by setting out to strengthen my ability, I granted permission to the entities to communicate with me. In this book, Ayn Rand further elaborates on the process, but let me add that the entities, rather quickly into our meetings, mentioned that I would receive material that would be beneficial to help people learn to be happier and would help bridge the gap between logic and the ethereal.

The experiences since have been profound and intense. I am in awe of all that I've learned and the great value of the experiences that I've had and continue to have. It's comforting and inspiring to know that we all have the ability to improve our lives, to live happily, and to enjoy ourselves on this physical plane. It's also a great assurance to know that we are eternal and this life is just one experience in the vast journey of our souls.

When I think back on this path of learning, I realize the huge commitment I made and the dedication it took, but oddly, it never felt like work. I remember times in my past when I was painting and I'd look at the clock only to discover that it was one o'clock in the morning. Time flew because I was engrossed and totally passionate about what I was doing. I feel the same way when I work psychically. I hunger for more and more information and experiences with this other realm. The sensations can be exceptional – physically, intellectually, and spiritually.

Physically, the entities "send love" to me during communications which I experience in intensity from a mild feeling of contentment, to complete euphoria. Having never studied the world of psychic communications before I began, these fantastic feelings were my first personal validation as to the authenticity of connecting.

Intellectually, I often experience such a rush of excitement when they convey information to me because the specifics are so profound that they enlighten and exhilarate me. I'm grateful to be able to satisfy my curiosity about virtually any topic.

Spiritually, the entities often contact me in non-direct ways, such as sending a symbol that has meaning between us. I love noticing these communications and when I acknowledge in my thoughts that I understood the message, they send me a great sensation of love. I also connect spiritually through a sense of "knowing." By receiving

2

memories of being in the energy realm or taking trips to other lifetimes, I remember things that are more important in life than just my physical existence.

As this process began, I was afraid – never of the process – but of other factors. What am I supposed to do with this material? Will people believe me? What if they think I'm crazy? I led a pretty ordinary life until then; receiving this material changed that.

My fears subside when I'm connected. I learned very quickly that I am never alone, unless I want to be. When I have a concern or fear, the entities expend great effort and imagination to help me overcome, face, or integrate it. They're very clever. If I don't "get it" at first, they try other ways to communicate the point. In the beginning, I was dense, I suppose, but now I easily recognize what they are trying to do. By being open to the guidance, I usually understand it faster.

I still have some occasional fears – but they are so minimal that I have a genuine sense of freedom. By connecting with what's really important, I understand more and more how trivial some earth worries are. Understanding why we are here, what the purpose is for physical life, and how to direct one's life towards fulfilling goals is liberating.

The fact that you're reading this book proves that you are open-minded, which will allow you to gain the greatest benefit from the material. It's my desire, and the desire of many entities, that you find immense value in the content.

This book was communicated to me through daily essays. Sometimes, the essays may not appear in what seems the most logical order, but there are reasons for the arrangement. Ayn had a body of material she wished to convey, but she also interacted with my thoughts. If she covered a topic and later found my thoughts wondering about it in more depth than she conveyed, she would add an essay expanding on a previous idea. I thought about reordering the passages, but opted to leave it exactly the way I received it for the reader to experience the material the way I did. Each segment is delineated with the date, time, and book session number.

The speed at which I received essays requiring no editing was astounding. One day in particular, I received about three thousand words in less than two hours. For anyone who has ever written a term paper – you may be able to understand how incredible that is. The only changes I made were in my own "receiving" errors, such as leaving out a word, misspelling, or misplacing commas. The content remains intact. If clarification was needed, I inserted my words in square brackets [ ].

At the onset of each session, the entities communicated with me until they were confident that I was connecting accurately. During this period, they often gave me information that was of value in my personal life, guidance that I cherish. The daily warm-ups and personal material have been removed from the public transcript.

I paused in receiving this book from September, 2005, until July, 2006. During this time, I explored other psychic areas in addition to channeling personal material and answers to my never-ending questions. When I reconvened in July, I didn't think to record the writing times the way I had with the earlier material. In the future, I'll format consistently throughout for those who find it useful.

Regarding use of gender throughout the book, Ayn expressed dissatisfaction with limits in our language. She used "he" and "she" throughout, but would have preferred her examples not indicate gender. Likewise, she felt limited by the English language with words such as "mankind," and "humanity." I don't think "feminism" was the compelling force behind her recognition of shortcomings in our language; I believe it was "globalism."

I have newfound respect and admiration for Ayn Rand. The things that matter to her *are* global and her enormous compassion radiates when she communicates with me.

To quote from within, "You have the gift of life in your hands; a life worth living." With sincerity, it is my firm desire that this gift changes your life and your thinking for the better the way it has mine. This is

… just the beginning.

About Ayn Rand (1905–1982)

Best known as the author of **The Fountainhead** *(1943) and the epic* **Atlas Shrugged** *(1957), Ayn Rand was one of the greatest visionary writers of the Twentieth Century. Rand was an influential intellectual, inspiring millions to understand and pursue her philosophy of rational self-interest known as "Objectivism."*

During her earth life, Rand summarized her views. "My philosophy, in essence," she said, "is the concept of man as a heroic being, with his own happiness as the moral purpose of his life, with productive achievement as his noblest activity, and reason as his only absolute."

Today, from the energy realm, Ayn Rand continues to communicate her visionary ideas free from earth encumbrances or misinformation.

May 27, 2005 3:33 pm   (First day of Book Writing)

Resourceful people often say that there is no end to what a human can accomplish. I am here to attest to that fact. Life on earth is magical, if only you reach for the tools that are buried deep within you.

Mathematics has proven facts that are primarily not denied. But what if I told you that even basic mathematical principles are false, that they are illusory? Would you believe me? Or are you so confident in math theory and hypotheses that you do not doubt their accuracy and relevance?

Not only is mathematics illusory, but so is science. "Proven" facts are no more proven or reliable than your dreams may appear to be. How can fallible humans, even collectively, be infallible simply as a consequence of walking into a laboratory? How often is information that is deemed "fact" later withdrawn or proven otherwise?

Results in scientific experiments are corrupted by the fact that scientists are human. Their thoughts, emotions, and expectations blend seamlessly with the experiments themselves, thus corrupting the outcome. As disciplined as a person may be, he or she is human above all else, and humans have the ability to emote, daydream, judge, and create. These qualities, wonderful and powerful in the game of life, simply do not lend themselves for non-corrupt evidence.

Feel free to interrupt. State your thoughts and contradictions aloud. Observe the rapidity with which your mind absorbs, connects with, or rejects information. You are simply reading a book teaching the true path to happiness and you cannot contain your mind to quiet down long enough to simply read. Your mind is interactive, and rightly so. A scientist's mind is also interactive. It does not rest on command, nor is the command to rest made to begin with.

What else can we observe about the "mind?" Where is it located? In the brain? If you lose your mind, does your brain fall out and your auto-response system cease to function? No. Your mind cannot be seen, touched, handled, contained, modified, or understood. It is intangible, yet it directs all your activities.

7

How little is known about one of the elements that makes you uniquely human. You cannot stop your mind from working; you cannot touch it. You know it is there, but you don't know where. You know that without it you could not function as a human being, yet little effort is extended to "know your own mind."

If experiments on concretes are fallible, imagine the impossible task of proving the characteristics and parameters of an intangible? The mind cannot be examined. Perhaps you are considering the reams of evidence that science has uncovered by observing individuals who have lost or damaged different lobes or physical components of the brain. What these observations connote is that different areas of the *physical* brain control different functions of the human being. Left unnoticed is a connection between the brain and the workings of the mind. One may not remember [occurrences] after damage to the brain, but does he or she still dream? Have the properties of the individual's emotions been altered, not observable behavior, but personal emotions?

The mind is elusive. But it is real.

What else is real that you cannot see or experiment on? Souls? Are souls real? Can science answer this question? Can a person live without a soul or can a soul live without a person?

The answers to the last question are "no" and "yes." A person cannot exist without a soul, but a soul can exist without the physical vehicle that you call the human body. How do I know that this is true? Because I am a soul without a physical manifestation. Karen Garvey has agreed to tell my story in an effort to guide humans to the path of happiness.

Could Karen have conceived the content of this book from her own mind? Perhaps. You are an intelligent being – you decide. I expect you to be an active participant in the reading, absorbing, and applying of the material contained herein, and you can begin by deciding for yourself if Karen authored this material or not. She has nothing to prove to you. Her goal in participating is simply to expose you to material that can and *will* bring you happiness, a commendable goal and one that provides the necessary conditions for me to communicate through her.

Read on knowing this: Your life will not be the same if you earnestly read and apply the content of this book. Your life will be better, happier, safer, and more enjoyable in every area strictly because of the messages in this text. What do you have to lose?

Simultaneously, observe the changes, overt and subtle, that occur in your life as you read and apply the content. Go slowly and allow new ideas to take root and flourish. You are the only one who controls the outcome of learning from this book. Participate, engage, think, challenge, and enjoy the process. You have the gift of life in your hands, a life worth living.

May 30, 2005 5:15 pm   (Book Session 2)

The curtain rises. You sit back content knowing that for the next two hours you will be stimulated and, hopefully, entertained by the happenings on the stage before you. Actors and actresses, playwrights and musicians, all play their role in bringing you an evening of enjoyment.

You are a spectator. Your body and your arms and your eyes and your brain all remain fixed in your viewing chair, yet your mind dances. You get caught up in the music, the sets, the lines, the costumes, the plot, and perhaps, the drama. So as you sit as a spectator, you are alive and active in your thoughts. Your body does not care about what transpires on the stage; only the mind is eager.

Why bother bringing the body at all? Because for your lifetime, your mind has affixed itself to the physical being. Or has it? Can you leave the body at home and go experience the play anyway?

The answer is not that easy, but this scenario demonstrates how separate the mind is from the physical organism that you call human. Which is human? The physical organism or the mind that affixes itself to the organism? Rather than answer these questions overtly, I will take you on a journey of understanding. Then you can conclude for yourself the answers to the questions posed.

Back to the same play. Let's assume it is a brilliant production radiating glamour, mystery, intrigue, sensational settings, and a delicious plot. You lose yourself in the production as it unfolds and wraps your senses in excitement.

Suddenly, in the second act, the lead actor has been replaced by the understudy. He is good, but not great, and his presence irritates you for the balance of the performance. Why was the actor replaced? Why did they not begin with him? Even continuity with the lesser actor would have been preferred to this awkward shift in the middle of the show. Should you ask for your money back because the change interrupted your pleasure? You want answers; after all, you paid very good money to see this program and it should not have been interrupted by a nuisance.

Your irritated attitude continues as you make your way back home, but eventually it fades. By the following day, the events that transpired seem less important and you lose interest in fighting for a refund. You go about your day's activities.

At work, you are fired.

Why? Was your performance not exemplary? Were you earning too much money? Did the boss hire his niece? There has to be an explanation for this action, and you intend to get to the bottom of it. The firing was unexpected, unwarranted, and totally unfair. You want answers.

Eventually, you wander home, lost in your passionate and pitiful thoughts. You indulge in blame, self-pity, confusion, anger, and sadness. What are you going to do? How will you pay your bills? Who will hire you? How can you find a new job quickly before your funds run out? Why you? The last thing on your mind is the play and your original desire for a refund.

How are you different from the actor in the first half of the performance? How are you the same? You were each taken "off the stage," regardless of the reason or the possibility of return. You are both performers in your own drama, only the actor is aware of his role and is compensated monetarily for it. You are not.

10

You have likely heard the metaphor that life is a stage. You are a performer in your own meticulously crafted play. How true. How much more true than you realize.

Your life is a play and you are the playwright. At any given moment, you could rewrite the plot, recast the fellow actors, or even turn a grim story line into a happy tale. The problem is that you don't know how. Why be unhappy if you could be joyful? If you could readily change the scenes from dismal to bright, wouldn't you? Is there any possibility that you would *choose* to be unhappy?

Think about the happiest person you know. Is it challenging to conjure one up in your thoughts? Focus on this individual and determine your attitude towards him or her. Do you want to be near this person we'll call "Happy?" Are you envious of Happy? Is Happy luckier than you? Richer, more poised of face, more intriguing, more highly educated? Do bad things happen to Happy? Does he or she get ill? Argue? Lose a loved one? Get fired? Get rained on?

Do you think Happy was born that way? Or is his or her life just better and easier?

Now think about yourself being that happy. How would people relate to you? Are you presently a complainer? If you were too happy to complain, what would you talk about with others? If there's endless drama in your family and you become too happy to care, what would the others do if you left the dramatic scenes to them? Would they resent you? Call you secretly to ensnare you into their folds? Could you resist? Would you remain happy without the drama?

Think about it.

Under this personal scrutiny, can you determine how happy you really are? And can you determine if you are ready to be consistently happier, regardless of circumstances?

All of your life is a play. You choose your roles, the plot, the twists and turns, and the outcome. Decide for yourself how you want your play to unfold. What do you really want?

11

Now let's begin ...

Set the stage. Who is present? What are you doing? Where do you live? Where do you work? Who are your friends? How do you spend your free time? What do you eat? Where do you sleep? What is making your life so perfect? And, more importantly, can this imagined existence be yours?

Living within the physical parameters as they exist in your life, you can recreate your play however you choose. Of course, if you are 100, you cannot make yourself 80, but you can transform the content of your day into a more enjoyable and consequential happening.

Did you ever hear of spontaneous healing? Miraculous recoveries? These occurrences are examples of individuals rewriting their plays. The medical community will often take credit, but true spontaneous healings are a reflection of the choice of the soul, not the actions of the stage actors. Some enlightened authorities will note the "victim's" attitude in the recovery, but for every example of a positive attitude accompanying a recovery, isn't there a greater number of examples of one with a positive attitude not recovering?

The medical community, as well as scientists, does not know how to research such findings. What enters the realm of the scientifically unexplainable becomes known as an anomaly. The conditions that brought about the spontaneous healing cannot be duplicated or understood, so others do not benefit from the lessons encompassed.

In time, you will understand these spontaneous events, but in the meantime, use the example as a benchmark indication that you, too, can rewrite the course of your life.

May 31, 2005 12:48 pm   (Book Session 3)

Heed this warning. Mercury does not cause brain damage. Simulated experiments indicate that small doses of mercury in rats did not cause any lasting brain dysfunction. Similar computerized simulations are now ready to be tested on humans.

Do you have confidence in the results of the simulated experiment? If you discovered that there was mercury in water, would you rest easy knowing that a simulated experiment showed no permanent consequence to the brain? Doubtful. Yet, that is what humans do every day. They trust and rely on the results of simulated experiments.

Every decision a person makes is "simulating" a result. If you choose one path, the result will be such and such. If you chose the other path, the result would be much different. As you stand at the crossroad of the decision, how do you know which path to choose? Which simulated result do you want to achieve?

The reason that your choices lead to simulated results is that you alter the results by the thoughts and beliefs you hold. Let's examine an example. You are choosing between moving or remaining in the city you now reside. You examine, endlessly, the factors and probable consequences of each possibility. You choose, making the "best" possible decision you can under the circumstances.

Now suppose you decide to leave. Your house is sold, a new one purchased, and you will begin a new job in three weeks. As you progress with the packing and preparations, you hear from your moving company personnel that many who have moved to your relocation city recently have been returning. Your moving company is now fielding calls from those who are unhappy in the new location and require a mover to bring them back.

What is your reaction? "This news is awful. I knew I should have stayed." Or is it optimism that your circumstances and attitude will make the transition smooth? Or perhaps you believe that the mover exaggerated the situation and is just making small talk without substantiating the claim.

The easy solution is to proceed with your plans regardless of what information you heard. But the doubt begins to take hold and paralyze your ability to effectively anticipate the move with joy. You are amidst a simulation of possible outcomes. Whereas you were previously confident that the move would be primarily rewarding, you are now feeling shaky and heavy-hearted as you continue with your plans.

13

What if you stay? What if you go? What if you go and hate it? The new possibilities play out in your mind with endless probabilities. You are simulating probable results. But are these results any more predictive than a computerized simulation on a rat? There is only one dependable predictive factor that will accurately forecast the future: your beliefs, not your thinking, but what you believe.

Do you believe that you are like the others who returned, because circumstances are similar if a person is moving from your current city to your intended city? Does the mere fact that they moved from your present location to the next location indicate that their lives can predict the outcome of yours?

If they return and you stay, you will all proceed with your lives. Based on the previously recognized similarities between you, does that now mean that you will have similar experiences back in your original location? Will all who moved and returned, or considered moving and opted-out, have parallel existences? Will you all live in the same neighborhood, have the same number of children, work for the same companies, face the same joys and tribulations?

Can you see how non-predictive factors really are when you think them through clearly? The risk in applying non-related factors into the equation of your simulation is that it can alter your outcome simply by altering what you *believe*. Before the mover told you of these other couples, you were content with your decision. Your belief was that those who made this transition before you were content in their new location as you would be. Now your belief about the possibility of being happy in the new location has changed. Clearly, if others returned, then this city must be the superior place to live.

Your *belief* about the shortcomings of the destination city can bring about the results that you fear. You will look at your new location with a filter of scrutiny as to why it is inferior. The negative aspects of the new culture, people, and surroundings will loom with intensity and the positives will appear negligible. The result of the change in your beliefs may actually cause a spiral of circumstances to send you packing back home.

Had you not heard the tale from the mover, you may have resided in your new location happily ever after, provided your other *beliefs* fit the simulated outcome.

The important lesson is to know what you believe.

Easier said than done. As we simulate events in our lives or set the stage for new acts, we often fail to recognize our authentic selves. From childhood through adulthood, most people cover their authentic selves under layers of masks. These masks develop, one after the other, in response to the actions of the people around us. At a very young age, we discover ways to obtain desired results from those we depend on. At first, the right cry gets the warm milk or the cuddly lap, but over time those cries become less effective. We discover new ways to "manipulate" the fulfillment of our desires. An extended cry with piercing peaks and valleys gets more cuddling. A panting cry may result in a faster response. Little by little, we alter our behavior to evoke action from those around us and even learn to use different behaviors for different people to get the same results. Sadly, the masks begin to appear. Cry "A" for mom; cry "B" for dad. We become disconnected from which cry we would have authentically chosen had we not needed to provoke responses.

The masks develop throughout life. Rarely can an individual remember his or her authentic self by the time adulthood is reached.

How do you remove the masks which hide your inner beliefs? First, be willing to work a little. Every change worth making takes some effort – you must be willing to extend some effort. If you are not willing to help become a happy person, then please put this book down and walk away. I cannot do it alone.

Now – let's take off the masks. Get out a piece of paper and a writing instrument. Assure that you will not be interrupted for at least twenty minutes. Turn off your cell, put the dog out, or use earplugs if you must. [If now is not convenient, wait to proceed until a suitable time.]

Any exercise in writing has but one rule. Do not censor yourself. Write freely without thinking about grammar, word choice, or what others would think. This paper is your private domain. There are no "wrong" answers or thoughts. For the next twenty minutes, answer this question: When have I been happiest and why? Write and write and write. Do not think about what you want to say or how you want to say it. Just write.

If you are reading this sentence, then your twenty-minute conversation with yourself is complete. If you did not write, then please do not read further until you have finished the task.

Thank you for your cooperation in helping you to be a happier person.

Look at your list. What do the items have in common? Were your happiest moments predominantly when you were a child? A teenager? A young adult? A new parent? Retired? Did the moments intersperse throughout the course of your life?

Were other people present? Would you have been as happy had they not been there? Were you traveling? Creating music or art? Working? Receiving recognition? Achieving a goal? Starting a new adventure?

Were the happiest times moments or periods of time? Were you playing a sport? Engaged in a physical pursuit? Or experiencing a sedentary reflective time?

What else can you discover from your list? Do you see any patterns? Does the list make you feel like the best is past? Or do you feel optimistic that happy moments lie abundantly ahead?

Your list answers the question, "Who am I?" When your masks are off, you experience your greatest moments of joy. Your authentic self is shining through allowing the real you to surface. Who are you? One who enjoys being alone or with others? One who needs escape from reality? One who creates? One who is talented?

The person that you are becomes clear in your happy moments. You are being yourself without worrying, without worrying about what others think, or the future, or the past, or work, or whether or not you are good enough or tall enough or rich enough.

You have seen the real you. Embrace the image and allow the feelings to surge within you.

Now that you know who you are, you are prepared to examine what your beliefs are. This step is trickier and also requires a bit of effort on your part. Once again, I respectfully ask you to pass this book on to one willing to participate rather than skip this step. I want to help those willing to receive help.

Go back to your paper and allow for twenty uninterrupted minutes again. Please feel free to pause and wait for a better time if now is not convenient.

Read through your list and, on a separate piece of paper, answer this question: What is not present in my list? Hint: Think about different people, your appearance, your surroundings, etc...

Go ...

Ahhh … you're back!

I am assuming you completed the exercise since you understand the importance of actively participating in your own happiness.

Look at your new list. Here a highly individualized analysis is necessary.

Who was not present when you were happiest? What does that tell you? Let me give you examples:

> My dad was not there. [Implies:] He makes me feel insecure.
> My children were not there. They are draining.
> My husband was not there. He wants things his way.

The second half of this equation in the examples above indicates what your beliefs are. The longer your list, the more you will understand what your deepest convictions are, your guiding principles.

Dig deep as you go through your list.

What was not present at your happiest times? Don't look only at the tangibles when you analyze what the absent items mean for you. For example:

> My job was not there. I hate my job.

What does this really say about what your beliefs are? You believe you cannot be happy during the periods of time when you work, even when you are not at the job? That you believe your life is stressful when you work? Do you believe that changing jobs would improve your life and why? Do you despise being controlled by someone else's schedule or demands or expectations? Are you too fearful to change jobs? What are you afraid of?

It is important to recognize patterns in your answers. Not all happy moments can contain an exact duplication of time, people, place, and circumstances; therefore, many variables will change from one scenario to the next. You are looking for patterns such as: "I was rarely at work or with work-related people." "Some form of art or creativity appears in most of my happiest moments." "I felt free."

The absence of a particular person consistently can be telling, even if that person appears intermittently throughout the list. Think about whether or not this person's presence added to your enjoyment, was inconsequential, or perhaps detracted from it.

The questions are endless and the more time you are willing to spend analyzing your list, the more you will understand your hidden beliefs which govern the outcome of your simulations.

June 1, 2005 11:40 am (Book Session 4)

Have you ever let someone do your thinking for you? Have you ever based a decision on someone else's opinion other than your own? If you said "no," then you are not being truthful with yourself. There are moments when you insert another's opinion in place of your own and are aware that you are doing so, but there are far more instances when you acquiesce to another's opinion without knowing it.

The media presents a foray of examples where another's opinion influences or supplants your own. Watch the news and you realize that murders and attacks are regular occurrences. You begin to believe that the murder rate is starkly on the rise and the perpetrators are becoming younger and younger. Do you check the statistics? Is murder on the rise? In your area? In your country? You may be surprised to learn that at the time of this writing, the overall murder statistics in your country are decreasing. Has that fact gained recognition?

In a frenzy for media market share, the reports of ill-doing are becoming more prolific and graphic, thus luring in viewers. The effect is that the general population believes that the United States of America is becoming an increasingly dangerous place to live.

Is this the only area that your opinion is influenced by the media? What about commercials? Carefully crafted to induce your desire and compel your purchase, these vehicles subtly and overtly influence your thinking. You may feel resistant to the bombardment of messages, and perhaps, largely, you are. But over time, the messages penetrate. Happy people have cell phones and nice cars. It is no longer a choice about whether you *want* a cell phone or not, but *which* cell phone to use. Yes, this [change] is [largely] a result of "progress," but the media hastens the progression, making you feel left out when you are not participating in ownership.

How should your hair look? Curly or sleek and straight? Is being bald in vogue or should you opt for an alternative? How thin should you be? Subtle shifts in the beauty choices that people make are pushed by the media. What clothes are "in"? How chunky should your highlights be? Are pants ankle length or to the floor?

Are you immune to these influences?

The media is not entirely to blame, nor is their influence entirely negative. For many, owning a cell phone *is* a smart choice. The key is to be able to recognize why you make the choices you do – to imitate or to be happy. Or worse yet, to imitate to be happy!

When the first caveman built fire, the other cave dwellers were envious because they understood the benefit of this new tool. They imitated their peer and consequently enjoyed an enriched life style. Imitation became synonymous with survival. The family that lived the most comfortably was imitated by others to increase their own level of comfort. Eventually, imitating "needs" became replaced with imitating "wants" and the two became intermingled. Today, people rarely can distinguish between the two and imitation is a prime motivator in the way individuals make decisions.

The fault does not lie in "wanting." As you will see in this book, wanting is good! The fault lies in not recognizing when a decision is being made independently or by the influence of others. It is not merely the attainment of material goods that is at risk here. The way in which you live your life, your morals, your religious beliefs, your character, and even how you choose to spend your leisure is bombarded by the influence of others.

Why is this distinction important?

Free is the life of the Independent Thinker. In a land where "freedom" is granted the highest honor of pursuit, it is astounding how much "freedom" is given up by individuals every day as they follow others without "deciding" for themselves if the idea, or action, or philosophy, or thought makes sense to them.

Why? Spend one week with the freeing mind of a two-year-old. Ask yourself "why" over and over and over again about everything you do. Be relentless in accepting only the tough answers that ring true. Persist!

Here's an example of a conversation you might have with yourself:

Why am I about to eat this donut?
Because it tastes good. (Dig deeper)
Because it's here. Because I need the sugar-rush. Because it's annoying to prepare a healthy snack. Because the donut is easier. Because one donut won't ruin my health. Because I don't want to think about my weight right now. Because I am stressed. Because it's free here at the office today. Because I have nothing else to eat. Because I have nothing else to do.

Do not give up until your response feels authentic, not a mask or a cover-up, or what you want to convince yourself of. Recognize the new "why's" that evolve from your responses.

Why am I going to Church today?
Because it's Sunday.
Why do I go to church on Sundays?
Because I was raised doing it.
Why do I continue?
Because I am happy when I am there.
Because I feel guilty when I don't go. (Why do I feel guilty when I don't go? …)
Because I love the community feeling there.
Because I would have to answer to GOD if I didn't go.
Because I would be sinful if I chose not to go.

Question not only your actions, but also your thoughts. When you read a newspaper and think about the article, question why your opinion is as it is. Is your opinion based on independent thinking on your part, or are you entertaining the opinions of others?

If you can diligently attempt to question your thoughts and actions for one week, you will train yourself to become an Independent Thinker.

For those readers who pride themselves in unearthing the truth as to whether or not Ayn Rand authored this book, let me add evidence. One reason that Karen was "chosen" to "receive" this book is because she is an Independent Thinker. Not a rebel, not a misfit, just an Independent Thinker in the truest sense of the phrase. We will give examples and, ultimately, it will be her decision if she chooses to include them in this manuscript. We respect her privacy.

When soccer participation is all the rage for families with children, she opted not to attend the annual out-of-state tournament with the soccer club. Although her children were considered to be valuable players and her family was frequently the only one not to attend, she did not succumb to the pressure of being a follower. Instead, she questioned why her family should participate and made the decision based on what was best for them. The teams had not excelled beyond local competition, the tournament was held on a holiday weekend each school year, and the expense would be similar to that of a different getaway. Her feeling was that the teams spent more time together than they could individually spend with other friends and family, and enjoying a pastime other than soccer would provide a well-rounded foundation for her children. She also believed that the sibling(s) of the participant would better enjoy an alternate weekend plan.

What is noteworthy about this choice is that it ran contrary to popular opinion. Although attending the tournament may have been the best decision for many families, it clearly was not for hers. Not certain of the outcome of her decision, she risked consequences: her child not being selected for the following year's team with tryouts just weeks away, being harshly judged by the other parents, or having her child feel left out.

Thinking independently at the risk of consequence takes courage. Going along with mass opinion without questioning "why" does not.

I was known on earth as being an Independent Thinker and there are many who believe that my ability to reason beyond mass thinking enabled me to encourage millions of others to enjoy the freedom that

23

independent thinking allows. My association with Karen is a testament to the value that I place on one's ability to think freely.

June 2, 2005 7:48 pm   (Book Session 5)

Reluctantly, I pursued leisure when I walked the earth. I preferred working. Leisure was a bothersome activity that distracted me from what I really wanted – to learn, to write, to advance human awareness. When I did enjoy some leisure time, my active mind continued to reflect upon the world happenings around me, seeking angles to examine or challenge. Leisure was for my body only; my mind rarely rested.

Even with my personality as Ayn Rand, however, I still maintained an overall life of balance – balancing work with friendship, family, and pleasure. I was the exception during my lifetime, the one who was considered the workaholic, yet I still had a more well-rounded life than many Americans enjoy today.

Why the frenzied pace? What are you running from? What are you hiding from? Why does a man or woman have to work until 8:00 at night to be considered valuable in business? I think that long hours are kept for two reasons: a lack of meaningful definition in one's life outside of work or as a form of escape.

The crammed hours do not end with work. Activities pursued fill the balance of time, usually without understanding their purpose. "Quality time" and "stolen moments" have become the phrases of the day. Do you believe that a frenzied pace serves your life purpose? Do you know what your life purpose is or do you have the time to ponder it?

Every life has a purpose. Every soul joins a physical body to fulfill an intended purpose. The short answer is that <u>you are on earth to love, create, and learn, in that order. There are no exceptions</u>.

We will examine each, possibly in a way that you have never thought about in the past.

LOVE

"All you need is love … love is all you need." - J. Lennon, 1967

Socrates, Shakespeare, Einstein, Lennon … the Greats over time have uttered memorable phrases, far-reaching, timeless, and often prolific, throughout the course of their lives. The thinking and philosophies are far too vast to evaluate in this forum, but we will acknowledge that the most profound, wise, all-knowing statement was the simple Beatles' verse, "All you need is love."

So simple, yet so accurate. The universal element binding all humans is love.

Has this thought or concept changed your life? You're probably questioning the merit of this book based on the simplicity of the statement, but bear with me as I begin to make you understand love in a way that you have never understood it before.

June 3, 2005 12:09 pm   (Book Session 6)

Love is patient … love is kind … love is never having to say you're sorry … love is a many splendored thing … love hurts…

What do you know about love? Common phrases, songs, messages, bombard you with misrepresentations of what love really is. It is not passion, nor merely compassion. It is not gentle and wise. It is not starbursts and judgement clouded by euphoria. It is not simple; it is not complex. It is not blind!

Love is an echo. Each soul reverberates with a unique energy that individualizes one human from another. This vibration is known as the **"soul's song."** No two soul songs are alike; they are as unique as a human fingerprint. When love is experienced, the one who loves echoes the other person's soul song. That does not mean that they mirror their image or imitate the song, but they reflect, through a sense you are probably unaware of, the soul song back.

What this means in the simplest terms is that one who loves understands the primary *essence* of the loved one. What makes him or her "tick"? What makes another unique, distinct, passionate, creative,

25

joyful, and special? Even identical twins have very different soul songs from one another.

Once one understands the concept of the "soul song," he or she may understand, feel, and reciprocate love. *But not before then.*

Being disconnected from the source of love, hearing one another's soul songs, causes a host of problems that are universal. These problems, all which stem from being disconnected, cause or have caused *every single* problem known to mankind.

Think about it. Every single problem, or wrong path, that humans have experienced from the beginning of time has been caused by people not understanding or reciprocating love in its true definition.

It is that simple.

In order to comprehend the simplicity in this concept, let's examine the problems that result from not hearing each other's soul songs. In close relationships, "love," as humans practice it, is widely distorted by attempts to satisfy needs. Each member of a relationship gives and takes in a balance of power. Some take more while others give more and, at other times, the roles may reverse. Ultimately, everyone wants to be loved for who they are, but they are, in fact, judged by what they do. When the balance created is not satisfactory to one or both parties, the "love" dies. What has really happened is that each individual's needs have not been met and the relationship no longer serves a useful purpose. "Love" has not died, if it existed at all to begin with. If these two heard each other's soul song, they cannot "unhear" it.

"Love" as you practice it, is usually a selfish endeavor. The other person's actions are viewed through the incessant filter of: "How does this affect me?" Parents filter interactions with their children. Lovers filter interactions with their mates. Children filter their view of siblings … the list goes on to include every relationship that exists: boss/employee, neighbor/neighbor, friend/friend, teacher/student.

The two parties fail to recognize the wants, fears, desires, dreams, hopes, cares, qualities, and talents of the other. They can't hear the other person's soul song. Hearing the song does not mean that people become wimpy doormats, giving everyone around them everything that he or she requests. It means that they "respect" the uniqueness of the other party. They know that he or she has complexities that direct his or her actions that all may not be aware of, yet they exist and they are real. Simply recognizing this fact helps people to act in a compassionate and respectful way. It helps them to communicate their own choices and needs in a clear and open manner. It brings people together in a level of understanding and respect that is rarely seen or strived for among humans.

Compromise, give and take in a mutually rewarding way, takes the ability to recognize that all people have soul songs. Even if you cannot "hear" the other person's song (you can't understand their complexities and individualness), recognizing that the song exists allows you to make choices and act in ways that are appropriately respectful.

Comprehending the concept of the soul song benefits families, neighborhoods, communities, countries, and the world. A perceived enemy suddenly has a soul song. You may not hear it, but you can respect it. An enemy nation is comprised of individuals with soul songs. To successfully correct the relationship damage that has been done in the human world, on the individual level all the way to the international level, both sides of the relationship must comprehend the concept. But in the meantime, the path for improvement can be paved by the one party with the awareness.

Ultimately, the soul song concept will be felt, understood, taught, and learned. The concept will burgeon with followers. Eventually, it will become a topic for childhood education. It will become as second nature as breathing. As this occurs, the world will slowly shift towards a day of peace and tranquility among neighbors and nations, among families and friends.

Imagine all the people …

Would you have imagined that John Lennon was one of the greatest thinkers in all of human history? His concept of love, his vision for peace, his lifelong dedication to teaching these ideals, separates him from most of the other great master teachers who have walked the earth.

As I compliment his attitude and his depth of understanding the true meaning of life while on earth, it is important for you to understand that I was not a John Lennon fan when I was inhabiting a physical vehicle. His message escaped me, befuddled me, and I cast his shenanigans aside as just another drug-induced hippie's need to emote. His "work" seemed fun but shallow.

It wasn't until after I died that I realized the greater value of his work than mine. He *taught* life, I merely pointed out human frailties. He wholeheartedly tried to make a difference in the quality of human life and comprehension.

John is now my dear friend. He and I are part of a group of several thousand entities who are dedicated to teaching humans how to be happy and live in peaceful harmony. Our methods may be suspect, but our aim is true.

I implore my readers to investigate the possibility of the truthfulness of these words on their own. Begin by studying Edgar Cayce and other unrefuted leaders in the ability to bridge the gap between our world and yours. Think independently. A blind follower is of little use in propagating the good intended in these pages. But a closed mind serves no purpose either. Allow yourself to be open to the possibility.

As often as I can, I will guide you towards your own self-investigation and give you information that will help to authenticate Karen's participation in this task.

Read up on THE SETH MATERIAL, remote viewing, channeling, and intuitives. Challenge yourself to discover evidence that supports the FACT that your life is not finite, the fact that your life is endless and your physical existence has a purpose. Why are so many ethereal pursuits prevalent and mainstream today? Because they are based on truth and truth is undeniable.

Stay alert as I and my comrades continue to take you on a journey of understanding the meaning of life as you have never heard it before!

June 4, 2005 3:27 pm   (Book Session 7)

The challenge lies in not just learning the material in this book, but living it. Humans tend to resist change even when it is beneficial for them. You can *know* that something is good for you, will make you happier, or even save your life, but the change is resisted anyway!

Please stop for a moment to appreciate the goal of living this book. Think about how you would feel if you were financially abundant, secure emotionally and physically, full of joy, able to express and receive mutually rewarding love from those around you, and felt optimistic and filled with a sense of well being. These are the benefits of living the messages in this book. Is it worth the effort? Please remind yourself of the goal and refer back to this page if you feel your dedication slipping. Day-to-day life has an odd way of interfering with people's ability to make positive changes.

Once you change, there's no turning back. You can not return to a lesser quality life. Awareness is like walking through a door that closes behind you. Right now you have opened the door to awareness and are peeping in, but shortly you will enter. Be fully prepared to have your life, and the lives of those around you, enriched!

Briefly, let me describe to you what "life" is like here. "Here" is an energy realm, not a physical realm as you know it. All of the negatives of physical life are absent and all the positives are enhanced, to the extreme. When you imagine nirvana, utopia, heaven, or any other imaginary "place" of well being, your thoughts cannot conjure an image positive or blissful enough to compare to the actual "here."

But please don't rush your arrival, either. As a soul, you made a very well contemplated decision to choose a physical life, and you should embrace and enjoy it to the best of your ability. Learn what you went [to earth] to learn, live as you intended, and be passionate.

The reason I am describing the essence of the positive energy that I and all other entities feel is because you are capable of reaching a similar state of euphoria on earth and we want to help you achieve that. "Feelings" or emotions are simply a measure of the energy emitted, the strength, density, and value of the energy. Picture a graph recording the power of music. When the graph is low, the music is quiet and subtle; as the volume increases in the music, the graph records in a thicker density and peaks to a higher level. Your emotions emit energy in a similar manner. Stronger emotions emit a dense, high level of energy, and weaker emotions emit a less strong, thinner, shorter energy.

Now imagine the same graph. The "x" axis and above record the positive emotions and the area below the line records your negative emotions. With this visualization you can see that the power of emotion is limitless, negative or positive, and the energy emitted by your feelings is clearly different – either negative or positive. Entities radiate at a dense, high level well above the line, whereas most humans exist within a narrow band range above and below the line.

The average human actually radiates the *majority* of his or her time in the region below the line.

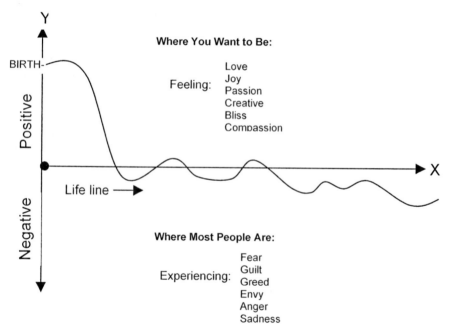

We want you to live the majority of your life well above the line!

Pretend for a moment that you are there. How does it feel? People love you. You love others. You feel happy and optimistic. You swell

30

with feelings of well being. You are upbeat, unstressed, full of good humor. Every day feels bright and fresh, a pleasure to welcome. And the good feelings never end. You may dip a little in range now and then, but overall, you emit bliss.

Can you *feel* it? Do you *want* to feel it? Decide now.

[pause]

Remember the abacus? All of math was represented on this simplistic tool where the beads were moved back and forth for counting. Mathematics complexity was limited to the number of beads on the abacus. No potential for trigonometry. No hope for the possibilities that calculus could introduce into human progress. Just some beads moving back and forth on a little dowel.

At the time, the abacus was advanced. The abacus was actually revolutionary in its day. Hard to fathom, isn't it?

Humans' ability to exist within their potential range of positive emotions is similar to the abacus' ability to allow humans to reach mathematics' potential. You are living with an abacus when you have the potential to live with quantum theory and beyond. Trade up. Throw away your abacus for some calculus, without the challenge involved in learning. Why not shoot for a bit of addition and multiplication? It's still a step up from merely counting.

How far are you willing to reach if the only commitment you must make is to practice the principals in this book? You decide.

Periodically, you will be directed towards supplementary material. The material is selected to hasten your growth and speed your process towards euphoria. You can opt to pursue the suggestions and reach for calculus, or you can remain within the binders of this book and settle for some multiplication and percentages. In either case, the rewards will be great, but obviously greater with a little more effort.

At this point, I would like you to read *Illusions*, by Richard Bach. If you have already read it, reread it. It takes on new meaning at different periods of your life. You can almost gauge your level of awareness by how many truths in the book you accept. At one point, some of the book's messages may read like pure fantasy, yet later, the concepts or lessons begin to ring true.

Do not be afraid that this book will become as trying as a master's level course. It will not. And the suggestions I make will be fun, never dreary or overly time-consuming. Give it a chance.

Why not walk with me to the path of joy?

June 7, 2005 2:04 pm   (Book Session 8)

Be still, my heart. Do I hear the sound of enlightenment coming from earth? It is a sweet sound, indeed.

If a white supremacist suddenly had the notion that blacks weren't that bad after all, would he be able to continue his "mission"? No. His life as he knew it, buried in a dark abyss of ignorance, would be shattered into the light. Interestingly, if a black person suddenly decided that all whites were bad after enjoying a life of cooperation and tolerance, would he be struck with "the truth?" This juxtaposition shows how humans have a natural, innate sense for truth. "Truth" hits them. Your metaphors depict this phenomenon beautifully. "I was hit over the head." "It hit me like a ton of bricks."

"Truth" is undeniable. Truth rings with realism that falsehoods simply do not carry. As you read this book, I challenge you to continually ask yourself, "What is true?" "Does this concept *feel* right?" The nature of the material does not lend itself readily to scientific examination, although I will do my best to provide what evidence I am able. You have within you a sense of what is real, buried deep within you, the original "you" that you were born with. Rely on this sense to corroborate the evidence that I provide. Your intuition is more reliable than the best scientific evidence, provided you know how to recognize it and train its capabilities to work with you in the way that it was intended.

Intuition has gotten a bad rap. It's all about "feelings" and girlie emotions. As Ayn Rand, I did not have much regard for it as a reliable

32

sense either. Intuition eluded me the way the profundity of John Lennon's concepts did.

But all that has changed. Now I *know*, beyond a shadow of a doubt, that a skillfully developed sense of intuition may serve as humans' most powerful sense of all. The reason is simple. Once you understand that your soul exists beyond your physical life span, you will recognize that you are "connected" to the "spiritual" or entity world. Your essence remembers the vast knowledge that you accumulated and carries it forth into physical life. Just as you become disconnected from your authentic self soon after birth, you also become disconnected from your source of wisdom. And just as you can rediscover your authentic self, you can also reconnect with the vast wisdom that lies within you. An example of this vast wisdom is when an awareness rings "true." You just *know* that it is right. You do not have to seek proof; you innately *know*.

The world is awash with evidence to support the presence of stores of wisdom and knowledge within people. I respectfully request that you seek information regarding "child prodigies" who excel at a musical instrument before the age of five, adults who suddenly speak a foreign language after a trauma, a language which they had not been exposed to in their physical lifetime, or persons with unusual knowledge of happenings in a different place and time. All of these occurrences are possible because of the knowledge the soul has gained over lifetimes. The "knowledge" is imprinted in the soul and carried from the entity realm into the physical realm, waiting to be detected, realized, developed and reconnected with.

Do you have any evidence that the soul is finite? None exists. Yet there is a proliferation of evidence that life beyond the physical realm exists. Why is that harder to accept?

For you diehard naysayers out there, I challenge you to submit evidence that the soul is finite. Submit it to a worthy, credible newspaper [along] with an open invitation for readers to refute your stance. Watch what happens.

Go off and do your own research. Learn about "psychics" who locate a missing person with whom they have no connection. Learn about "near-death" experiences and the unquestionable similarities among the

33

reports. There is obviously more to the physical life than meets the eye, or ear, or hands ....

From this point on, I will assume that you accept the premise that the soul is infinite. Let's continue.

How can you develop your intuition? The beauty of increasing your intuitive sense is that it not only gives you more power over your reality, but it also serves to confirm that the facts spoken in this book are truths. I do not want to be patronizing but, once again, I remind you that the progress you make in increasing your level of happiness is dependent on your willingness to participate in the activities in this book.

Begin with a dream log. For the next thirty days, record what you remember from your dream life each morning before you begin your day. I know it sounds like work, but bear with me. If it were not a valuable strategy for discovery, I would not recommend that you spend your time this way.

Many people claim that they do not dream. This presumption is false. Everyone dreams. The difference from one person to another is their ability to recall their dreams. You can increase your likelihood of dream recall by making this simple suggestion as you enter your pre-sleep state, "I dream. I remember my dreams and I will recall them when I awaken."

In the morning, before you listen to the radio or put your slippers on, grab your log off your nightstand and write whatever you can remember. At first your records may be brief, but they will increase over time. Do not be concerned with grammar, handwriting, or vivid details. Just write down the basics as quickly as you can.

Begin to watch for patterns, hints, or elements of a predictive nature. You may, for example, dream about peanut butter and later see a new ad similar to your dream. You may experience déjà vu and trace the experience back to a like dream experience.

In addition to looking for predictive material, search for material of a helpful nature. Perhaps you have a problem that you are seeking a solution for. Check your dreams for possible ideas. Dreams work out possibilities while you sleep in order to help you make better choices when you are awake. As you examine your dream log over time, you will begin to notice these remarkable elements of your dream life.

People who log their dreams regularly have a tremendously improved capability of predicting events. Not in a creepy, scary way, but in a subtle helpful way that enables them to live an enriched life. As you begin to notice the predictive nature, the predictions will be about non-personal, inconsequential happenings, becoming more personally beneficial as time goes on.

Dreams, like intuition, are often overlooked as superfluous, yet they are more valid and consequential to your happiness than some silly physical maneuverings that you regularly undertake. Take, for example, the habit of listening to others for advice on how to live your life. When you *acquiesce* to another's opinions, you are relying on a resource that is not as dependable as the knowledge that you have within you. Sure, listen for opinions or to share the tribulations of a problem, but make your decision based on what you know is right for you. Your dreams already help you uncover your best course of action; you probably have simply not yet realized it.

June 8, 2005 12:18 pm   (Book Session 9)

Damage to the cerebral plexus often shows discord in the anterior lobe.[1] What is startling about this discovery is that there is no known connection between the two until the damage occurs. What this evidence suggests is that even what scientists believe to be factual is not.

---

1 What is meant here is a "scientific" sounding hypothetical. I did not use a real example for several reasons. First, it may be "proven" true then untrue then true again during the life span of this book, convoluting the point. Second, I do not want Karen debating issues in which she has no knowledge. And third, a true example that I might offer in terms of brain activity is difficult for Karen to receive. The art of receiving psychically requires that the receiver have some basis of knowledge or vocabulary in the area in order to accept details, and Karen does not possess a foundation of knowledge about the brain.

What becomes of such contrary evidence? The original facts as they were known continue to be taught and recognized, rarely stating the contrary evidence. Is the stance on the theory of evolution now being challenged? Highbrow support against Darwin's original theory is growing in light of new evidence contradicting significant portions, primarily that man evolved from ape.

These examples should remind you to continually question what is accepted as factual. I can cite hundreds of examples where a fact was withdrawn, contradicted, or discarded as having no basis. Humans have the awesome power of reasoning. This power comes with the responsibility of being exercised. Exercise your power of reasoning by continually questioning what is widely accepted around you.

On the most simple of human levels, consider gossip. How many people question juicy pieces of scandalous "information" about others? Gossip is often repeated as a pleasurable pastime! A story, likely invalid in the first place, becomes even more distorted and grotesque as it travels from one set of ears to the next.

Why don't you slam down the gossip? For most people, repeating the tales makes people feel important; it makes them feel like they are accepted. Being accepted by others is the primary motivator in many choices that people make. So great is the lure of acceptance that people will risk damaging another's reputation and, in some cases, their life path simply to fit in.

Gossip is a loose, inconsequential distortion of the truth compared to the establishment of great institutions that misrepresent facts to promote their agenda. When an institution is based on faith, the distortions become vulgar as the truth is manipulated for a self-serving purpose. Yet, millions accept these "truths" as fact simply because they were always taught these "facts." They are too afraid to challenge the status quo, or they are too ignorant to listen to their intuition.

What is the point and how is it relevant to the material in this book? First, one of the single most difficult self-limiting flaws to recognize is when an individual accepts blindly the opinion of another or [that of] an institution in place of thinking independently. Although this book guarantees that you will find greater happiness upon successful implementation of the ideals contained within, it may also, and hopefully *will*, cause you to question many of your long-standing beliefs. The intent is not to persuade you to accept a particular philosophy or way of thinking. It is merely to incite you to question, evaluate, investigate, and analyze your current rationale and to be open to the possibility that not all that is accepted as "truth" is, in fact, true at all.

Free is the life of the Independent Thinker.

[1:11 pm long pause]

Treat others as you would want them to treat you.

Noble, but silly at humans' collective level of awareness. There are people who take pleasure in being treated subserviently. Does this mean that the individual should treat others as subservient to them? Rather impossible. If you are doubting this paragon, think about someone you know who does not want a managerial role at work. There are many who prefer the role of worker to that of leader. Isn't this person pleased, then, when they are in a position of subservience? Now, can this same individual successfully treat his boss as subservient while remaining in a position of subservience? And since the intent of the phrase is to be kindhearted to others, isn't it unkind for the employee to treat his boss as subordinate?

Thinking independently takes effort. You can literally dissect every phrase and every institution to unmask its inconsistencies.

It is easier to build than to tear down. Once you accept and validate life's basic truths, you can easily build a successful life with the truths as the basis. Life is about love, creativity, and learning, in that order.

We examined what "love" really means. Now let's look at "creativity." Like intuition, creativity is not given great credence in your society. Yes, there are certain masters at their instrument of choice who are exalted, but primarily, creativity in day-to-day life is not recognized as the true virtue that it really is.

To be creative is analogous to being an Independent Thinker. It represents the freedom to express your authentic self, uncensored by

37

the opinions of others. All great advances have been founded upon creativity. The works of the Wright brothers, Alexander Graham Bell, Albert Einstein, Henry Ford, Thomas Edison, and the likes, were the product of astutely creative minds. Their creations (notice the root word) were possible only because they were creative and independent thinkers. How many times were these Greats told that what they were trying to achieve could not be done? Could not that thinking permeate their judgement and inhibit their development? These men stood out because they thought independently. They did not accept another's opinion as their own. In fact, their own hundreds of failures, which reinforced the dire opinions of others, did not hamper their independent thinking, the creative belief that what they set out to accomplish could be achieved.

All greatness is founded upon independent thinking.

Therefore, all greatness is founded upon creativity. Souls choose physical life as a way to creatively try out solutions to problems and to creatively expand the individual and collective experiences of mankind. Not to "do unto others as you would have them do unto you," but to reach beyond a "kindness" reciprocity agreement.

Why have so many humans lost their way in the soul's intent? Sadly, as an infant loses its connection with its unique self, so does the soul become disconnected from its purpose. Life has a way of interfering with the path, so to say. Children, at the youngest ages, learn to adapt to the beliefs of those around them, being exposed to more and more off-target notions as they age. The massive sea of misinformation engulfs and clutters their minds. It happens to nearly every human, with few exceptions, to some extent or another.

Helen Keller was an exceptional example of one who was not compromised by the beliefs of others, perhaps protected by her own blindness and deafness. She did not absorb others' beliefs that being blind and deaf in any way meant that life could not be productive, meaningful, passionate, and creative. Her prolific quotes live on beyond her as a testament to the beautiful Independent Thinker that she was.

What most people don't know is that Helen Keller *chose* her physical life, including the limitations that she rose above. Her quest as a soul was to increase the awareness of humankind to the best of her ability and she chose her "handicaps" as a vehicle to achieve that conquest. And succeed she did.

This last paragraph will raise more questions than it answered. A soul does not have a clear definition of the physical parameters in which it will exist. Instead, it sets forth a "quest," an ideal that it wishes to achieve. The billions of probabilities that occur in any given situation help the quest to take shape, while the soul directs the progression through the choices that it makes in the physical realm. When I discuss the unfortunate disconnection that separates a person from its authentic self, I am indicating the cause for a person losing "sight" of their initial quest.

A soul also "attracts" in the situations, people, and events that will help the quest to take root and reach fruition. If the soul becomes disconnected from its intent, as most do to some extent, it will then begin to attract in the events, people, and situations that will help for their replacement path. This fact explains the crux of why people have either relatively happy or unhappy experiences, and also is the basis for why one's "luck" may change.

Let me reiterate the progression.

The soul chooses a physical life with an intended "quest." The soul/ physical vehicle, or person, then attracts in the events necessary to fulfill the quest. The person often becomes disconnected from the quest, or the quest becomes buried in layers, by the thoughts, actions, and feelings of those the individual is surrounded by. As this disconnection occurs, a person loses "sight" of their mission and "chooses" an alternate path that reflects the new ideas that have been learned from others. At this point, the person attracts in a new set of situations to reflect their new set of beliefs.

Challenge yourself to think about the staggering applicability of these facts. A terrorist, for example, is born, like all souls, with a virtuous quest. (For simplicity only, since your language does not contain a singular non-gender specific pronoun, I will use the male identity in my example.) He is born into a family that is saturated, generation after generation, in misguided, grotesquely distorted beliefs. As the young mind develops, all signs of tolerance are promptly squashed, and the boy begins to subconsciously understand that any possibility of "normalcy" within this unit will include adopting their belief system. The sad part of this progression is that the little boy is not aware of his change in values or ideals. His brain is not mature enough to independently assess the messages of those around him or to determine the validity in the beliefs.

As was stated previously, acceptance is a primary motivator for most human actions. His desire to be "accepted" and, far more importantly, to be loved allows for the slow contamination of his original intent. His "quest" mutates into a myopic, pathetic existence where acceptance requires maligned thinking and no possibility of independent thinking.

The incredible observation in this scenario, as well as in any cult-like organization, is that the desperate need for acceptance (with its basis being the need for love) is so great that it exceeds the natural intuition that would disallow bringing harm to another.

We have come full circle. The need for love, the understanding of what love really means, is the most important element of human existence - with the power of creativity a close second.

[2:43 pm]

June 9, 2005 12:22 pm   (Book Session 10)

Wonderful news!   Your soul is inhabiting a body that it enjoys. Remarkable, rare, and yet I am not surprised. You always struck me as the kind of soul who knew what he wanted. And there you are, trim, handsome, well-constructed, fit, glowing with excellent health. Ideally constructed specimen of a human. What's that you say? Your calves are too thin? Your tongue is larger than average? You can't quite hear as well as you'd like? That is quite pitiful; from all outward appearances, you seem like an ideal physical specimen. How could you possibly find fault with your vehicle?

Ahhhh, yes, entities sometimes forget the quality of humans that always seeks the negative. You could have beamed as I commented on your appearance and physical prowess. Yet, instead you found fault.

How can people train themselves to do this less so?

First let's examine which physical properties on earth humans have some measure of control over. Every one of them.

Humans collectively determine the weather, the pollution, the crime rate, the outbound happiness, the subtle geographical changes that occur, even the rate of decay. The implications and proof for this phenomenon are beyond the scope of this book, but suffice it to say that human thoughts and beliefs pattern to form events, situations, weather, disasters, and porcupines. Yes, porcupines. The energy emitted by people's thoughts is so complex, it carries with it a nearly infinite range of possible effects. When "like" thought waves coincide, they strengthen allowing the effect to grow. Simplistically stated, humans "create" the world around them, from the plants and flowers, to the radios, to the animals, to the earthquakes, to the heat emitted from the sun.

The whole of your experience is created by your thoughts, your neighbors' thoughts, and the thoughts of those who existed before you. A growing regional feeling of angst, worry, listlessness, and agitation will, over time, have enough magnitude in the collective energy emitted to cause an earthquake. The smaller the "disaster" the less "like" energy was bound together, and for a shorter period of time. The collective energy of a region can be reversed or redirected at any moment. If a shift in mass thinking occurs, the energy the inhabitants emit will change its intensity and its direction.

This information exceeds the grasp of 99.9% humans, but is being stated as an illustration about the way people create their realities. People do not "ask for" disasters, but they form changes in the earth's structure and weather patterns that reflect the aggregate level of emotion of a given region.

Make that 99.99% of humans. Even Karen cannot grasp this concept, and understandably so. She is wondering why an earthquake would occur on an uninhabited island.

Massive stores of energy travel great distances. An earthquake in an uninhabited region could be the collective result of the thinking of those within a thousand-mile radius. It is important to understand that energy builds up and builds up until there is a physical "explosion" in weather or occurrences in nature. The explosion usually returns the region back to a neutral level. However, if the force was not great enough to redirect the pool of collected energy, another correction will occur.

The world is the stage for humans to play out their soul's intent. Over millions of years, the world reflects the changes in humans' thought patterns, ideals, and intent. Many physical disasters are actually brought about by the collective agreement of souls to choose the trial as a learning experience. Thousands of souls, for example, will choose to be born into a particular region where the souls' original intent has gotten far off track. Together, their energy will effect a disaster enabling the fundamental correction of the direction of the souls' paths. The devastating loss will cause the people to return to the basic necessities of a meaningful life: to love, to create, and to learn. The misdirected paths will quickly revert back to the true intention of the soul.

As sad as the deaths seem to humans, those who perish actually chose, while in the entity realm, to contribute to the collective learning experience of humans. Although most physical beings do not recall this agreement, the agreement alone provides for a very peaceful release of the physical body. The "sacrifice" made by these souls was not a sacrifice at all since souls do not die. When the agreement was made to choose physical life for the purpose of bettering humankind's experiences and purpose, the choice was made willingly and with an "open heart."

Some survive the disasters, while others perish. Whether or not a physical being will survive, suffer injury, or die is determined by the soul's path once living the chosen physical life. As you have learned, the infinite number of probable outcomes to any situation will alter the path of the soul based on the choices made.

As the world becomes smaller through developments in travel and communications, disasters affect far greater areas than [they] had previously. On the path towards significant enlightenment among vast numbers of people, this "global downsizing" is beneficial, allowing far greater numbers of people to benefit from the lessons learned through human struggles.

The good news is that as humans' awareness increases, they will be able to learn and grow in awareness from non-negative experiences as readily as they presently learn from negative situations.

The ultimate goal of all souls is to enable the development of the soul through happiness. This concept will be discussed in further detail when we examine the soul's source.

We are going to take a look at the underpinnings, consequences, and intended results of a real-life disaster to illustrate the concepts: the tsunami in Southeast Asia in December of 2004.

Southeast Asia was undergoing a transformation from old-world to modern in its technology and culture. The advances were largely limited to the wealthy, who existed balancing precariously between two worlds, their traditional way of life and a modernized life which held a great allure as an exciting, exotic way of life. The two groups were at odds with each other, not capable of communicating the appeal of each other's choice to one another. The disparity between the groups rose, and ultimately, as any poorer group eventually comes to believe, the modernized lifestyles began to appear more desirable than the traditional ways. Nothing much else had changed, except exposure to comforts and riches that began to taunt the poorer classes.

Over time, battles ensued, figuratively and literally, as different groups tried either to preserve their way or to retaliate for their feelings of envy. Children became pawns in the battle of confusion. The energies emitted by the people of the region grew, particularly of the children who were harmed in a life of poverty, slavery, and prostitution. Although the percentage of population physically involved in the torments was small, the knowledge of the depth of the torment was widespread. Little or nothing was done to correct the imbalances; even the government turned a blind eye to the plight of children.

43

Had the facts not been largely known and ignored, the energy of those immediately involved may not have amassed to a great enough level to cause a physical disaster of that magnitude. However, the act of ignoring the responsibility of protecting those who could not protect themselves, in human terms, added a significant amount of "like" energy to the energy emitted by those tormented.

The ensuing disaster served many corrective purposes. The children, whose souls had "chosen" this physical path to help better the awareness of humankind, "sacrificed" their lives in disproportionate amounts. The effect is that the region, as a whole, is now forced to recognize the importance of children, and to admit the need to protect their safety and their liberty. It may seem perverse that it is not only those who mistreated the rights of others who suffered, but the growth of the human soul does not depend on, need, or benefit from punishment. The "wrongdoers" are not punished; instead, the region is given an opportunity to fundamentally change the maligned course that it was collectively traveling.

In addition, this disaster enabled a worldwide "coming together" or meeting of the minds. Few examples in history demonstrated such an outpouring of generosity, love, and support as this one. Survivors became ambassadors of sorts, teaching others the value of life and reminding others of meaningful priorities. The region has an opportunity to recover, physically and to the level of the soul. The soul's original intent has an opportunity to flourish and develop in ways that would not have been otherwise possible.

The byproduct of the event, so far, is one of great growth in human awareness. The outcome potential is continually affected by the choices that humans make. Will one pilfer or profit? Will others sacrifice to help the communities rebuild? What is the collective reaction and actions of humans?

To illustrate the potential for growth or stagnation of the collective human awareness, remember the news stories about what amount of donations each country's government was contributing. The act of comparison, the mere act of comparing one government's generosity to another, duplicated the underlying imbalance preceding the tsunami

44

itself. Groups against groups, not cooperating for a common goal. What was the purpose of this comparison? To allow one group to feel superior to another? A feeling of superiority of one group over another has contributed to all wars throughout history. If the intended result of the tsunami was to create harmony and human awareness, this behavior of nations ran contrary to the intention. Luckily, the amount of energy emitted by this battle of perception was dwarfed by the great energy emitted through human kindness.

This macroscopic illustration demonstrates how groups of people affect their surroundings, conditions that are largely out of your immediate control. But what you do control through your thoughts and your beliefs is the circumstances of your day-to-day life.

[3:08 pm]

June 10, 2005 12:42 pm   (Book Session 11)

When was the moment you realized that you were different? At birth? Simple, yet complex. Was it at age three? There was a moment when you understood that you were not exactly like everyone else or *anyone* else. You can probably not remember the exact moment, because you knew it always from before you were born until now. And you always will know it even after your death. There is no soul on earth exactly like you. There is no soul *off* earth exactly like you.

Interestingly, you are aware of this fact, yet you likely ignore it. Humans spend vast amounts of time, money, and energy imitating one another. If you are unique, why do you want to be like another?

Then there are those who differentiate deliberately. Anti-imitation. Those persons intentionally reject mainstream expressions and mores in an attempt to individualize themselves. The motivation is not to show uniqueness, but to capture attention, attention that will fill the void of a lack of feeling loved.

So if you are the same, you are denying your identity and if you are different, you are denying your identity. How can you express your identity? The answer is through creativity. Your appearance does little

45

to outwardly demonstrate your identity, unless you design your own clothes and wear them proudly. Even then, what influences your choices, the desire to fit in or the desire to stand out? Unless the answer is an exact "neither," then you are still challenged in your ability to show the creativity [that reveals your identity].

Creativity has long been associated with the arts ... music, visual arts, graphic design, virtually any form of expression that can be seen or heard. The aspects of creativity that have long been forgotten are the more subtle, less recognizable expressions. Have you ever heard an NBA announcer exclaim, "And he is one of the most creative players on the court!" Or perhaps big news about a scientific breakthrough, "We credit Ms. Sanders with her extraordinary creativity in spearheading this startling discovery!"?

What about a mom who raises her children with a creative eye? A woman who has the ability to absorb and reflect back the needs and individuality of her children and skew her parenting to their individual uniqueness? Doesn't such a skill take creativity?

Creativity can be demonstrated by anyone who "creates" a new path, unharnessed by external influence. True creativity is based upon passion and joy, not saddled in angst or revulsion. An intuitive individual can detect whether an expression of art was created through joy or out of pain. Look at art and listen to music. Which pieces make your heart soar, and which clamp down your spirit, literally making your skin crawl? Those created in joy express the inner soul, the joyous origin of a person. Those created in rebellion and hatred merely express a soul hidden in layers of misguided direction. You will arguably consider forms of art that assault one's senses as being creative, but not the "creative" that we are discussing in this book. The creative power which is essential to the growth and expression of the human soul is based on positive origins.

There are billions of examples in art that fall between the expression of pure joy and pure angst; however, have you ever noticed that those based on the purest of either expression are the ones that become timeless or revered for their greatness? Take The Righteous Brothers' *Unchained Melody* vs. the movie, *The Exorcist*: One lilting and able to carry one's mood to a brighter level, the other, dark, macabre, and resulting in

46

a tightening of one's mood. Both timeless classics, one created in joy, the other in angst.

You can almost see or feel or hear the joyousness or joyless-ness of the soul creating the art.

Mama Cass, formerly of the 1960's group *The Mamas and the Papas*, was one such individual who expressed her identity through art. Although her physical appearance created an image of a tortured soul on earth, she was, in fact, full of great joy and great love. Her vocals and music reflected her joy, unbounded by the influence of others. Cass succeeded with an anti-societal physical vehicle when few could, a testament to the strength of her vibrational energy, her love of self and others.

These passages may confuse those who believe that art must be created through pain, or those who believe great works are produced by tortured souls. According to the modern day definition of creativity, they are, in fact, creative. However, the creativity that is essential to the expression of the soul's original intent, that is to love, create, and learn with the intent of increasing the awareness of oneself and humankind, is only expressed through joy.

An important side note about creativity: As you have learned, external influences often redirect a person off his or her original path. As that soul attempts to return to its original intent, the physical being may "create" in angst, and the act of "creating" serves as a form of therapy. The desired result of the "therapy" is to help the soul uncover the layers that have buried him or her from the original purpose. As such, the "therapy" can be positive; however, the greater likelihood is that the "creations" will have a twofold negative effect. One is that the person will become entrenched with the expression, causing him to tighten the grip of the layers that surround him. The second risk is that the "creations" will also tighten the grip of the layers that surround those exposed. Plainly stated, expressions created in pain risk keeping others in pain, or keeping others from feeling their joyful soul.

So pervasive is the belief that great art comes from tortured souls, that many artists will subconsciously block their creative energies when their lives are smooth, unencumbered, or happy.

47

The creativity that is essential to the growth in human awareness is always founded upon joy.

For those of you who want to develop or increase your positive expression of creativity, remember that it does not take any particular talent. Positive creativity can be expressed in mathematics, literature, parenting, gardening, music, dancing, sports, writing, talking, dressing, and even thinking – if the positive thinking is converted into action.

If you *feel* positive about what you have created, if you get "lost" during the time of expression, if you *feel* light-hearted or unstressed while creating, then you have successfully expressed your soul's original intent. Another way to judge if you have succeeded is to assess the product of your expression. If one person or more has a happy moment or a happier life as a result, you have succeeded.

The purpose of human life is to love, create, and learn, in that order. There are no exceptions. With that said, I must add the exception, contradicting myself for clarity. (Let's call it a "clarification" rather than an exception). The clarification is that the true definitions of "create" and "creative" must be understood to mean coming from a positive origin.

With that point understood, the purpose of human life is love, create, and learn, in that order. There are no exceptions.

[long pause]

Elephants walk the earth, stomping hard, leaving footprints in their wake. Like these mighty and gentle creatures, the mighty and gentle "Greats" leave indelible footprints in their wake.

We, [the entities and I], call a "Great," one who affects, positively, the wave of human awareness and leaves the world a better place than it was found. The vibrational strength of Greats is so strong that they are not easily separated from their purpose. The energy that they emit is a powerful protector from the elements of influence that will attempt to permeate the intent. You have heard expressions, "Nothing will stop her, " or "He can do no wrong." These expressions describe the force necessary for Greats to endure [persevere].

48

One such Great is with me as I write this passage, Benjamin Franklin. His achievements are well documented, his quotations live on, but lesser known was the quality of his character. His influence reigned beyond his accomplishments; he affected, positively, the lives of those he came into contact with. He left the world a better place than he found it.

Other Greats in my midst are Henry David Thoreau, Benjamin Disraeli, Albert Einstein, Cass Elliot, Edgar Allen Poe, Elizabeth Browning …. There are many, some of who have "written" through Karen. In common, we still hold the trait of trying to help humans create a better world. Our vision, and hopefully yours, is a peaceful civilization worldwide which fosters creativity and the positive environment necessary to promote future growth of human awareness.

We have come to an apex. We have reached the moment when we are ready to affect, positively, human awareness, and the nature of humankind's current awareness will allow the assistance to be received. You are on the precipice of the human dream: to fulfill your life's desires while contributing to the betterment of the human experience. Some describe this period as the "Age of Aquarius," others simply recognize an underlying ideal in human interaction. Call it what you will, but the time is now for you to further your understanding for the purpose of fulfilling your soul's intent.

I will introduce you to, or reconnect you with, your original source. All souls have a "vibrational level" which reflects their level of awareness. "Old Souls," as you may have heard the wise among you described, vibrate with greater intensity than newer souls. The reach of their energy has a more powerful affect on the world around them and with this power comes the responsibility of using it in a positive way.

As you "progress" in the development of your soul, your soul vibrates with greater and greater intensity. During each lifetime, you love, create, and learn to a certain degree, and the products of your accumulated experiences advance the development of your soul. As entities, all souls vibrate with only positive intensity, and this intensity is what people aspire to achieve on earth. Imagine your absolutely happiest moment ever, and that "feeling" or vibrational level of the energy you emit does not compare in its intensity to how strong the energy is here. Our

49

happiness feels stronger and we do not experience unhappiness. This ideal is what souls attempt to achieve on earth and the more positive energy emitted by a person, the closer he or she is to achieving that goal.

The greatest energy of all, ALL THAT IS, vibrates with a level of energy so great that it cannot be put into human language. Imagine all the energy of all of the stars amassed and the power of the energy that radiates. ALL THAT IS has an energy greater than that. As our souls develop, as our emitted energy grows in intensity and strength, we get closer and closer to the level of energy emitted by ALL THAT IS. The reason souls aspire to get closer and closer to this ideal is that ALL THAT IS "feels" an indescribable, pure state of bliss. There is no pain, no remorse, no sadness, no fear. The energy of ALL THAT IS is one of pure love and acceptance and beauty. Imagine feeling that positive all the time! You, by practicing the principals in this book, can bring yourself closer and closer to that feeling, or in other words, to happiness.

[3:55 pm]

June 12, 2005 1:00 pm   (Book Session 12)

You drown your sorrows by choosing to keep them afloat. Think about the metaphor. To "drown" something, simply ignore it. Leave it alone. To pay attention to it, you are preventing it from drowning, or keeping it afloat. Humans tend to "give in" to their sorrow, almost savoring the pain. The pain is a powerful sensation that makes them feel human and alive, albeit sad. Can you achieve such a state happily? The truth is that most humans presently can achieve a greater degree of sadness than that intense degree of joy. They are also more practiced at sustaining it for much longer periods of time as well.

Why the cross-firing? A misfiring of synapses created by digging a deeper trench on the sad path? Too much focus on the negative creates a path of ease for thought to readily flow down. It's easy to re-travel that pathway, but more difficult to carve a strong trench for happiness simply because it is unworn.

Can you manually or physically correct this misfiring? It takes effort and dedication since embedding oneself in negativity is familiar, therefore comfortable. If you are willing to extend the effort to retread the pathways, to make the happiness path the natural course and allow the tides of time to lessen the negative path, I will teach you how to do so.

[break 1:26 pm; resume 1:50 pm]

Rather than give you step-by-step instructions, let me tell you a story. There once was a little boy named Miguel. He stopped along his path frequently to examine a shiny stone or a brown toad. The world captured his eye and his attention, and focusing on someone else's quest was challenging. Such a young boy was free of the encumbrances of grown-up responsibility, and his heart was light with the magnificence of the world around him.

One day on the way to the village, Miguel saw a thorny toad, one of such rare beauty, he could see nothing else. His mother kept her brisk pace as Miguel bent down to follow the path of the toad. Several strides ahead, Miguel's mother sensed her young son's absence and turned abruptly back to discover him chasing a toad. Angered by his persistent idling, she handed him her heavy basket of wares to carry along the way. It was not the punishment that prevented Miguel from wandering off again, it was the basket. He focused on holding it steady, not spilling its contents, and bearing its heavy load. He could not see the toads or the shiny stones.

In your lifetime, many people have handed you baskets. You were inclined to put them down because they were not fun to carry, yet due to external forces, you carried the baskets. It seemed the more able you were to bear the load, the more baskets were handed to you, until the moment when you rarely had idle hands.

Maturity and increasing responsibility are necessary for the development of self-sufficient adults. But how can you learn to carry baskets with a light heart? How can you learn to carry some baskets and put others down? The mere act of carrying an undue number and weight of baskets teaches the brain that the emotions associated with the burden are normal. It is normal to feel pressure to accomplish. It is normal to

51

feel less than happy or free. Gradually, the shift from happy to unhappy occurs.

For the parents guiding the young, the solution is easy. Watch what you put in the baskets and how much you are asking the child to carry. There is a mixed tendency today towards postponing the teaching of self-reliance and responsibility while also directing children towards outcomes that reflect the desire of the parents. This combination creates young adults who are moderately incapable of self-sufficiency, but, far worse, are relatively incapable of making up their own minds, of choosing their own path.

Parenting should focus on guiding children, especially adolescents and teens, towards figuring out what they want and why. Not all decisions should be unilateral. By allowing your child to participate in the decision-making process, you are teaching them to develop a lifelong ability to know their own minds. Obviously, not all decisions can include their participation, but many can. Consider, for example, a choice a child must make attending a cultural program with their grandparents or attending a friend's birthday party. Assuming you approve of either choice, ask your child questions as he examines his choices. Continue gently posing new questions until the child can figure out what he really wants and why. Allow your questions to remain neutral and unbiased. For example, "Why do you want to go to the party when you already spend so much time with your friends?" could easily be asked; "Is there a reason you want to go to the party instead of the concert?" Continue to ask questions until the child determines, for himself, which choice is best and the consequences for the choice.

What you are doing is handing your child an empty basket and asking him to either put it down [by guiding him towards discovering what he wants] or to fill it with the contents of *your* choice [by deciding or influencing the decision]. Do not replace sound judgement with this technique. You have the capacity to think. If your child repeatedly avoids the grandparents, find out why rather than forcing his attendance. He may have a very valid reason that you are unaware of. Trust your instincts in his choices as well. Often a well-reared child will make a seemingly inappropriate choice for a valid reason.

Quite simply, teach your child to think for him or herself. Do not unduly burden them with your choices. Learning independent thinking is a skill that needs encouragement to flourish.

Back to you. How can you balance the struggle between freedom and responsibility while carrying the necessary baskets? Remember the objective: to enjoy more happy moments than moments laden with negative emotions.

Listen for the rush. Listen when your senses tingle with anticipation or you just can't get your mind off an event or a project or an idea. Do not dismiss the thoughts with your burden of responsible actions that you must take. Listen and determine why you feel passion about this concept, then make the time to pursue it. It may mean you drop a basket, or empty one out, but doing so will enable you to begin to replace unhappy moments with happy ones.

Examples help to solidify ideas.

You have a creative problem at work. The situation is slightly off-course from your normal job description. Why does this "problem" capture your attention? Why do you become excited as you analyze different solutions in your head? Your instincts are guiding you towards a change in direction. Perhaps you have become stagnant in your current position. Your desire to solve the problem beyond the scope of your position is your authentic self, pushing you out of an area of comfort or security. Grab the passion and run with it. Create a meaningful course of actions that will allow you to segue from your current employment into the new area, whether within the firm or externally.

There are a million reasons why you "can't" do it, but there is one far more compelling reason why you should. You create your reality by your thoughts and your beliefs. You can choose to believe that "safely" is the way to play, or you can believe that your risk is small in comparison to the risk of suffocating in a job you are no longer stimulated by. You can balance responsibility with risk by diminishing the risk through positive beliefs.

Believe you will fail and you will. *Believe* you will succeed and you will.

53

A powerful theory in modern times is the "Power of Positive Thinking." The missing element in that widely recognized theorem is the inclusion of the "power of positive *feeling*." You can think all you want, but if your thoughts do not help you emit an energy of excitement, of enthusiasm, then they will not proactively change your reality.

Remember the example. You felt an excitement contemplating possible solutions; you *felt* excited! It is those positive *feelings* that can change your existence, not the positive thoughts that preceded them. Listen to your own clues. Your mind is giving you clues continually as to what will make you *feel* enthusiastic. Your authentic self wants to be happy. Don't ignore the signals even though the burden of others' baskets has caused you to do so.

Can you cite one example of a Great whose name lives on in history who did not feel passionate? Passion is the lifeblood of human happiness. Follow your passion. Although not all who made their mark in history were happy, they were passionate about something. Passion is the precursor to creativity and, as you know, creativity is one of the three essential ingredients for human fulfillment. The historically known Greats who were not happy were missing one or two of the other ingredients: the understanding of and ability to love, or the ability to learn from one's life.

[3:41 pm]

June 13, 2005 12:28 pm   (Book Session 13)

The story of Miguel shows how easily we are led off our natural path of choosing our own direction. The exercise in finding your authentic self through the examination of your happy moments will guide you in discovering what you have forgotten. You are carrying too many baskets and they are not filled with enough things that you enjoy. Without the luxury of dropping every basket and running, try to put a number of them down. Don't take the easy way of just dropping one insignificant item, like a once-a-month supper club. Look hard at the list to discover where you can modify your schedule to make room for fun.

Evaluate why you participate in all the activities on your list: for pleasure, obligation, to avoid guilt, to please someone other than you? If you are presently raising children and their activities compete for your time, evaluate those activities as an open-minded family and chisel your family obligations down to a manageable level, one that allows for pleasure, recreation, hobbies, relaxing, and doing absolutely nothing. Those moments when the schedule is empty are when your relaxed mind can love, create, and learn to its greatest capacity.

If you are like most people, accomplishing this goal is easier in theory than in practice. Your schedule is packed with superfluous activities which you and your family (and your society) have deemed essential. Did you survive childhood without travel baseball? Without four practices a week for sports and instruments? Without another game or tournament, religion classes, and tutoring?

What is the goal? Children can be exposed to a variety of opportunities without each becoming an obsession, consuming exhaustive amounts of money and time. When you listen to your children's soul song, you will hear their passion. Help them to follow their passion or interests in a way that is not replacing the magic of living a well-rounded childhood. Once the children move out of the house, will you better remember the thousand tournament hours you spent on fields, or will you remember the times when you laughed together, created together, baked together, or read together?

There is an occasional child whose passion is so great that it consumes their thinking. Helping that child pursue her dream may be a commitment that you and your family choose; however, it is an onerous decision where the rewards and consequences need be carefully evaluated.

Those without children consuming their time also harbor a variety of misconceptions about the importance of their activities. Many Americans, for example, believe that they must work long, long hours to earn the respect and income that they desire. The corporate days of nine-to-five are slipping away, replaced with a competitive mentality that equates work with life. BlackBerries, cell phones, and email have created an atmosphere of work and personal lives blending together. Where does one end and the other start? Gradually, respect for time off

55

has lessened to the point where an employee is virtually corporate property. And what does a person receive in return for this loyalty, sacrifice, and availability? Love? Are you irreplaceable?

An interesting phenomenon to observe that you can detect independently is the reports of "life evaluation" after a near-death experience. Universal accounts report that those who "return" to life after being medically deceased realize the importance of family and love, as well as the insignificance of work and material possessions when they return to normalcy. The interchange with death has a common effect of causing the "traveler" to reassess his or her priorities, often choosing the pursuit of love and pleasure dramatically more.

I will agree that changing priorities to ones inconsistent with priorities valued in society is challenging. It is not easy to be the first one to say, "Let's cut back on the soccer;" "Work should not consume my leisure hours;" or "I have better things to do with my time." Trends change, however. What was vogue twenty years ago in societal patterns is barely recognizable. As individuals begin to claim back the right to choose how they spend their time, the pendulum will swing to that direction.

There is a societal overload that is prevalent around you today that is beginning to take a marked toll on the well being of its citizens. Stress levels are at an all time high in a period enjoying the greatest level of economic freedom, freedom through technology, and freedom of choice. Watch the pharmaceutical ads to see what people are taking to cope, to relax, to live "freely."

Phobias abound. Why the rapidly increasing number of people with anxiety or phobia? Phobia is a response to control. Individuals with subconscious feelings of lack of control over their personal lives use phobias as a method to exercise control over what they do, how they do it, and whom they do it with. Anxiety is another subconscious symptom that arises to help individuals gain control over their events, situations, and schedules.

It is simpler for the body to create needs which must be physically obeyed than it is for people to willingly and knowingly take control over their choices. The body responds with symptoms to protect the person from further harm. The actual process is complex beyond explanation in this level of writing; however, humans have summed up this process eloquently when they talk about the mind-body connection.

The body responds with what the mind needs. As simple as contracting a mild two-day virus when a person is overloaded and needs down-time, to far more complex injuries and illnesses to enable the person to solve more fundamental and grave issues. When the symptoms are correctly interpreted, the body can be restored to maximum health. The symptoms will persist if the underlying need is not recognized. This fact is the basis for spontaneous healings, as you know them.

All challenge, medical or otherwise, is an opportunity for learning. This process extends far beyond finding the "silver lining" in a bad situation. This process can actually be circumvented by understanding and practicing the principles in this book. You can learn without negative challenges. Wouldn't that make you happier?

For now, look for the opportunities for increasing your personal awareness when faced with negative situations. Soon you will be able to see a decided decrease in the number and frequency of your challenges.

Each disharmonious event should cause you to ponder: *Why? Why do I need this challenge in my life right now? What benefit does this event have for me?* Seek an answer that "rings true," one that your instincts tell you is cause for the struggle. Determining how a challenge can correct an imbalance in your life helps you to reconcile the challenge and overcome it far more quickly.

Let's explore an example. Your house is flooded. There are an infinite number of possible causes for the challenge, but let's cite a few underlying currents that may have contributed.

> Do you have a need for attention? Perhaps you feel under-appreciated, invisible, unloved, or unlovable. A crisis draws protective and helpful people to your side, leaving your soul awash with the *necessary* feelings of love.

> Are you encumbered by material possessions? Having or collecting or owning material objects is not wrong. Allowing them to possess you or become a burden is, however,

57

detrimental. A flood can rid you of encumbrances and renew your spirit with the priority of what is really important to you.

You fundamentally believe that life is a battle. This is a common core belief. Many individuals will attract in crises that validate that the belief is true.

Your house as well as your neighboring community is suffering the same fate. The community as a whole may be in desperate need of relief from pallor, apathy, poverty, or lack of direction or unity. A community-wide crises draws in radiant energy from surrounding areas, men and women who are compassionate and trained to offer physical and emotional aid. This assistance brings a renewed sense of vitality in the community as the residents see their value through the eyes of others. In addition, all natural crises provide the opportunity to build community, to get people out of self-absorbed concerns and bring them together from the common place of pain and for the common cause of rebuilding and assisting one another. If you have ever helped another expecting nothing in return, then you know that there are far fewer feelings of satisfaction known to humankind.

These scenarios are just a few of the possible causes for the challenge of a flood. Not only are the possibilities endless, but the combination of causes are infinite. It is up to you to examine the challenge unfalteringly until the cause or causes are clear to you. Your understanding of the underlying need for the challenge will allow your awareness to develop beyond requiring such a physical manifestation again.

You are on your way to comprehending the "learning" portion of the important life elements. Amassing knowledge of facts is not the learning that we refer to. Learning as a critical element in the process of life is to increase your awareness of how and why you manifest your reality, and contribute to the reality of others, in the way that you do. Lessons that are ignored will be repeated, through the same representation or differently, until the lesson is learned.

As I have previously stated, you have the capability, as all humans do, to experience growth through positive circumstances rather than through negative events.

58

June 14, 2005 10:59 am   (Book Session 14)

Take the angry energy in the world and turn it. What could be accomplished if the passion were changed from destruction to construction? If each person did their part to construct a better world, overnight humanity would collectively reach its quest. Let's give a moment of thanks to the people who do just that. They bring hope and enlightenment to the world beyond their physical existence.

The world needs a day to honor these citizens. A day to recognize and revere the accomplishments of those enlightened individuals who see beyond the shadow of their physical bodies. Let's pick a day to celebrate the dedication of those who are motivated to leave the world a better place than they found it, who strive for the betterment of humankind. April 30th shall be the day of honor from this moment on. Every person will do one kind deed for someone who helps others. Bake a cake, send an email, take out their garbage, hang a balloon ... choose one act to show respect for the admiration you feel for a helpful person. Contact someone from your past and let that person know how he or she affected your life.

We'll call it THE DAY OF KINDNESS and encourage people to exert a little imagination and effort to show their respect. Choose anyone who has touched you by demonstrating kindness to you or to another. For more impact, choose someone you do not know personally, but at a minimum, choose someone who won't expect the honor.

Oprah Winfrey's *Random Acts of Kindness* movement exemplified the concept and the effect we wish to achieve. Hallmark can create a line of cards to get the ball rolling. Use your imagination to achieve worldwide recognition for [participation in] THE DAY OF KINDNESS.

[pause]

William Shakespeare was a Great Thinker in his time. Can you think of any other creator of art who is studied in public schools centuries after his or her death? Many authors created great works in literature, why the profound, enduring interest in his? The answer lies in his prolific

59

ability to comment on society's ills while enticing the reader to engage in the plot. We now see such wrongs as the betrayal of Caesar as an obviously maligned act, but in Shakespeare's day, the thinking was revolutionary.

Few works have illuminated the senseless and harmful aspects of prejudice as *Romeo and Juliet*, a story which endures through the ages for its simple and evocative truth. *Romeo and Juliet* remains the world's most frequently re-told story, through its representation in theatre to the modernizing of the message through stories such as *Westside Story*.

Perhaps it is time to consider the bodies of work that endure the test of time. The common essence that they hold is truth. Humanity has an instinctual affinity for truth and, as such, regards highly the tales in which truth resides. Even THE BIBLE holds many enduring truths, even if the historical retelling of the events is misrepresented. The romance that surrounds the "idea" of the Holy Grail is a further testament to humankind's passion for truth.

Were one able to analyze, succinctly and clearly, the works of all past Greats, a complete book of truth and wisdom could be possible. Aside from the massiveness of the endeavor, however, the human factor would corrupt the integrity of the project, just as THE BIBLE was corrupted through intentional or unintentional human mishandling.

The book you are holding avoids the pitfalls of human frailties by eliciting the assistance of souls who no longer have the capacity to lie, propagandize, or err. Truths stand tall and obvious to those in the energy realm, not shrouded in layers of human mishandling.

In reverence to the magnificence of human's ability to reason, however, I continually invite you to investigate or contradict, with evidence, the claims herein.

[1:06 pm]

Some semblance of truth is not acceptable to the entities. Truth stands victoriously independent and has no equal. The transition from a physical realm to our energy realm elicits a quick cognition of what is real and what is not, what is true and what is false. There are no misunderstandings.

Besides the feeling of euphoria that we experience, perhaps the best aspect of our realm is freedom. Freedom to think, act, and be whatever we choose. The foundation for all freedom is truth, therefore, our freedom is guaranteed by our inability to misunderstand or misrepresent truth.

Your soul *knows* what is true. Layers of corruption have often masked the truth from your conscious mind, but peeling off the layers of others' opinions and demands will allow you to recognize truth again.

An individual dons layers of protection against truth if living in falsehood represents the physical being's choices. For example, a person engulfed in the "mind control" of a cult has permitted the control to take place in order to fulfill a need much greater than freedom. The person has an all-consuming need for acceptance and love, two needs that are seemingly addressed by the organization. It is easy to recognize when a person has been persuaded or controlled by a cult-like organization (even those who emerge from the haze of manipulation are shocked at how clear the persuasion was), yet thousands of examples of the manipulation of the mind exist which humans do not or choose not to recognize.

Some examples may shake the core of your belief system, a system that you have adopted to serve the nature of your reality, so I will begin with examples less startling. Observe the increase in ADD or ADHD diagnoses in children. Drug treatment proliferates, often mildly sedating a disruptive child under the guise of enhancing the child's focus.

What is really going on? The diagnosis and treatment are simply Band-Aids for symptoms that are more appropriately addressed through the proper response to a child's soul song. Children are often raised haphazardly without a clear understanding of what the child needs, from proper nutrition, to exercise, to caressing, to love, to patience, to stimulation of the intellect. When a child's soul song is not heard, ADD and the like may emerge as a protective symptom to elicit the correct balancing elements that he or she needs. Unfortunately, the response often exacerbates the unaddressed problems that initiated the

61

"disorder." As with many pharmaceuticals, the drug therapy may cause more harm than the good that was intended. In addition to pharmaceuticals falling in the category of fallible scientific study, they are not tested on children and cannot, therefore, be guaranteed safe.

What does a child need? Love beyond all else. Unconditional love and acceptance combined with gentle and consistent discipline and guidance. They need a balanced diet. They need to have their minds and their bodies engaged and stimulated. They need quiet and security. They need respect. They need their soul songs heard so that their individual beauty can be honored.

Doubt, question, or believe – the choice is yours. Investigate freely the instances when a child was "cured" of these "disorders" without the use of unproven drugs. Or believe the statements because your intuition, your knowing-core, tells you that they are true.

June 15, 2005 10:38 am   (Book Session 15)

Elected officials have largely lost their way. Not all, but most, no longer recall the passionate purpose of democracy. Saddled in corruption, misuse of funds, and misguided allegiances, they stumble into an environment where only the unfit survive. By unfit, I mean by the standards of the Founding Fathers. Their purpose was altruistic, noble, passionate, forward-thinking, groundbreaking, revolutionary, exemplary, and rooted in timeless principles. Seldom in history has a group of Greats assembled for such a large purpose.

How did the paths of government officials go so astray? Greed? Opportunism? Power? The path of deterioration has been slow, but the officials are not entirely to blame. Citizens contributed to every immoral step that was taken. Rather than stand on principle or fight for what is right, individuals, one-by-one, served their own purpose instead of the higher good.

Yet, it makes sense. Humans are judged largely by their material possessions and the status of the company they keep. If a person knows that his purpose will be furthered by aligning improperly with those who can assist, the temptation is too great, especially when the alignment is legal. Here is the basis for political contributions and the subsequent funds becoming a serious source of democracy veering off its intended path.

What began as an opportunity for the average person to compete for political position in the same arena that the wealthy do, spiraled into an out-of-control system of greed, power, and legal bribery. The observations are not meant as social commentary of the wrongdoing of people today. I'll leave that job to my works in literature that still roam the earth. Instead, my intent is to show how askew human's understanding of the nature of their reality has gotten, with the expectation that the course can be corrected.

As it has been proven that the war against drugs must be attacked from a demand perspective (not until there is no demand will there be no drug sales), the same is true with the war against corruption. Not until the demand for fortune at the expense of another is curtailed will corruption become void.

How will this hunger be curtailed? By allowing humans to understand, once again, how they create their own life circumstances. Why is Bill Gates widely demonized by the American public instead of exalted for his genius, ingenuity, passion, perseverance, and artistic ability to create wealth for thousands of fellow Americans?

Bill Gates created his reality. He did not use illegal or immoral actions to amass an empire of productivity, creativity, and prosperity. The prosperity that he has created is not limited to himself; it extends far beyond his own personal wealth or even the wealth of his key employees. It reaches to the level of every employee who works for a critical supplier of Microsoft resources, and to the communities that each company *and* each supplier company resides in as the employees spend their paychecks on food, cars, banking services, libraries, roads, etc. The economic gains realized by his efforts are explosive. His life is synonymous with the authentic purpose of democracy. Rather than criticize his bank accounts, Americans should be relentless in their pursuit of understanding how he achieved such greatness. Look beyond his intellect, his education, and his background, and find out how he *feels*. What is his attitude? What is his outlook? What are his expectations? You can learn more by studying his frame of mind than by studying his physical background.

Why do two seemingly similar people have such entirely different realities? As an example, two Midwesterners with similar upbringings, similar skills, and similar appearances arrive in New York for their big acting opportunity. One gets discovered and the other gets sent home. Is it just luck? Coincidence? What is different?

Their belief systems. One is eager, passionate, almost desperate to achieve, whereas the other is eager, passionate, and filled with a *knowing* that she will succeed. A deeply rooted belief that she has all the talent and "good luck" and determination needed to succeed. The one back home had a belief system deeply entrenched in doubt and the "realistic" idea that not many succeed. Without realizing it, she met her own expectations by joining the majority who do not "make it" in the business.

You can learn much from those who succeeded before you, if you ask the right questions.

Questions must be designed to uncover beliefs rather than just backgrounds or circumstances. What made you think you could do it? How are you different? Are you optimistic generally? Could you see yourself in a different profession?

"Stars" generally share the same essence in their answers. They *always* knew they would make it. They never lost hope. They never lost sight of their goal. They were passionate in their imaginative methods of reaching their desires. The parallel energy that they emitted with the strength of their beliefs attracted in the right people, opportunities, and circumstances to allow the dream to reach fruition.

Greats are not easily distracted. That is not to say that stars or those in the public eye are Greats; some are and some are not. But the true Greats remain steadfast in their belief in an idea and in themselves.

The key to their success is focus. Have you ever tried your hand at a task and succeeded, whereas at other times you failed? Think of a time when you botched up something that you were typically skilled at: you missed the goal, you burnt dinner, your art was uninspired and dull, missing the mark. How was your mood or thinking different that day than on all the days you succeeded?

The difference in the way you felt emitted a different energy than that when you were "on." The difference between the gold and silver Olympians is just a matter of attitude, or the emission of strong "positive" energy. By emitting an energy in slightly greater strength than the opponents, the gold wins the medal over the medal contenders. How strong is the energy that radiates from the beliefs of the person who was ranked seventeenth and pulled out in front to take the gold?

Surprisingly, this energy can be measured. I'll put the idea out there and leave it to brilliant Americans to discover how. Hints: The greatest strength of energy emitted by humans is in the area about six inches in front of their chests. Also, a measuring device does not have to come into contact with the body. As a matter of fact, touching the body may corrupt the measurement. The energy will change depending upon the way a person *feels* or emotes.

You don't have to be a seismologist to crack the code. Virtually anyone can build a measuring device to detect the energy emitted by a person. And that's my last hint. Or is it?

[1:15 pm]

I'm walking on sunshine, oh yeah ... and don't it feel good? –Katrina and the Waves

A simple 1980's lyric summarizes your entire purpose. *To feel good.* To experience the powerful energy emitted when you love, create, and learn to your greatest capacity. What is fascinating is that strong emotions that are created from a negative source emit an energy exactly opposite to that emitted based on a positive source. The strength can be the same, therefore the ability to attract similar energies in is equivalent, but the pulsation of the energy is opposite. The phenomenon is similar to the bipolar properties of a magnet; one repels and one attracts.

Likewise, positive versus negative sources of energy behave oppositely. Positive emotions and beliefs will attract in positive people, events, and

65

circumstances, and negative emotions and beliefs will attract in negative people, events, and circumstances. The degree to which the attraction occurs will depend on the strength and consistency of the energy emoted. For example, if you are extremely happy for an extended period of time, you emit positively charged "antennae," if you will. These antennae will seek like "antennae" and attract them back to you. An invisible "string" is attached to each of your antennae and will pull you towards it [like people, events, and circumstances] when the antenna bonds with a like antenna. The effect is that you and the person emitting antennae with like properties will be drawn to one another.

This extremely rudimentary explanation is the basis for the way you create your reality, and also explains "coincidences." Coincidence is merely a word that describes the attraction of like antennae.

Consistent and prolonged emission of negative emotions such as apathy, sadness, or rage will attract in people and circumstances that will enable the emitter to justify, subconsciously and outwardly, the continuation of the negative emotion. This vicious cycle creates an incessant pattern of negativity that not only perpetuates, but also acts to reaffirm the person's belief that life is angering, or sad, or senseless.

[1:50 pm]

June 16, 2005 9:59 am   (Book Session 16)

Advanced scientific data has often disproved long-held beliefs about the church, yet the two opposing ideologies co-exist in relatively harmony. This was not always the case, as the lives of Galileo and Sir Isaac Newton can attest to. Scientific postulations were often considered blasphemous and great strides were taken by many to suppress the evidence as it was reported. How did this fractionating reconcile? Throughout history there remains the unexplainable. The questions of triviality could be answered by science, while religion strengthened its hold over the answers to the unscientific questions. Yes, the earth is round, but why are we here? The human heart is a muscle that transports blood around the body, but what makes us *feel*?

As long as "unanswerable" questions remain, faith will reign dominant over the possibilities. Religion will explain the unexplainable by claiming to know truth.

Interestingly, not only do societies live harmoniously balanced between science and religion, but individuals do as well. A scientist, one dedicated to assuming nothing in the pursuit of truth, will embrace faith as a personal comfort for the trials that occur in life. There is a need and a passion to have answers. To understand the meaning of life, to have support for the idea that life is not finite, that human existence matters for a purpose. Not all faithful followers accept the advances of science, and not all scientifically-minded persons embrace religion, but the odd crossover, the mixing of vinegar with oil, is so prevalent that it is worth examining.

A deeply religious woman contracts cancer and battles the disease through modern technological advances, yet prays and asks for the prayers of others to help her battle her circumstances. Is this not incongruent? To ask of science and religion, in equal pleas, for a cure?

Does her faith lie in God or in man's medicine?

If she accepts the fact that science can produce a cure, as she does by her pursuit of medical intervention, then why does she not accept the "facts" that science purports contrarily to the teachings of her religion? She has faith that God created man, yet science claims that another origin for humankind exists and, at a minimum, man evolved from simple species. She selectively accepts and rejects the findings of scientific discovery, accepting those that serve her purpose and rejecting those that question her faith.

Which will cure her, science or faith?

You will find the answer in this book. In the meantime, challenge yourself to detect and examine inconsistencies in your own thinking.

Live without electricity for a week and you will quickly discover your dependence on this scientific discovery. Be a purist. Do not limit your ban to just electric power, but on any source of power that emerged as a product of electricity; that means no batteries. What time is it? Do you own a wind-up analog timepiece? What's for breakfast? No toast, no waffles, unless you have a hand-held, cast-iron, stovetop iron that you will flip over your gas, non-electronically ignited stove. Oh, your orange juice is in the cellar, a lovely lukewarm just the way you like it.

[break 10:50 am – 11:27 am]

Replicating the simplicity of past generations, you can get an idea of the limit in choices that were available of how to spend one's time or to earn one's living. Advances in technology broaden opportunities and expand thinking. Although many reject advances for the threat that they supposedly pose to civilized culture, in actuality, advances have promoted creativity and independent thinking. Advances often explain the previously unexplainable aspects of human existence, and also serve to provide new paths of learning and discovery for those willing to embrace them. How many people now work in a profession of computer technology? The software engineers, information technologists, website designers, manufacturers of hardware and software, and so on. Is it possible that the number and income of these professions over the past two decades exceeds the job loss total of manufacturing jobs in America?

As one group fights to preserve a passing way, another group boards the train of progress and flourishes creatively on its rails.

While many argue for the benefits of the simpler way of life, progress continues as it pushes antiquated thinkers out of its way. The world changes, with or without consent of all its members.

Those who reject progress eventually die off, leaving generations of new people ignorant to the past simplicity. They may study times, but they cannot truly comprehend the world under those circumstances. You may be thinking, "How did I survive without my cell phone?" while today's children may not have even seen a rotary telephone.

And through it all, religion prevails, standing as monument to the simplicity of older days, fiercely clung to in hope of providing a stabilizing force through dramatic change. It serves as the one constant that can be depended upon. But the power that religion provides has always existed even before the advent of organized religion. Religion

68

has largely obscured the purest source of power – the power within each individual.

In prerecorded history, humans embraced a bond with nature and a oneness with the universe. They understood their purpose and lived in peaceful coexistence with neighbors and nature. The presently hidden sense of intuition was the most developed and accurate of all the senses. Over time, through the calculated misguided manipulations of historic predecessors, humans began to rely on others' opinions and power in place of their own. This process has continued through today where wisdom and truth and direction are sought from without instead of from within.

A very simple example of the passage of power and thinking is that towards the medical diagnosticians. Although there is a corrective movement presently encouraging patients to partner with their health care providers in the diagnosis and treatment of imbalance, more prevalent is the likelihood of Americans to replace their judgement and intuitive beliefs with that of those in the profession. With a surge in popularity of Eastern medical philosophies, the interest in whole-body healing is increasing rapidly, but the vast majority still relinquish their power and inner wisdom to those educated in Western medicine.

Why is disease, chronic and terminal disease such as cancer and heart ailments, less prevalent in Eastern cultures? With the massive quantity of intellect in the United States, cannot society detect and imitate their success? Why the slow support of holistic techniques in lieu of invasive, costly procedures, if each has the support of successes?

Culturally, the people of the United States are embarking on a movement towards regaining their power. The trend, which was propelled in the 1960's, encourages citizens to think for themselves, not necessarily to reject all of the advances of modern technology, but to discover and support the power within.

This books aims neither to agree nor disagree with modern institutions or choices; its simple goal is to encourage you to think for yourself.

As I often hear Karen say to her children, "If you haven't seen it with your own eyes, or heard it with your own ears, then you have to assume it isn't true." Her teaching is to encourage her children to think independently, particularly in respect to gossip, but the idea behind the questions is to challenge always the "facts" that are presented around you. Her "gut" feeling guides her choices more ardently than a well-cited argument in the local newspaper, because she trusts her instincts to detect truth.

She has regained the power lost.

June 17, 2005 12:45 pm   (Book Session 17)

What an extraordinary day! The sun is bright and blue skies abound. The air is misty with a cooling breeze taking the edge off the intense heat. Breathe it in! Feel it all around you. I feel as good as the day. I am warm and sunny and filled with good cheer. There is nothing that can ruin this day.

Especially if I tune out the people on earth. Can't they just enjoy this day? It's such a perfect day – why do they fret so? Everything is a problem. Complaining all around. Oh, the interminable man-made suffering. What a bore!

When the world around them is aglow with magical nature and heavenly people all whispering their soft goodness ... hould they shout to be heard? Why can't people just be quiet for a little while to hear the soft sounds? The sounds of the whispering souls. The sounds of the peaceful earth sighing a hush of gladness.

The magic is all around you, if you just stop to listen.

You do not have to be lost in nature to commune with your soul. When you learn to hear the softness, you can commune with others. You will hear the soft and radiant sound of their soul songs, longing to be noticed, to be appreciated, to be heard. Just be quiet long enough to listen.

Some people need to listen to the quiet of a person lost before they can hear the soul song. Their absence carries their song long after they are gone. Through the whispering winds and the hollow rooms, the song is clear and undeniable. At that moment you understand the essence of the person gone. Why couldn't you hear it while they were alive? You would have been kinder, more patient, and braver. You would have had the courage to speak your truths, to share your personal ideas and beliefs and quiet quests.

Find your authentic self and share it with others. Everyone wants the moments of being touched by another, a moment when you know that they understand you.

The layers that mask the authentic self also prevent the real person-to-person moments. Presently, sadness and pain peel back the layers deeply enough to allow authentic human moments to occur, but society and individuals can learn to experience this bonding without pain.

[1:56 pm long break]

Camouflage, worn by troops to protect from the enemy. Why is it worn by civilians? Are all people enemies? Do you have to layer your soul in protective outer clothing to protect yourself from harm?

Until people learn to hear each other's soul songs, the camouflage deflects the unkind actions of others. In an attempt to protect the soul from being hurt, layers upon layers of camouflage hide the authentic self, the part that is most vulnerable to pain. Yet even with protection, the hurt penetrates. The camouflage only hides the pain; instead of keeping it out, it keeps it in.

As more and more people learn to understand the beauty of the essence of every person around them, then, and only then, will the camouflage be peeled away. And burned! For this en*light*enment cannot be returned to a state of darkness.

How can you start the process? Let me give you an example. Danielle learned an important lesson. Not one to despise many people, she was surprised at the depth of her anger towards an acquaintance who had wronged her. When, days later, she would be thrust into a situation with Lisa again, she felt dread. A friend suggested that Danielle simply greet Lisa with a smile and "How are you?" She did just that.

The surprise was the outcome. Lisa's face lit up and she smiled in return. She seemed relieved and Danielle could feel the negative energy between them fade. In that moment, she recognized Lisa's soul song. She understood that, as misguided as the woman's actions were, she was acting out of ignorance. Not only did Lisa lack awareness, but Danielle understood that her personality was camouflaged in a misguided attempt to get the attention or appreciation that she craved. Danielle realized that it was pitiable that Lisa could not feel loved without surrounding herself with drama.

There are two lessons that can be learned from this scenario. First, you can defuse your enemy by showing appreciation. It is hard, I know, but worth the challenge. As you witness your adversary stumbling to regain composure, you will actually be able to feel the energy between you lighten. Even if you have to fake your first action, the results are the same.

The second lesson is that all unkind acts by people are misguided attempts to get approval, recognition, acceptance, or love. When you realize this fact, acting kindly to your adversaries becomes less difficult.

Every unkind act can be boiled down to a simple insecurity, a feeling of being less worthy than others. Even the most maddening displays of pomposity and arrogance are slick camouflages for feelings of low self-esteem. Think of a bully/victim scenario. The bully lacks awareness about how to make others value or accept him for who he is, so he forces others to take notice by pushing others around. The victim releases energy which the bully picks up, deflating the victim and empowering the bully. The exchange of energy is measurable. Each act of cruelty between people results in the culprit extracting energy from the victim.

By being kind in return, the energy is restored to its proper owners.

The physical exchange of energy, if not properly restored, serves to increase the energy of the bully which had previously been depleted by others. A person not properly loved, energized, and respected as a child will develop methods to steal energy from another in an attempt to compensate for what was missing. Should others hear this person's soul song, the need to replace the lost energy would disappear. If the person is accepted, loved, and appreciated, he will no longer need to usurp power from others.

These absolutes vary infinitely from one person to another. One may be critically abused as a child and be fully restored through the understanding of one person, whereas another may be less severely harmed and require the unconditional love of many over long periods to become fully restored.

I can write volumes about the exchange of energy and the complications of the soul that ensue from a lack of proper unconditional love in one's life, but the important lesson is twofold:

> An unkind person is not acting unkindly for reasons directed personally at you. They are attempting to overcome a particular lack.

> You can help towards the restoration of a person's energy by acting kindly. Being willing to hear a person's soul song, or simply acknowledging that it exists, will assist you in this challenge.

Again, as more and more people acknowledge one another's soul songs, the camouflage will be discarded, layer by layer, until all authentic selves can shine through. As the collective human awareness spreads, *all* camouflage can be burned for there will be no need for war.

[3:09 pm]

June 19, 2005 11:25 am   (Book Session 18)

Perplexed by the bombardment of messages, the boy stared out the window and let his mind wander. Everybody was pulling him in different directions. His mother wanted him to hate his dad and his dad wanted him to move in with him. His grandparents had even gotten really weird. Sometimes he felt like he was a Gumby doll being stretched in every direction. He wished they would all just leave him alone. He gazed outside and remembered playing in his Radio Flyer. His dad would pull him in the wagon down to the ice cream store and they'd get doublescoops with chocolate sprinkles. He'd trail the wagon back, throwing anything he found worthy into it. And they'd race back home.

Sometimes they'd laugh and wrestle and throw a ball around. Mom would bring cookies outside and smile.

Now his life would never be the same. All his good days were memories and he hated the stupid grownups for ruining his life.

He got up, grabbed his jacket, and ran out the door to find his friends. It was the only place he felt normal anymore.

Who is listening to his soul song?

If the parents would just breathe deeply and think about him from his perspective, not as a pawn in their battle of hatred and revenge ... just take a deep breath and think. Look into his eyes. Remember something from their own childhood that brought them peaceful happy memories. Isn't Billy entitled to those feelings? Security, freedom, happy days lying in the grass pulling blades and watching the clouds?

Perhaps the parents never had their soul songs heard either and that's why they can't hear his. They tried and tried to get each other to hear their song, but they never could, and the marriage spiraled downward as each found other layers of camouflage to hide a misheard heart.

The parents who can't hear their children's songs were not likely heard as children themselves, but that can change. As an adult they can recognize the lack and replace it with honest love from those around them. If they hide beneath the camouflage, they muffle the sound of their song, but when they peer out from underneath it with a tender heart, others can hear the song and learn to love them for who they are.

Try looking at your life and your relationships. How honest are you with those you try to love? Can you see patterns of behavior that you and others use to avoid truth? Little dancing games where you avoid any real human connection for fear of getting your heart trampled on.

74

Let love in. Only when you feel love can you know what it is like to love another without playing games. To have your soul song heard is to let yourself hear another's.

If you fight, ask yourself why. Why am I angry? What is it that I really need? Do I feel unappreciated? Unloved? Misunderstood? Like a doormat? What is really going on here?

Every argument has a root. It is so simple to slip into a pattern established by all the previous arguments and allow this one to escalate, but it's so difficult to break the pattern, to determine the root of the pattern of behavior and stop it. Don't let the familiar cycle engulf you. Don't get trapped into interactions that are less worthy than the meaningful life you were intended to have.

Stop. Listen to your answers. Listen to your opponent. You'll be surprised to see how human, compassionate, and likeable he or she really is if you just listen. He is fighting his own unknown complex pattern. Fighting to be heard. Fighting to be recognized. Fighting to be appreciated. Every person in every fight has the same battle. They want to be understood. They want to be accepted. They want their soul songs to be heard.

It is that simple. Listen to the answers to your own questions and then take the time to listen to his. "What's really bothering you? Why are we fighting? What is it that we each really need? How is it that I feel, which leads to this type of fighting?"

Practice makes perfect. When practiced with one person, it becomes second nature with another. An astute mother instinctually understood this fact when she would make her young children stay together in a room until they worked out their fight. Instead of taking sides or listening to a blow-by-blow of the argument, she would tell them that they could not come out until they solved their problem. Sounds a little silly with one being only a two-year old, but it worked. She felt that their relationship was their responsibility to learn how to honor.

Sometimes they needed a little push or guidance, but they usually worked it out.

What would you do today if you knew that tomorrow was your last day on earth?

If you can settle into that mind-frame, you will understand how to hear your loved ones' soul songs. Let the idea of your impending passing envelop you and imagine how you would spend this day. Would you fight? Would you have any need to fight? No – all that would matter is the essence of you and the essence of those you love. You would feel them, hear them, touch them, and understand them like you have never done before. You would hear their soul songs.

Just like with other states of awareness, you could never become unaware again. Just imagine you then lived the next day and impending death was no longer a threat. The sounds of your loved ones' souls would remain with you. You would understand them and act more appropriately towards them, honoring their essence. And in return for your new actions, they would treat you more appropriately as well. The viscous cycle of negative behavioral patterns would be lost and replaced with a quiet, respectful, knowing, understanding of the importance of each other. And you don't need years of therapy to get there.

In school, humans don't pass a course when they receive an "F," yet they allow "failure" in their relationships. Relationships, which are more important priorities than any book learning, can be allowed to fail.

Public school education often teaches balancing a checkbook, basic cooking and sewing skills, how to use a computer, and so on. Students learn survival skills to allow them to live independently in the real world, but they never learn how to live in a real world of people. They are not taught how to make a relationship work, how to understand and respect another's needs, how to love in a healthy way that honors both parties.

The tide is turning. Programs are cropping up which attempt to teach tolerance and mediation, but more is necessary.

June 20, 2005 2:39 pm   (Book Session 19)

Respect yourself and respect others equally. This sentence is the basis for all harmonious and successful relationships. Establish a connection beneficial to all.

How do you learn to stop thinking of your needs first in a relationship? Tell the truth.

Telling the truth does not mean eliminating lying. It means, determine what you want and expect before an interaction, and clearly let the other person know during the conversation. In a land where intuition has taken a back seat to all other senses, how can you expect someone to read your mind? Give others the benefit of the doubt; they cannot possibly always know what it is that you want.

By speaking truthfully, you may not always get everything you desire, but you and your counterpart can clearly identify your goals and work towards them through compromise. Let's look at a work situation as an example. You ask for a day off and you are told "no." You are furious because you work hard and haven't had a day off in months.

How do you react? Do you go back to your department and complain, mope, and slow your work pace? This reaction is normal, but what if you tried to discuss your feelings instead? Say to your boss, "I understand that it's busy, but I haven't had time off in awhile and this is important. I have worked hard and accomplished so and so. Is there any way that we can work together to enable me to take this day? I can work through lunch or come in a little early if necessary. What do you suggest?"

In most cases, the immediate reaction of a superior is to stop and rethink her first reaction. Suddenly, listening to your intelligent debate, giving you the time off doesn't seem that unreasonable.

This situation does not imply that you should remain in a position where your needs are clearly never met, but in an ordinary work environment, compromises can be made and the needs of both parties can be met. It takes patience and understanding. Patience because the technique may be new and understanding because it is helpful to understand the other's perspective when approaching him with a request. By recognizing that the other party is a person with needs and concerns of his own, you can usually avoid one-sided edicts.

As a boss, you can use the same technique when addressing your staff. Assuming an employee is diligent, listen to his requests carefully before you make a rash decision. Mutual respect can help you avoid and eliminate all conflicts.

Respecting others' soul songs is not challenging once you practice. Even people you dislike behave in unlikable ways because of some needs in their life that haven't been met. When you approach a person who fits this description, try to remember that you are the one that is more aware of the nature of human behavior. You have a leg up! Use your awareness to your advantage by allowing the other party to be heard and accepted. Listen and you will find the underlying reason why the person is disagreeable.

The incentive to get along with your peers, your subordinates, and your managers at work is clear. You spend a lot of time there, you care about your success and the success of the company, and you enjoy having job security and opportunities for growth.

What is the incentive to work as diligently on the relationships you have at home? Unfortunately, many leave the best of themselves at the office and forget about the importance of building healthy relationships at home. It is not just important to hear your spouse and your parents, it is especially important to hear your children. Parents often take their leadership role, their parenting role, to mean that they are the dictators with all the knowledge. Or, contrarily, the trend is to allow the children to make most of the decisions.

Parenting takes work and thought. Think before you speak. Think before you react. Why is this matter important right now? What is best for everyone? Talking and listening calmly will often result in a mutually beneficial solution. When you *must* disappoint your child through your decision, explain why. "I'm not comfortable with you sleeping over someone else's where I don't know the family."

Being truthful helps them to accept your decisions. If you partner with them at an early age they will learn that you make your choices based on what is best for them, not to be mean or to punish or to control. As the decisions get weightier, you have a proven record of compromise and reasonableness that cannot be refuted. This means you learn to balance the "noes" with "yeses" when appropriate.

The essence of all relationship building strategies is, once again, understanding the fact that the other person has a soul song. Even if you cannot hear it, acknowledging that it exists helps you to be open-minded and compromising.

Unless you choose to work alone and live alone, learning to respect everyone's soul song benefits you as much as it benefits him or her! Your relationships will naturally become more harmonious and your cooperative attitude will send the message that you accept the other person. As you now know, acceptance is a prime motivator in all interactions and choices that people make.

Funny upside – people who know you will like you and they won't even realize why.

Establish the connection.

[4:37 pm]

In fact, all you do can be improved through the use of respect for others' soul songs. Your interaction with the cashier, the librarian, the gas attendant, the musicians, the media, the planter, the mechanic, the bosses can each be smoother, more pleasant, and more advantageous to you by demonstrating respect for their individual-ness.

Did you ever hear of the ripple effect? An act of kindness ripples waves, which get larger and larger as they move away from the original splash. When Cynthia's local grocery store shut down for renovations, she noticed a woman who was probably in her late eighties or early nineties walking her familiar route to the store. Busy at the moment with children loaded in the car, Cynthia paused to think about how the store closing would affect this woman.

She stopped the woman, introduced herself, explained the store closing, and offered to buy her groceries until it reopened. She wrote her number on a piece of paper and handed it to the woman. Now, in Cynthia's mind, it would not be an easy task to help with indefinitely, but she felt it was the right thing to do.

A few days later, Cynthia received a phone call from a neighbor on her block, Elise. Since she had just moved to the neighborhood, Cynthia and her family didn't know Elise or many neighbors. Elise called to thank Cynthia for the wonderful gesture that she had made for her grandmother, who lived in an apartment at Elise's house. She then invited Cynthia and her family to a party the following weekend, which they attended and met wonderful neighbors. Cynthia's children even met and played with kids that would be on their bus, making the new school and bus experiences much easier for them.

It turned out that Elise's grandmother knew the store was closed, was well taken care of but walked most days simply for exercise and to get out. She didn't need the help that Cynthia offered, but the mere act of offering led to a wonderful ripple effect for her and her family!

Stories such as this one are commonplace. When you respect others and show kindness, your kindness is rewarded immeasurably and in unexpected ways. This fact demonstrates how acknowledging others' soul songs benefits all.

Establish the connection, even for just a minute.

[5:04 pm]

June 21, 2005 2:18 pm   (Book Session 20)

Helpless Victim

Interestingly, many will read this book and believe that they are exempt from the law of attraction. They will convince themselves that their lives are different, that they didn't manifest the series of unfortunate events that regularly occur. "Yes, most people I know create their own reality, but me, I'm different. I am a helpless victim. How can I possibly want to have this chronic illness, or my kid taking drugs? I didn't ask to be hit by that car!"

The error in this thinking lies with the fact that you do not specifically *want* negative events to happen. They occur as a consequence of misguided beliefs. Your beliefs have continually been distorted by the distorted beliefs of those around you, especially in childhood. You did not choose to have your awareness contaminated. But now as an adult, you are suffering the consequences by attracting in events and circumstances and people that reinforce your new misguided beliefs.

Have you ever witnessed a parent being grotesquely overprotective of a child's safety? Hovering, shouting out "what ifs," and nearly suffocating the child's natural tendencies? This child, who was born with the ability to remain safe and happy, carefree and not fretful, learns that "life is dangerous." He begins to believe that injuries are common and expected and that he cannot rely on his own senses to guide his actions in avoiding pitfalls. When this child breaks his arm, is he to blame for attracting in the injury based on his beliefs? No. He has layers of padding over his innate senses that may have prevented the injury. Is his parent to blame? No. The parent is acting on his belief system, which has already been convoluted by others.

This example is simplistic and supposes a direct cause and effect between the parent's behavior and the broken arm. Although this chain of events may be the root, there are an infinite number of other variables that may have contributed to the injury. For example, the parent may not be demonstrative with affection. Suppose, typically, this same parent shows positive emotions to those injured or sick. In a subconscious effort to release those emotions to him when he may be feeling unloved or invisible, the boy attracts in a broken arm. The parent then affirms his own belief that the world is dangerous and injuries are likely, and also demonstrates affection to his son to his greatest capacity.

Once again, this occurrence is a simplified explanation of the possible causes for a person to attract a negative experience into his life, but it demonstrates how a person is not to blame for those events. Shedding the layers that corrupt one's belief system is the first step towards living a life that primarily attracts in positive events and people.

81

When you meet a hypochondriac and witness the maneuverings of the parent, it seems self-evident as to why the hypochondriac became the way he is. Finding the hidden cause of other limiting behaviors may be more challenging, but all non-happiness-producing circumstances are rooted in a faulty belief system.

When you examine your limiting beliefs, it is unnecessary to blame the person or persons responsible for leading you towards faulty beliefs. Remember that their beliefs were unduly corrupted as well. You should ultimately feel compassion since you understand how your layered beliefs adversely affected your life.

Becoming aware of your ability to attract in the circumstances of your life can be scary. You may go through a period when you are afraid of your hidden feelings. The good news is that you can begin, immediately, to alter your beliefs to begin to produce a lifestyle that you prefer.

Begin with simple problems or circumstances that irritate you. Ask yourself the interminable question, "Why do I need this (or him/her) in my life right now?" If you are willing to be honest with yourself, you will detect the truthful answer. When you hit upon the truth, you will recognize it.

At this time, I would like to direct those who would like additional information to read *Love, Medicine and Miracles*, by Dr. Bernie S. Siegel. This book wisely recognizes the connection between illness, or *dis*-ease, and a person's beliefs.

Every event and person that you attract in to your life serves a purpose. Did you ever notice that you were extremely close to someone, but somehow you drifted apart? Or perhaps you know someone whose company you enjoyed and suddenly spending time with him or her seemed burdensome. The reason for this universal phenomenon is that you attract in what you need based on the level of your personal awareness at any given moment. Sometimes the purpose is completed and you simply move on. At other times, you manifest your personal growth in awareness that the relationship provided the opportunity for and the other person stagnated. You needed to move on voluntarily while the other clung.

Ideally, in a relationship that you value, both parties will continue to grow in awareness and allow the other to do so as well. This ideal can be met more readily if each party is aware and responds to one another's soul songs.

The Law of Attraction as we describe it is an important component of the human's need for learning. As you know, life is about loving, creating, and learning, in that order. The learning comes from the events, people, and circumstances that you attract in. You can change the tendency of attracting in the negative to attracting in the positive by examining and altering your belief system.

A person unwilling or unable to learn a lesson that is presented will attract in more opportunities to learn. Examples are valuable sources of support. A young man we'll call Ted contracts leukemia. His father is an alcoholic whose level of dysfunction is severe and his mother attempts to compensate with extra compassion and displays of affection.

Ted's friends and neighbors are horrified by the news and by the deterioration of his condition. They rally around him, hosting fundraisers and offering endless support. Temporarily, his illness recedes. He, as well as his mother, enjoys the love that he receives from those around him while his father remains in his protective haze of alcohol.

Again, this scenario is simplified for illustration purposes, but it is a true story.

After years in the patterns of this family, Ted's illness was attracted in as an opportunity to help the family learn what is important. The family is at a crossroads. The father has an opportunity to realize the value of the members of his family and the joy that they bring him. He can opt to quit alcohol and *live*, or continue to drink and escape. There is always a choice.

No one realized the gift that this opportunity provided. The father was unable within his present level of awareness to learn the lesson and stop drinking. Instead, he used his son's illness as an excuse to escape further and his condition worsened. As his father drank more, and was unable to communicate his fears, hopes, and love to his son, Ted's conditioned worsened as well.

Was Ted to blame? Was the dad to blame? Was the mother to blame? The answer is no. Each of these people acted to the best of their ability with the level of awareness that they had at the moment. After Ted's passing, Ted understood instantly the purpose of his physical life and learned valuable lessons that expanded the level of awareness of his soul. During the balance of their lives, the parents will continue to learn lessons from the life of their son, but others may be disregarded. Upon their own deaths, they, too, will understand the purpose of their lives and that of their son's. As a result, the overall learning of their souls will increase dramatically, far more rapidly than if they had been unencumbered by his illness.

The lesson for the father is apparent. Love is the most important emotion or action on earth. A person who is unable to love himself is unable to love another effectively and will often choose some type of escape to avoid the lesson. The escape will be substance abuse, workaholism, illness, recklessness, busy-ness, or so on, but the most important element of human life will not be embraced: to love oneself and to love one another, or, in other words, to hear one's soul song.

Every person who is caught up in a cycle of escape and avoidance, of not allowing love, is given numerous opportunities to learn the lesson of the importance of listening to each other's soul songs. You probably know of people who have had a crisis that changed their lives. For example, think of one who survived a heart attack and changed their relationship with others as a consequence. The heart attack served as a wake-up call to the lesson that was learned. Another example is a person who suddenly and unexpectedly loses his job. Panic ensues and, during the recovery period, the person decides to take a risk and start his own business. The opportunity (the job loss) provided the vehicle for the man to live creatively and passionately as he would not have chosen otherwise. Assuming he did not love his job and felt trapped in the position, his change honors his soul song. He was given an opportunity to change his beliefs about job security and his new beliefs manifest new found success. And he is happier.

[4:48 pm]

June 22, 2005 12:00 pm   (Book Session 21)

Why do you think you can't have it all? A happy home, a career you love, an abundance of money? You knew you could have it all when you were born, but what happened since then?

Think about it. "Only the good die young." "Be careful what you wish for." These and other sayings reflect a superstitious attitude towards happiness that many harbor. When was the last time you saw some mother's back break when her child stepped on a crack? Maybe you jump over the crack sometimes for fun, but you don't really believe that your mother's back will crack if you step on it. Do you? Superstition taken too seriously can lead to obsessive and compulsive behavior. (Actually there are an infinite number of causes for this behavior, or "condition" as Americans term it.) Believing the silly sayings, which indicate that the good will soon turn bad, is another form of superstition that can lead to silly behavior.

By being skeptical about your "entitlement" to good or long-lasting happy feelings, you can actually send your "antennae" out in search for items to validate that nonsensical belief.

You were born on earth to be happy, loving, and prosperous. Decide now not to let anyone else's notions or beliefs contaminate the path that you are entitled to.

Life is meant to be fun, a JOY, full of pleasure and warm, happy feelings. Let that thought penetrate. Get it into your mind. Know it. Feel it. Do it. Feel happy. Free yourself of manmade encumbrances. Let your essence and ability to have joy shine through. If everyone else wants to sabotage their happiness, let them. But don't let them make you.

Free is the life of the Independent Thinker.

You have the freedom to reject silly ideas, ideas which have no basis in fact. Do not believe any adage without confirming it with your intuition!

Time for a momentary contradiction. I will give you an adage that you should memorize, even if you don't believe it, simply because it is true. The purpose of life is to love, create, and learn, in that order. There are no exceptions.

What time is it? Time to take your life into your own hands. Think, think, and then think some more. It doesn't cost you anything and it doesn't waste time. There is really no downside to thinking, but you have heard plenty of evidence about the downside of not thinking. Giving up your precious gift of reasoning is like going through life with a blindfold on. Or diving into a pool without water because someone says it is safe.

You would check that it was safe and within your best interest to jump or not jump, wouldn't you? Treat your whole life with that mindset. Listen, reason, evaluate, and allow your intuition to assist.

I, and my fellow entities, want you to be happy. When your positive vibrational energy increases, ours does too. Just as money as an economic commodity increases as it is circulated or spent, so does the vibrational level of others increase as another's increases. One popular idiom in your culture is that if you want to have a happy marriage, spend time with happily married people. Not only are positive life habits picked up through such an association, but the high vibrational level of the happy couples is also.

By surrounding yourself with others whose vibrational level is high, you can increase your own. And the reverse is true as well. When a child is chastised for "hanging around with the wrong crowd," what the parent doesn't realize is that the crowds' negative vibrational energy can actually reduce the member's energy. The parent is not simply protecting the child from harmful actions and attitudes, he or she is protecting the child from harmful negative energy.

As humans successfully comprehend and apply the principles behind "love, create, and learn," they will increase their positive vibrational energy as well as the positive vibrational energy of other humans and entities.

This point brings me to an interesting side note of which you should be aware. As I have explained, entities want humans to be happy and this fact is true of their loved ones and humans in general. For those of you who are experiencing grief, please know that your deceased loved one does not want you to be unduly sad. Although they recognize the need to express sadness, disappointment, or even anger, they also know that these emotions serve the purpose of allowing you to learn. Learn what you must, but then move on. Allow yourself to be happy once again.

Sometimes just by knowing that your loved one wants you to be happy is enough knowledge to allow you to move past any regret, guilt, or anger that may be cementing you to your grief. If you do not feel freedom in this understanding, then ask yourself why you need to cling to grief if the grieving seems excessive.

Since the matter of grief is such a powerful deterrent from human's ability to feel joy, I will elaborate on the factual process of death. When a person dies, he experiences a separation from the physical vehicle. This separation can occur long before the body ceases to function at the moment when the soul lets go. No soul lets go before it is ready. The lessons that the soul intended to learn were experienced regardless of the age of the individual. You may not know what the person's life intent was, but that is irrelevant. Upon the moment of death, the soul understood its purpose and peacefully and blissfully released the human body.

After death, or separation, souls embark on a journey of discovery. They reconnect with their essence and all the earthly masks and layers disintegrate. They are in their pure state, once again, one unencumbered by human challenges and misunderstandings. They also experience a brief evaluation period when their soul recognizes the lessons that were learned on earth and integrates the lessons into the awareness of the soul. Separation automatically induces a higher vibrational level for the soul as the lessons are integrated. Not all lessons were learned on earth; often the results of physical actions are apparent only after separation.

Nor are every soul's intended lessons the same. The soul chooses basic areas of growth that it wants to embark on before choosing a physical life and then pursues those lessons. When the job is over, it's over, whether earth beings are ready or not.

The important lesson for you, the earthling, to understand is not how this process works, but just that it does. When anyone dies, they are blissful, knowledgeable, vibrating at an extremely high level, much higher that you have ever experienced on earth, and they want you to be happy. They, your loved ones and all entities, want you to love, to create, and to learn. They want your life to be filled with joy and prosperity. They want your vibrational level to be as great as possible on earth in order that you may feel the level of total joy that we feel.

Suffice it to say that your language does not even contain language strong enough for me to explain how wonderful we feel. Your "orange" is a dull gray to us. The vividness of our spectrum exceeds your ability to grasp.

So if you want to honor your loved ones, enjoy the positive memories of their lives, be happy that you shared a physical existence together, and be joyful once again!

One more lesson: your loved one can communicate with you on some level. Most often, they communicate with humans through dreams, but other "signs" occur as well. Use your capacity to reason combined with your intuition to listen to their soul song across the realms. And let them know that you are okay.

Please do not cling excessively. Let them go. They have opportunities in our realm that are exciting and rewarding. They will hear your anguished pleas if you persist, but they truly just want you to be happy.

Since the first humans roamed the earth, there has been a natural curiosity about what happens after death. Thousands of theories and religions have cropped up to offer explanations. I will do my best to explain to you what does happen with the hope that you will better understand the purpose of your life.

Choosing a physical life on earth is only one of the many ways that a soul can grow in its awareness and vibrational level. The quest is universal: to reach higher and higher in the vibrational level or, in other words, to become happier and wiser and happier and wiser.

The ultimate goal is to vibrate as close to the vibrational goal of ALL THAT IS that is possible.

Growth can be accelerated through a new physical life or by attending schools of thought here in our realm. Entities with the vastest knowledge become master teachers and entities choose to learn under their tutelage. As the master teachers teach and the students learn, both entities' awareness and vibrational levels increases. Think of how excited Annie Sullivan was when Helen Keller understood the sign language symbol for "water." Not only did Helen's vibrational level increase, so did Annie's. Any time a human or an entity brings another to a higher level of awareness, both increase their vibrational energy.

Many Greats who walked the earth were master teachers. The powerful level of the vibration of their souls allowed them to increase the collective level of awareness of many on earth. They may have been askew from all true facts, but their message rang clear. They improved humanity by increasing their vibrational levels.

As I evaluate my most recent physical life, I am pleased that I caused millions to think independently. For that, I am grateful. The component of life that is most important, to hear one another's soul song or to recognize that it exists, escaped me. Although I practiced a degree of recognizing others' soul songs on earth, I was often judgmental, failing to comprehend the concept that every one is doing the best that they can within their present level of awareness. I do not "regret" my life's choices for I understand that I, too, did the best that I could on earth. And besides that, entities cannot feel regret!

Most Greats were not capable of teaching all three essential components in one lifetime. That task is overwhelming. I focused, unknowingly, on learning and creativity, in that order. And yes, I just implied that I was a Great. No false modesty here! The truth is that humbleness is not a trait that entities possess either; we are simply honest. According to my definition of a Great, I, as Ayn Rand, qualified.

For fear of leaving out someone that you recognize as having had the ability to teach all three key components of life, I will not list those few individuals who were capable of achieving the nearly impossible. Listen to your intuition. If harm was caused to another in the name of teaching, then rest assured that that individual not only was not one of those few who qualify, but he or she was not a Great at all. Greats innately know not to harm another.

Keep your eyes and ears attuned. Keep your intuition sharp, because there are Greats among you now who can change, for the better, the course of humanity. If you happen to meet one, tell them I said "hello" and please enjoy their company. But remember, too, that even Greats are not infallible. Use your gift of reasoning even with them!

To excite you further, I will tell you that there has never before been a moment in history when as many Greats inhabited the earth as there is today. During the next few decades, you will see a subtle shift in the ability for more and more individuals to think independently, the precursor for humanity to increase their collective awareness and vibrational levels.

You have been born into a very exciting era in history, one that will leave humanity better than was started. One more incentive to be happy!

June 23, 2005 11:20 am   (Book Session 22)

Hexagon Station: Six ways in and six ways out. Which way do you go and what do you do while you are in there?

Every decision you make has choices. When you are deciding, you are standing in Hexagon Station - the land of immobility. You can't do anything in the station but wait. And think. And choose. Eventually you pick a door and go through it. When you move, when you choose, you live. Choose and live. Choose to live. Life is not meant to be stagnant. Standing in the middle of the station, nothing ever changes. It's boring. Get up and move. What's the worst that could happen? Just pick a door and move through it.

90

Anthony Robbins is a worthwhile read for those of you who are stuck, stuck in the same job, same deleterious relationships, or stuck in the same frame of mind endlessly. Pick up a Tony Robbins book for the push you need to get unstuck. Life is not a spectator sport.

I want to revisit the notion of Greats walking the earth. It occurred to me that you would like me to mention at least one Triple Great that roamed the earth. A Triple Great is one who was able to raise the level of awareness and vibrational energy of humans on earth in all three critical areas: love, creativity, and learning. Abraham Lincoln was one such man. You may believe that the act of war, or his participation in the Civil War, brought harm to others and he is disqualified. This is not true. A person cannot be a Great when he or she intentionally brings harm to another. Lincoln's actions were in defense, not offense. He did not invade with the intention of others learning of his and his people's superiority. He understood that all humans were equal. The war cut him to the core, but he existed in an era when no option existed.

Lincoln was a simple man. He was a Great man. He was simply a Great man.

You understand his magnificent actions in the abolishment of slavery, but examine some of his lesser-known qualities. At a period in time when women were considered second class, Lincoln respected women as equals. His understanding of the existence of people's soul songs extended to all: blacks, whites, women, and Southerners.

Deaths of loved ones near to him prepared him to accept the casualties of war. Had he not experienced human grief to that level, he may not have been able to withstand the effects of war. Just as other Triple Greats needed to adjust their methods or their stance to effectively teach during the period that they walked the earth, Lincoln was forced to do the same.

Not only does earth have more Greats than ever before, but you also have the most Triple Greats that ever lived at one time.

At the time of this writing, June 23, 2005, one presently lives in Taiwan. I will not name names ... I trust your judgment and intuition to determine who the person is. It may take decades for you to complete your determination, but you can do it. Look for someone who heightens the collective awareness of people in the areas of love, creativity, and learning.

You, if residing in the United States, also have Triple Greats living closer to home. Enjoy the opportunity, as it is a rare one.

Now back to Hexagon Station.

If you are stuck, get unstuck. Pick one small action and take it, whether it's making a phone call, sending an email, researching possibilities, or looking over a course catalog. It only takes one small action to have your momentum shift. By placing your energy behind one action, you shift your future thoughts and energy in that direction.

After your one small step, take another. Then another. Go slowly at first and you will realize that movement and direction is not that scary. Stagnation is scary! As you act, you will well up with pride, for a single action can change your life for the better. There is a ton of support available to you. Just look for it at your local library or on the Internet. You will find what you need.

Whichever door you choose in Hexagon Station, you can discover a happier world and a better life. Just make the decision to open the door.

Can you name a Great who lived in Hexagon Station? Can you name someone you admire who lives in Hexagon Station? People often pause there to catch their breaths or to recuperate from excitement, but they move on if they choose to live.

[long pause 1:08 pm]

Standards. Raising your standards.

Religion and law are founded upon the principle that people will not do the right thing given the choice. Laws regulate nearly every human behavior, reflecting what society considers acceptable at any particular time in history. Religion offers tenets which must be obeyed to avoid

"Hell" or some other dire consequence. As a fortuitous reward for the religious leaders and the lawmakers, they could control the people. And they still do, under the guise of what's best for everybody.

Over a long, long, long period of time, humanity can become self-governing by increasing the collective level of awareness until all understand the existence of others' soul songs. In the meantime, it is somewhat beneficial for humans to have external guidance as to what is and isn't acceptable and, for many, laws and religion fulfill that purpose.

Now is the time for you to privately evaluate your standards or your "morals," as civilization likes to refer to it. What behaviors are you willing to accept in yourself? What behaviors will you not accept? Which actions will you avoid because they are illegal and you fear reprisal? Which actions will you avoid because they *feel* wrong? Which actions will you avoid because you fear repercussions through your religious beliefs? Which actions will you take to win approval in your belief system of worship?

Take some time to seriously think about the answers to these questions. Your evaluation is private and no one need know your responses. The importance of this exercise is for you to self-determine what your personal code of *right vs. wrong* is.

Here are sample questions to help you think with breadth in this area:

- Would you kill someone? Stab someone? Hit someone? When? Why?
- Would you insult someone? Disregard someone in need? Act meanly towards a family member? When? Why?
- Would you dump garbage in an empty lot or park? Would you throw a wrapper out the car window? A cigarette butt? Would you empty your ashtray in the parking lot? When? Why?
- Would you lie? When? Why?
- Would you steal? Would you cheat on your taxes? When? Why?
- Do you return phone calls or not? Respond to invitations or not? When? Why?

Are you guilty of little non-victim infractions? Have you committed illegal acts? Have you committed sins? Can you feel your energy level

93

dip when you contemplate these three questions? That is because they imply judgment. Ignore judgment in this exercise. Try to think honestly about where you draw your personal lines in conduct for your own reference regardless of laws, mores, religious beliefs, or external opinions.

Then raise your standards. Every time you behave in a way that is more beneficial towards neighbors and nature than you would normally behave, you increase your vibrational level. You control this method of making yourself happier. For example, if you would normally step over an empty water bottle on the field, pick it up and toss it out. You will feel pride.

If your cashier is slow and you find him irritating, smile and be nice anyway. You will feel proud.

Keep challenging yourself to raise your standards. Most people believe that if there is no consequence for a less-than-kind-action, then there is no harm done. The harm is done to your vibrational level and, therefore, to the vibrational level of those around you. The more you can increase your level of vibration, the more you will increase your level of awareness and of your happiness. Such a simple way to become happier.

Perhaps in speaking to your husband this evening you uncharacteristically initiate a friendly, supportive, and compassionate conversation. Don't allow him to shift the conversation back to a normal negative encounter; keep your strength up and persist. After a few interactions like this one, your relationship will grow and reconnect. Your vibrational level and his will increase. And you might even hear his soul song along the way. Be nice.

There are additional benefits to raising your standards. You model exemplary behavior for others who may catch the bug. You will accumulate days, then weeks, then months and years in which you have no regret. Everyone has regret or has made mistakes. By raising your standards and acting accordingly, you will live from this moment on without additional remorse or regret. That is a peaceful, happy way to live. Then let the rest of your past [negative actions] go.

When all of humanity raises their standards and their level of awareness and vibration, laws will not be necessary. Think about what else will not be necessary.

[1:54pm]

June 24, 2005 3:22 pm   (Book Session 23)

Memories are a collection of simulated probabilities that occurred. Think of them as a collection of experiments which shows outcomes depending on the simulated events, people, and situations that were used. The object of an experiment is to learn, just as you are to learn from your experiments called memories. Not all your memories will be positive, just as not all experiments have favorable results, yet you can learn from each.

Since the objective of reading this book is to become a happier person, you will learn to distance yourself from your negative memories and enhance the outcome of the positive ones. As you learn these techniques, you will rid yourself of the guilt and regrets that impede your ability to feel joy today.

Everyone makes mistakes, some grievous. If you had to choose, you would not make those mistakes again. That means you learned. The mistakes served a purpose by allowing your soul to become more aware. Let it serve its purpose by learning the lesson and letting go of the negative aspects of your memories.

One way to accomplish this goal is by exercising your freedom to control your thinking. As long as you are certain you extracted the valuable lessons that you needed to from your experience, then start to control your thoughts about them.

Visualize the object or scene of your embittered memory as very large and possibly loud. With your eyes closed, picture the scene decreasing in size until it is so tiny, you can barely see it. Imagine you are taking off in an airplane. See how the objects on the ground get smaller and smaller? That is what will happen to the scene in your memory – it will fade in size until it is barely noticeable.

Then IMMEDIATELY turn your attention to a positive memory. Think about a wonderful vacation, an accolade, or a special person. Think about something that makes you incredibly happy and focus on that memory for a long while.

As I told you, there is an easy way to measure the energy you emit. When you are experiencing a negative memory, your energy has a pattern opposite to that of when you are happy. Some people, those in touch with their intuitive sense, can detect the energy and the change in energy without any tools.[2] The detection of this energy, positive or negative, accounts primarily for why you sometimes instantly dislike or like a person. Your intuition is either picking up on the energy that they emit, or you intuition is experiencing a previous encounter with this person from another lifetime.

Souls travel together. It is very common for you to meet again those from a previous life. The reason is that the souls are drawn together by a similar vibrational level in strength and pattern. When born into another life, the energies attract one another towards each other again.

Throughout your lifetime, the people who you bond with most readily, those who you are most comfortable with or feel connected to, likely have a similar vibrational level as you. Others, who your self intuitively repels, even a member of your own family, likely have great variations in their vibrational patterns and strength. It is vital to recognize that those you feel repelled by still have soul songs. Even though their energy is different than yours, that does not mean that one of you is "better" than the other, simply different in the energy emitted.

People who commit egregious acts are still people with soul songs and their own vibrational energy. The masks and layers that piled up on them throughout their lives hid their pure soul so deeply that the soul song is nearly undetectable. There is no such thing as a "bad" person or a "good" person. Every soul is born in a pure state of bliss awaiting

---

[2] [Email energy@TheAnswersUnlimited.com for details about how to detect the energy you emit when you are thinking of a happy moment versus when you are thinking of an unhappy moment.]

life's layers. Some are fortunate to have few layers and masks thrust upon them, while others are so severely assaulted with layers that negative behavior appears at a young age.

And every person has the ability to shed the layers at any moment. With approval, recognition, appreciation, and unconditional love, even the hardest-worn layers can be chiseled away. No one is beyond help. It is just the incorrect help that prevents the layers from shedding.

I make this point for two reasons. Obviously, the penal system is incapable of assisting wrongdoers in removing the damaging layers. In humans' collective state of awareness, removing offenders from offending again may be necessary. A rare person imprisoned is capable of removing the layers independently and, without knowing why, the parole board senses the change and may release the offender. When this occurs, the best possible outcome in your terms has occurred. It is more likely, however, that the offender cannot unmask the soul song independently and, to make matters worse, the conditions of prison actually increase the layers, worsening an already sad state.

Remember that the third most important factor in life's game is to learn. A criminal act, with or without penalty, accelerates the learning process. For those who do not learn the lessons on earth, they will reconcile or integrate the lessons after death. But the lessons will be learned. The lessons will usually teach a soul the importance of each and every person's soul song. He or she will understand the impact that his or her actions had upon every affected individual.

As the lessons are integrated in the evaluation-after-death period, the soul grows in awareness and vibrational energy.

Awakening after death precipitated by abusive actions on earth is the most challenging way to grow in energy. Just as you are capable on earth of growing in awareness through positive experiences instead of negative ones, the departed soul is encumbered by the negativity of the past actions and appreciates and recognizes the beauty and ease of learning through positive experiences. The consequence to the soul after separation from the physical body is that an unresolved negative action may take longer to integrate than the positive ones. Those experiences carry a great weight of learning and their weightiness usually take longer to integrate.

After the integration period, a soul is able to reach its high state of pure bliss. The extent of the blissful feelings experienced will be determined by the intensity and pattern of the soul's energy, but in every case the bliss will be greater than the previous time that the soul was in the energy realm. To rephrase that concept, regardless of what vibrational level you are on at any given moment, your vibrational level will be greater after integration than it was before you were born.

Most of the information that you just read is new to you and the concepts are challenging. I will restate some key ideas as simply as I can. The purpose of a soul is to grow in awareness, thus to vibrate on a stronger and stronger level. A soul in the energy realm, where I am, enjoys the great feelings of a high, intense vibrational level and aims to continuously increase that wonderful feeling. One way that the level can be increased is by choosing a physical life on earth.

On earth the soul's only purpose is to love, create, and learn, in that order. Masks and layers unwittingly hide the soul's intent; the more layers, the more hidden the intent becomes.

Upon death, or separation, the newly departed souls experience an evaluation period when they integrate the lessons learned during the lifetime as well as the lessons postponed until death. Those souls with lessons ignored on earth will experience a longer period of integration than souls who learned the lessons while on earth. As a consequence, the state of bliss that will be experienced is delayed until the integration is complete.

Through this process, start to finish, birth through separation, the soul grows. After each lifetime, a soul always vibrates at a higher level than before the lifetime, which is one reason souls choose physical life.

If you want to maximize your state of bliss after separation, then do your best to learn the lessons that you were intended to learn on earth. Further, have more fun, lighten up, enjoy your freedom, and love, love, love, and love some more.

98

Remember, also, that since "to love" and "to create" rank higher than "to learn" as the purpose of human life, you will experience the greatest surges in your vibrational level, *therefore your happiness*, when you LOVE and when you CREATE!

Quite frankly, by recognizing and respecting that every person has a soul song you will increase your eternal level of vibration far greater than any single accomplishment that you can achieve. Not only will your bliss be greater in my realm, but you will experience more happiness while on earth.

Those who know Karen understand that, although she dislikes some people (she's only human after all), she has a tremendous capacity to understand that every person on earth is doing the best that they can within their present level of awareness. What she did not realize until recently is that she can be free of judgement of other people because she senses that everyone has a soul song.

It is noteworthy as well, that recognizing the existence of others' soul songs does not mean that you become a self-sacrificing, timid, withering, people-pleaser. Becoming a doormat or aiding others for no personal gain is not a worthy pursuit. Even if the gain is that you *feel* good about yourself by helping, then that is beneficial. However, if the incentive is merely to adopt an attitude of martyrdom expecting others to praise and exalt you, then your actions will not serve the purpose of increasing your level of vibration. If you are to grow in awareness from these actions, you may have to wait until after separation for the lesson to be learned. But the upside is someone got helped along the way and if you want to help someone while seeking growth in awareness, then good for them!

Although the material that you have just read will take time to understand, digest, and absorb, I do want to add an addendum. If you lose a loved one whom you did not adequately demonstrate your feelings of love for while the person was on earth, you can still send the love after separation. Do not dwell on this issue. Simply tell your loved one that you love him or her. Say it aloud. They will understand and you will feel better. Remember, entities do not have the capacity to pass judgment; therefore, they cannot feel angry or remorseful towards anything that you did or did not do while on earth. By letting them know that you love them, you are merely assisting both of you in moving towards your next moment of joy.

As I said, do not dwell on this issue. Your loved ones have a much greater awareness of the causes for all happenings on earth than you do, and those happenings are far less significant than you believe. Feel peaceful and let regret go. Your loved ones do not benefit from your regret and neither do you.

[5:15 pm]

June 25, 2005 12:53 pm   (Book Session 24)

Freedom rings true.

After the party, think about what you've done. Did you enjoy yourself? Did you drink too much? Did you have any meaningful conversations with anyone new? Did you get excited about a new idea or adventure? Unless you're in the singles market, chances are you did not make any meaningful new connections. You likely did not meet someone who you will see again.

Why is it so hard to make connections that enhance the quality of your life? Kids seem to meet new people all the time, but adults are guarded. They regularly pass the time with new people without making contact again.

Now imagine being on a deserted island. Are you happy to be alone? All your worries are far behind and there's plenty to eat. Doesn't it feel great to be away from all the annoying people? No one to answer to; no one to ask permission of; no one whose needs come before yours. What a relief!

How long do you think you could enjoy that life? A day? A week? A year? Would you miss the touch of another person? Would you miss certain people, but not others? Would you miss people in general to laugh with, talk with, play with, or dream with?

Now imagine that six years of aloneness have passed. You have played every imaginable game of solitaire and even invented some new ones. You haven't spoken a word in years because there is no one to speak to. You do not think that you will ever be rescued and those who knew you have likely moved on by now.

Then suddenly a rescue plane lands and takes you back home!

After a good shower and meal, how do you feel? Do you think you will ever think the same about people again? Will you be more tolerant? More eager to meet new people and make connections? Isolation has a way of awakening you towards the preciousness of other people. How can this lesson be learned without living on a secluded island for a period of time?

If your purpose on earth is to love, create, and learn, then it seems self-evident that you should value people. In your culture, there have been many advances that have improved humanity's collective awareness, but one change risks adversely affecting the human experience. There is a trend which is causing a decrease in neighborliness and community. Individuals are more focused on their individual and familial needs than in the past. The effect is less closeness or less appreciation for neighbors.

As people became increasingly mobile, their roots become shallower. Gone are the days of barn raisings, community picnics, and helping one another selflessly. Mobility is not to blame. A strong community welcomes new members. It is the attitude of self-pursuit that is at the core of the problem.

As connections become less rooted, and friendships and families become more fleeting, humanity as a whole will seek ways to reconnect. Presently the trend in America is to create community through strife, not through joyful traditions of the past. For example, as each new couple wed, communities would gather for days in celebration. Each family contributed food and wares, easing the burden of any one family. The festivities were joyous and anticipated with glee.

Communities celebrated life in ways that were not connected to a newlywed couple's beginning as well. They hosted harvest festivals and spring cotillions, hoe-downs, and quilting bees. Although passages are still marked with celebration in modern society, the connection and bonding experienced has lessened.

[long break, probably 45 min.]

When was the last time you brought over a bushel of peaches to your neighbor, or shoveled his walk because you could and he couldn't? When was the last time you sat on your front porch enjoying mint juleps with your neighbors?

All is not lost. Many still live in a neighborly way that encourages connection, but increasingly, community bonding comes in the form of tragedy. The death of young people brings hundreds or thousands to funeral homes. Some are so severely shaken from their state of introspection that they bring meals to the family in loss or host fundraisers. People let their masks fall off during these times. Their souls songs shine through and they connect on a human level rarely experienced.

The ripples of compassion are felt long and far. Suddenly, fences are mended and people forgive one another in earnest. They feel the tightening of human bonds with their neighbors, loved ones, and those in loss.

These tragedies heighten the community's awareness and therefore, strangely enough, heighten their vibrational level. This same result could be reached through positive events if people would allow themselves to open up to human contact, to willingly discard their masks and permit authentic interaction with one another.

What can you do? First, find your authentic self and share it with others. Turn off your cell phone on line in the grocery store and converse pleasantly with others instead. Join or start groups where your passion lies and actively participate in the groups you do belong to. Recognize common bonds. Don't all homeowners' associations have the common bond of wanting a beautiful community at a low cost? Recognize and build upon the commonalties instead of focusing in battle on the differences. Understand that all people are doing the best that they can at their present level of awareness and work towards understanding the existence of their soul songs.

By attuning to others' soul songs, you can almost intuitively know best how to interact with them. Some people really need to be left alone at times, whereas others crave interaction.

Share yourself and honor the soul song of others.

[3:51 pm]

June 26, 2005 7:30 pm   (Book Session 25)

Change. I love that word! It conjures equal feelings of positive and negative. It always incites a reaction, one for those resistant, and a different one for those in favor. A very strong and powerful word, "change."

Why can't you? Change – that is. Why can't you change? What is holding you back? Fear, inertia, baggage, familiarity? What makes you stuck like glue to the way things are?

Can you imagine, even people in reprehensible conditions would often prefer to stay than to risk the unknown of change. Why does a woman stay within an abusive relationship? Why does someone remain in a clearly dead-end job? Why do college students subconsciously try to stretch the experience to five years? People would rather deal with the known than the unknown in most circumstances.

One of the best human explanations for this trait that I have come across is Tony Robbins' version of pain verses pleasure. Humans are motivated by two factors: the avoidance of pain and the pursuit of pleasure. These two factors compete for attention, with the stronger winning the battle. For example, if a smoker considers quitting, he subconsciously evaluates which feeling will be stronger, the pain from not having cigarettes, or the pleasure from not smoking. If he enjoys smoking as an excuse to exit social situations, he will add this loss to the pain of overcoming the physical and emotional addiction. Next, he will evaluate the pleasure he will receive from quitting: perhaps a longer life, the ability to breathe more freely, the potential of a new job that doesn't allow smoking on the campus. Unknowingly, he will weigh the strength of each outcome and choose the path that brings the greater of the two: avoidance of pain or the attainment of pleasure.

Understanding this principle allows you to leverage your success by putting more in the pleasure column of evaluation than in the pain column.

Make a two column list. Write "Attain Pleasure" and "Avoid Pain" on the top of the columns.

List everything you can possibly imagine that goes under each heading. Keep thinking and writing until you've exhausted your possibilities.

Then rip up the "pain" half and throw it away. Do it. Don't just think it – DO IT! Carry around your "pleasure" half and read it often. Read it aloud; read it before you go to bed. Write it on your bathroom mirror and on your desktop. Think about it when you get a chance. Make the list your single-minded purpose.

As you read and reread the list, let the feelings grow and take hold of you. Let them permeate your senses. Feel the pleasure. Look forward to the pleasure. Picture yourself enjoying the pleasure. If you practice this exercise diligently, you will leverage your success. Suddenly, the old habit or negative pattern will seem completely unacceptable.

This method works. But I can't make you do it. If you want to change, if any part of you wants to change, you must make the effort.

If you can't do it for yourself, then do it for humanity. Remember, your increase in vibrational energy increases the energy of those around you!

Let me take a moment to comment on the fact that I have now recognized Tony Robbins' success twice in this book. He has supporters and he has those who believe he is a quack. The latter are living on a lower vibrational level than the former. Their awareness level is simply not as advanced as those who sense Robbins is benefiting humans. Some dislike Mr. Robbins because they are in the public health field and must hold on to their belief system about change being an arduous process with extensive evaluation. These individuals, when faced with information contrary to their belief system, must reject the information (or bearer of the information) in order to continue to operate within their long held beliefs. Interestingly, aren't they hesitant to change or to consider change?

The truth is that Anthony Robbins is increasing the collective awareness of many humans, thus fulfilling the soul's intent of increasing the vibrational level of humanity. Further, he is focusing on teaching people, in a creative way, to love themselves. To rephrase, people are creatively learning to love.

[8:59pm]

June 27, 2005 12:48 pm   (Book Session 26)
Jordan, Michael.

What did he do for the sport of basketball? He brought excitement, magic, pulse, and energy. He introduced the sport to a whole new generation of fans. He became an idol and role model for boys looking for a mentor. He showed young people that dreams can come alive, that hard work and determination and confidence can help you carve out a great life. Jordan learns from his mistakes and integrates the lessons while maintaining his integrity.

Perhaps you are not "great" at any one particular skill, breaking records and pursuing a passion with unrelenting vigor. But you can be "great" to the people you come in contact with.

Here's a true story, one similar to a situation you have probably witnessed in your own life. Two first-grade teachers retire. One was basically nasty throughout her tenure. The other was passionate, inspired, and most importantly, listened, as best she could, to her students' soul songs. On the day of the year-end festivities, Teacher "C" for "Clueless" did not receive a retirement send off or acknowledgement. At the same event a few yards away, Mrs. "G" for "Got it" was surrounded by gifts and homemade goodies from those who understood her contribution. She received letters from former students and parents from years earlier. The show of affection for her was sincere and heartfelt, yet the stark contrast between the two teachers' last day was almost painful to witness.

There are several lessons to this story. First, Mrs. C thought she did a good job. She thought she was well-liked and, as sad as it seems, she did the best she could at her level of awareness. She was now at a crossroads. Facing retirement may be daunting enough, but now she also had to face the critical shortcomings that she had as a teacher. The opportunity, as painful as it was, gave her two choices. She could do some self-evaluation to determine the difference, or she could make a flippant excuse to herself to explain the unjust outcome.

I won't tell you what she did; I'll leave the ending to your imagination.

If you are faced with a challenge such as Mrs. C's, you will integrate the lesson one way or another for the growth of your soul. The hope of entities is that you will integrate while inhabiting your physical body for several reasons. First, your vibrational energy will increase, thus increasing the vibrational energy of those around you. Second, each new step to a new level of awareness remains fixed. You cannot unlearn an awareness. Third, you are opened to the opportunity to modify an unaware behavior in all your future encounters, thus having the wonderful gift of improving your vibrational energy and that of others on earth.

Take your lessons and integrate them. Then decide to vibrate on a stronger level through positive actions.

The situation with the two teachers can be witnessed in any profession or any neighborhood or any family. Examine two doctors, for example, one abrupt and distant, another friendly and compassionate. Think about two different families moving in your neighborhood. Now picture the different send-offs they each receive. Some are welcome to go, whereas others are welcome to stay. Which teacher, doctor, or neighbor do you want to be? Let your authentic self shine through and be the one that others admire, respect, and love.

The choice is yours. You can be the Michael Jordan of your profession, your neighborhood, and your family, or you can be the Tex Reed, forgettable.

Stimulate Growth

I and my compadres have given you numerous reasons to evaluate and improve your ability to love, create, and learn. Now let me give you one more: You alone are responsible for your life. If you turn ninety and look back with remorse or regret, you are the only one responsible. Just as I implore you to honor the responsibility of having the gift of reason, I also implore you to take the responsibility for the development of your life seriously as well. Make your life on earth count. Make it important. Make it worthwhile. You need not touch the lives of thousands or even dozens to make it count. Just be the best person that you are capable of being.

Relatively few people try or succeed at that goal. As the messages in this book and other similar venues reach more and more people, the numbers will increase.

Economic Development

You have nothing to lose and everything to gain by following the prescription for happiness outlaid in this book. As one additional incentive, let me explain to you the theory of abundance. Since few on earth do not wish to increase their material wealth, know that you can increase yours by completing the exercises contained herein. You can utilize what you've learned about your antennae to your advantage in seeking and attracting wealth. The law of abundance postulates that an increase in abundance creates more abundance. Just as Bill Gates' genius has turned into a multitude of ripples in economic growth, so does growth in abundance for you increase the abundance for others. Abundance is not finite, nor should it be feared. Money and material wealth grow, individually and aggregately.

Forget vows of poverty, or envy and disgust for those who seemingly have more than you. Their success does not increase the probability of your failure. According to the accurate law of abundance, their success actually increases the likelihood of yours.

Let's examine "corporate greed" as many enjoy terming it. As we saw through the example of Microsoft, their abundance has a tremendous ripple effect creating opportunity, wealth, and abundance exponentially.

Now consider other corporations that earnestly create goods and services. Provided that they are not a monopoly, which has its own set of rules, the corporation will profit to the extent that people are willing through the free enterprise system. If people are willing to purchase a good at the prices that are being collected, then the demand exists at that rate. If the goods are priced too high, then demand will decrease until it reaches a level that triggers a market correction. The company chooses to decrease production, thus decreasing supply, reduce its price, or leave the market. The free enterprise system enables all to succeed at the level that the consumer is willing to commit.

As I continue with my scenario, I would like to preface the balance with a remark. This example as a support for my conclusion assumes that dishonest measures of bribery, theft, embezzlement, and fraud do not take place.

Think about the owners, creators, or contributors of successful companies. Their income is frequently dependent on specific indicators of financial success. The premise behind bonuses is to act as incentive for the members to be as creative in the pursuit of corporate success as they are able and to be rewarded for that creativity. If the members are rewarded financially, doesn't that indicate that the company has prospered? When a company prospers, think about all the economic ripples it creates, not just for the suppliers and through the employees' paychecks. Growth means larger facilities, more taxes incurred, additional rent or purchase of real estate, more consumption of supplies, more need for landscaper and janitorial services. The list goes on and on.

Now peek at the pay which the members received as bonuses. What happens to those funds? They are used to increase purchases, pay for education, consume more goods and services. They are also used for additional savings and investments. Investments stimulate the economy further and savings are then used by lending institutions to support loans, which in turn enter into the economic corridor as well.

What is the downside? Growth helps everyone.

With the basis of the free enterprise system understood, let's look at the law of abundance in effect in a way that you may not have imagined.

Let's assume that two companies manufacture and sell Wompits. Company C enjoys profits and squirrels them away, paying the employees the minimal amount necessary to keep people working. Company G enjoys profits and shares them, literally and figuratively, with the employees. The employees feel appreciated and value the company. They feel connected to the success of the firm. Their passion for Company G induces their peak performance and maximum expenditure of creativity. As a result of the abundance of good energy and wealth, the company prospers beyond the level of Company C.

Company C employees feel unappreciated and undervalued. The company plugs along, but the atmosphere is one of lack, not abundance. There exists no passion or incentive to create greater prosperity. The minimum output necessary for the firm to remain competitive and viable will be expended.

Back to Company G. The amount of abundance shared with the employees is actually less than the amount that Company C hoarded from profits. And to make matters worse, the disparity between personal fortunes will continue to grow in this model, as the cycle of growth, attracting abundance, sharing abundance, and increasing productivity continues for Company G.

The moral of the story is that even though profitable companies increase economic growth in ripples, profitability combined with an atmosphere of sharing and appreciation will attract in more abundance, therefore greater benefits for all involved.

By listening to the soul songs of employees, companies realize better profits. And that is a fact.

[3:32 pm]

June 28, 2005 6:40 pm   (Book Session 27)

Strategies exist for overcoming just about any malady or uncertainty that you can imagine. Volumes have been written about every illness, dysfunction, or mishap that can occur. You can read about them, seek opinions, and learn all you can, but in the end, the decision is yours. What strategy do you use?

The best and most certain remedy is to eliminate the challenge before it occurs, similar in theory to preventive medicine. Stay healthy through well-care and stay happy through malady avoidance. The choice is and always has been yours.

We, the entities and I, are not suggesting that you stay in Hexagon Square. There you may avoid challenges, but you will ultimately whither away and die … of boredom if nothing else. What we are suggesting is that you take matters into your own hand, literally.

Your stage has been created by your thoughts and the thoughts of others. All physical properties have been "agreed upon" throughout history and by millions of people. A bear is a bear and not a whale. A sunny sky is blue; a cloudy, grey or white. They have all been created with such conviction that they would take centuries and centuries to change, and only if the change was thought up, or "agreed upon," by millions. This concept exceeds the scope of this book but I will use it to illustrate a point. For those of you who require or desire additional information regarding the creation of the physical properties of the world around you, please read *The Seth Material* and series of related books.

Within the "agreement" of physical properties there exists certain "laws." One which you are familiar with is the law of gravity. In this section you will learn how to change the physical manifestation of the reality around you up to the point of these laws. For example, if you have an addiction, you can change that. If you have high body fat, you can reduce it. But you cannot exceed the physical limits that the "laws" have set forth. For example, you can overcome a systemic illness, but you cannot grow back a limb. You can soften the appearance of your face, but you can't restructure it. Not during this lifetime, anyway, without the use of surgical alterations.

110

Other than those "laws," you can change anything or transport yourself behind the expected limitations. Before I continue, let me tell you, or remind you for those who already understand, that time and space are not laws. A physical life must play out in an imaginary space and time in order to allow the realm of growth that a physical existence is capable of. Only those with advanced knowledge of physics can understand the scientific explanation for time and space as you know it.

Hundreds of studies or reportings have cited examples of people "transcending" space and time. Most accidentally stumbled across their ability to enable the mind to leave the physical attachment of the body, yet others intentionally sought for the controlled separation to occur. As a reminder to stimulate your curiosity, please research the findings of Edgar Cayce in addition to well-documented experiences in remote viewing and past-life regression.

All knowledge is available to all people at any given time, as long as the individual knows how to "tap into" it or seek it. Edgar Cayce's prolific body of work confirms and validates this fact and, thanks to the diligence of his protégée, the value of his discoveries is still accessible through the Association for Research and Enlightenment (A.R.E.).

Did you ever notice how some people seem to have mini-crises all the time? The car breaks down, sewer backs up, and the like, while others seem to enjoy relatively crisis-free lives? Usually unknowingly, the latter have manifested a problem-free existence though their belief system. Sure, everyone, even the most aware souls on earth, has occasional mishaps, but there are many who live from trouble to trouble. And when a crisis passes, they half-heartedly expect the next one to be around the corner.

[8:16 pm]

July 1, 2005 2:54 pm   (Book Session 28)

Ponder this point. In the nearest three galaxies to yours, no life remotely resembling yours has been discovered. Does that mean that none exists? Some of you wish they did and others wish they didn't. Yet, universally, almost everyone has a slight or strong inclination that the possibility exists.

What do you think?

Even a slight glimmer of curiosity or belief indicates your open-mindedness. Please apply that happy curiosity to the reading of this book. Doubt is healthy, but a closed mind shortchanges you of enlightening life experiences.

What I'm about to say may sound crazy ... but keep an open mind. Throughout the course of your physical life, you regularly travel away from your physical body to different places and times. Previously, I have hinted at the power of the dream experience, but now I will tell you that dreams are far more potent than you may have imagined.

As you develop your dream log, you will also develop your ability to steer your dreams toward positive life issue resolution. In some cases, you may regress to a past life era and learn a practical strategy from what you witnessed. Your experiences in your dreams are as real as your "real" life and far more capable of accurately depicting reality. During the dream state you are actually separating from your physical body and exploring other possible realities. The movie-like scenes that you view are actual experiences that fragments of yourself are engaged in, either now or in another time. These movies are visual pictorials of "other" lives, depicted in symbols that your present self can understand. The symbology of dream-life is complex and beyond the scope of this book, but you should know that symbols chosen are uniquely selected for your interpretation. A book is not a book. A book is a representation of the belief that you associate with books. If you are excited and intrigued by books, then it may represent the coming of a grand adventure. The dream may be predicting that you are at the exciting beginning.

If books represent drudgery and boredom to you, then the symbol may be indicating that you are in a rut or bored with your life. One symbol

112

may have endless interpretations depending on, and corresponding to, the individual casting the dream. It could require years of evaluation for you to begin to comprehend a symbolic individual dream interpretation, yet you can use your intuition to extract the value of the dream even without having the ability to understand each symbol. The more important the message, the more reinforcement or layering of symbols the dream will have. For example, a dream with a book may also contain a key. The key may represent what you need to unlock in order to begin the adventure.

The actual dreams cannot be remembered since they occur within realms that your human consciousness has not experienced or does not remember. As a consequence, the subconscious neatly organizes the messages into pictures and sometimes words. Your alternate selves travel to find solutions to your current issues and return to you a set of symbols to allow you to apply the knowledge gained.

This concept is not only hard to grasp, but it is difficult to explain in your language as well. The important points for you to know are that your dreams are essential in assisting you in increasing your awareness and solving your questions; symbols are not universal, therefore a dream symbol interpretation book must be used with caution. Trust your own interpretation of the message and as you begin to see your success in doing so, you will reinforce your skills and accuracy.

Every new skill takes practice. This skill is worth the effort.

In order to "receive" this material, Karen practiced the skill daily for almost three months. If you would enjoy understanding the process behind this skill, I encourage you to investigate the multitude of information, evidence, and case studies about "automatic writing." Practicing was not always convenient, yet look at the rewards. Practice interpreting your dreams and you can expect a valuable reward as well.

Since we are on the subject of automatic writing, I will give you additional details about Karen's receipt of this book. After years of assessing Karen's potential ability to act as a conduit, we (the entities and I) initiated contact. Our means was to stimulate her husband's idea to "play" with a Ouija Board. If you have ever had an experience when a thought popped into your head and you know you didn't

113

intellectualize it, then you understand how we contacted him. He spontaneously "decided" to buy a board. The idea was not outlandish to him since he had read about Jane Roberts' initial contact with the Seth personality through a Ouija. His wife had already shown evidence of being able to recognize her strong intuitive powers through what is often termed "psychic hits." Psychic hits are nothing more than coincidence or intuition being interpreted correctly. Everyone has the ability; some just recognize it or develop it more than others.

Their initial experience with the Ouija was atypical of usual experiences. After a brief interlude with departed loved ones, three sessions in all, they were contacted by Mama Cass Elliot. Of course disbelieving, they put her through the ringer to prove the authenticity of her claim, asking endless questions, attempting to trick her, and validating the truth further by seeking answers that they did not know the answers to, yet could verify.

I was the next entity to contact them and they "assaulted" me with the same level of proof seeking that they had used with Cass. After two weeks of contact with us and other entities from this mission, we suggested that Karen try automatic writing.

Reeling in disbelief, they lived in a temporary state of "suspended animation" as they maintained complete normalcy in all areas of their lives. Karen's talent at completing the conduit necessary for her to "receive" information from me became evident quickly. She was sent a tutor, my dear friend, Pat, who worked with Karen for two hours a day. Her lessons included receiving nonsensical words, essays, misspellings, incorrect words in sentences, and using words in a context that she was not familiar with. On occasion, she was not given a particular word, which she left blank, then the word was transmitted later and she went back to add it. Throughout training, Karen confirmed the accuracy of the content through the Ouija. She improved to an accuracy level of over 96% in less than two months and was nearly ready to begin.

For those of you interested in attempting the process of automatic writing, you should understand the alignment of like energy of the transmitter with like energy of the receiver is critical. What this means in real terms is that not just anyone can receive from any entity, and some humans can't receive at all. The match between transmitter and

114

receiver is so complex that it is difficult to explain. Also, there is no such thing as an "evil" entity. Any entity that communicates with humans has but one goal, to increase the awareness level, thus the vibrational level, of one or more humans.

In this mission, some entities have a transmitter/receiver connection with one person, Karen. Her energy is configured differently allowing this process to take place. Do not be disheartened, however. There are thousands upon thousands of entities who wish to communicate their wisdom through humans and, through your willingness, you are likely to connect with a very nice one!

And then we began. I gave Karen two days notice that I would begin the transmission of this book. Her dedication is fierce and progress has been rapid. On occasion, we have even allowed "guest" transmitters to express an idea in their own words, with me coming through to finish the content.

The entities are having great fun! We are cautious and remind Karen often that she is receiving accurately by putting forth evidence that confirms the truth for her. Constant revalidation is reassuring for her and gives her confidence to continue.

For those of you who remain skeptical, think about angels. Or miracles. Or God. Or Heaven. Or interplanetary beings. If you have so much as the slightest, tiniest belief that any of those are real, then apply your open-mindedness to this issue. I will not yet tell you which of those other ethereal ponderings are based on truth, but I will tell you, beyond a shadow of a doubt, that life beyond human physicality is wonderful and we aim to increase your vibrational level!

[5:45 pm]

July 2, 2005 11:00 am   (Book Session 29)

Circumstances beyond your control are not. Beyond your control, that is. Perhaps your past belief system has gotten you into a mess of trouble, but you can still reel it back in before it gets too bad.

Systematically redefine the circumstances. If you don't stop to think about what is going on and why, the path you created will seem to spiral out of your control. You have the power to change your patterned reaction to situations. You can halt detrimental progression of a problem simply by acting differently than you normally would. This tactic will not stop the problem from ever resuming, but it will pause the downward spiral long enough to allow you to rethink the cause and solution.

For example, your child falls and severely scrapes his knee. Injuries of this type are common for him. What is your normal reaction? Are you calm, indifferent, accusatory, or panicky? What are your beliefs about the injury? The child is clumsy? Foolish? Adventurous? Needy? Careless? Typical?

Ordinarily, a scraped knee does not warrant much attention to your thoughts and beliefs, but the fact that his injuries occur frequently indicate that it is time to examine them. Often, a child's recurring circumstances has to do with his desire to attract in the fulfillment of his own needs. As a parent, your needs are most intertwined with his.

You run to his side with a bit of hysteria and rush him into the house. You call the doctor and debate about whether or not to take him to the hospital. Any outsider could easily determine that the injury is not critical enough to warrant intervention, but you continue with your crazed response.

What is going on here? Your overreaction is reinforcing a pattern that has developed. Your belief system is comprised of fearful scenarios of "what ifs." Your thoughts automatically take you to the worst possible outcome and you react accordingly. Your son picks up on this undue dramatization and he learns that injury is an excellent way to elicit a great amount of attention from you. You feel useful and like a good parent, so everybody gets a little something out of the drama. The needs satisfaction extends beyond the present moment. You take him to the hospital and you receive more attention from the staff there. Later, you retell your story and your listeners reinforce your belief that your reaction to injury makes you a good mother.

116

As the boy grows, your behavior will contribute to him developing one or more patterns of his own. He may increase his rate of injury and need for attention through medical dramas, or he may grow weary of your over-protectiveness and go to great lengths to avoid the permeation of your belief system to contaminate his.

A child of overprotective parents may have a very strong vibrational energy that repels the contamination, but what is more likely is that the child will develop a trait of neediness and persistent injuries and illness. He or she may also lose the ability to clearly determine the level of severity in dramatic circumstances.

Now suppose you decided that this would be the moment when you would stop and think. You scoop him up and gently say, "It's okay. Let me take a look." You calmly take him inside and clean the area. All the while, your panic is under the surface, but you hold steady and do not reveal it.

Ultimately, you discover that the injury is not severe and you bandage his knee and send him back out. You fight back your fears and let the knowingness of everything turning out fine to wash over you. You realize that your fears were unfounded; he did not get a rare bacterial virus through the cut and his knee cap was not broken. He can walk and run and play and laugh unburdened by your previously misguided beliefs.

The next time a similar situation occurs, you will feel more like you act. The previous panic that welled under the surface will subside and you will begin to believe that life is not dangerous, with evil germs and scary villains lurking at every moment waiting to plunge. Your energy during challenging moments will increase in its positive strength, the negative panicky energy decreasing.

Your child will recognize the healthy attention he receives, attention in proportion to the situation. He will feel secure in your ability to attend to him and not be burdened by your needs. He will not have the need to increase the number or severity of injuries or illnesses he attracts in because an incident rate above normal will not gain him any fulfillment of unsatisfied needs.

It is important for you to remember that, although your past behavior was detrimental to your son, you are NOT to blame for the development of your faulty beliefs. It is a worthwhile challenge to attempt to determine how your unfounded beliefs came to pass, but with an eye towards recognition and improvement, not blame. Do not blame yourself or others for your or others' faulty beliefs.

You were born to be a well-functioning unit. You were meant to be happy and healthy. Those states are *natural;* illness and unhappiness are unnatural states that arise through the layering of the soul's intent through others' false beliefs. If this message is repetitive or redundant in this book, it is because you need to understand it.

Scraped knees will eventually turn into chronic illnesses if the misguided beliefs are not restrained or, better yet, corrected. You absolutely attract in or repel away your circumstances according to your belief system. If you were considering marriage, wouldn't you want to get to know your mate *really* well? After all, that person will have a major impact on the course of your life. Is that union one that will make you happy?

Mates may come and go through break-ups, divorce, or death, but your relationship with yourself lasts for ever. Why not examine your beliefs with the same intensity that you examine a potential mate? Your beliefs have a tremendously greater impact on the course of your life than any mate ever will! Your system of beliefs will even guarantee the success or dissolution of the relationships you choose by guiding the attraction. You will attract in mates that fit the current need level of your belief system.

When you peel the layers back and allow your soul song to be heard, you will likely attract a mate that will complement your need for a happy, healthy life. And the good just keeps getting better! In a soulful relationship, you have the ability to raise healthy, well-adjusted children as well.

Take a look at couples where one parent clearly believes that he or she is superior in parenting skills. Suppose, for illustration purposes, that this person is a man. He feels cocky in his ability and disgruntled with hers. Perhaps he should instead wonder what need he has that would attract in a mate with inferior parenting ability. Maybe his convoluted belief system which drew in the mate to begin with is now continuing to mask her soul song, thus encouraging her layers to wear thick. Perhaps by peeling his layers, he can help her extract hers, thus allowing both to improve their capableness.

The point is, do not judge loved ones. They are doing the best they can at any given moment with the set of beliefs that they presently hold. If your loved ones have not read this book, then they are not likely aware of this process, and therefore, cannot yet remedy their present state. Every person on earth can remedy faulty beliefs. As you improve yours and peel away your masks and layers, allow others the privilege to do the same without reprisal. Be patient. Your layers are not completely removed if you feel compelled to judge others. Judgment indicates a lack of awareness of the process of the layering of souls. A lack of awareness in any area of personal development indicates the presence of a layer, or two, or three .... Resist instructing others how to remove their layers unless you are a highly trained ambassador of this mission (more about that later), or you have the true capability of demonstrating, through your own example, how you successfully removed your layers.

To a receptive person, simply point out how you succeeded. Stop talking as soon as they become guarded, distracted, submissive, or agitated. You will absolutely know when your listener is ready to hear you. Likewise, you will absolutely know when he or she is not. By eliminating your layers, you allow your intuition to strengthen. This intuition will guide you towards understanding when, where, if, and how you can assist in the enlightening of another.

Have you ever met someone who has read every self-help book on the market and is still a mess? Don't become one of them. Use your intuition responsibly and strongly to determine if you are, in fact, able to assist others, or if your desire to help is to feed your layer of control or your layer of neediness.

Whatever you *believe*, not *think*, will determine the nature of your reality. Examine every area of your beliefs as vigorously as you would a potential mate. As I have said, your belief system has a far greater affect on your ability to create a happy life than any relationship ever can.

119

[break]

If you have come this far in this book, you have a strong intuition that truth lies within these pages. Your ability to use the information to construct a purposeful, happy life depends largely on your willingness to perform the exercises contained within, to accept the fact that you create your own reality (good or bad), and to commit to being an Independent Thinker.

Those who meet that three-fold criteria are eligible to become Ambassadors of the Mission. I'm not fond of that terminology, but at least it conveys the point. Actually, the words are capable, but American nuances associated with the words distort their true meaning to a degree.

Ambassadors will be recruited, among those willing and eligible, to assist in disseminating the critical information in this book and others to come. The thousands of entities involved will select and train the Ambassadors. You cannot apply for the position; you must have a level of awareness and a vibrational level that match the requirements. If you found this book to be of value as a reinforcement of your positive ideals already in action, or if you readily applied the content successfully, then you likely have the capacity to become an Ambassador.

Ambassadors of the Mission, or AMs, will have specific job duties. The level of time and dedication you are willing to commit will determine your tasks. There is no obligation to become an AM or to commit any particular time. As a matter of fact, a requirement of employment is that you must *want* to perform any task that you undertake.

AMs are neither leaders nor followers. They do not tell others what to do; they simply guide others toward their own inner wisdom. They can answer questions asked or pose questions unasked, but rarely can they answer questions that they themselves posed. Understanding that past sentence is an essential element of being a successful AM.

AMs will have an opportunity to earn a vigorous living at this job. The more abundance an AM realizes, the more abundance will be realized by others. This fact can be convoluted by misguided beliefs. In no way should "tithe" or any semblance of homage be paid to an AM in an attempt to gain wealth. AMs should not be worshipped. They should be loved and respected because everyone should be loved and respected. They should be valued for their awareness and ability to enlighten others. They should be admired for their capacity to increase human vibrational levels.

AMs do not represent a religion or a church or any other manmade institution. They represent truth, independent thinking, and the voice of love, creativity, and learning. They represent intuition and happiness, health and fun. They represent the new human experience.

For those curious, I will outline a brief description of the process. Potential AMs need only state in their thoughts the desire to be selected and believe that they are capable in order to be chosen. They will be given clear instructions and guidance through their training process and learn tools for communicating with an entity. A selected AM can quit at any moment, or can choose to disseminate the wisdom privately and without personal acknowledgment. Every AM will increase their personal happiness and wealth and health. It is impossible not to, since the successful implementation of the material contained within is a prerequisite for the job.

The method of communication between an entity and an AM will be individual. The entity or entities will examine your vibrational energy and all the other impossible-to-describe elements necessary for the successful transmitter / receiver relationship. An adjunctive component of the primary form of communication will be lessons you will receive in your dream state. You will be given a specific method to allow an entity to teach you while you sleep.

Your privacy will never be compromised because, quite frankly, entities do not care AT ALL about your physical activities, thus we do not attune to them. You can pick your nose or eat out of the ice cream box. We don't care. The only thing we attune to is the level of your vibrational energy and your relevant thoughts. The process is virtually instantaneous and completely non-invasive. And the pleasures and rewards are vast!

[1:54 pm]

121

You wouldn't get angry with a character in a book for long, would you? A good writer will design the plot to entice you to feel attachments to the outcome and the storyline. You will root for some and despise others. When the book is finished, do you remain angry with the villain? Of course not! You knew it was just a piece of fiction. You were gripped and escaped reality for a fun romp. But shut the book and reality is back. Right?

Not really.

Not at all, to be precise. Your reality is no different than the book you just read, except that you cast the villains and the angels. You choose the plot, the twists, and ebbs. If you don't like the villain in your story, then change what you believe. Until you are adept at doing so, practice this skill: When you have a negative interaction with someone, take time to step back and ponder. If you can't do it immediately, do it soon, like on the car ride home from work or while you're taking a shower. The typical mindset when reconvening your thoughts to the villain will be to replay it over and over and over until your heart rate increases. What has this thought process accomplished? To anger you repeatedly, often to a greater extent than the initial action. Why would you do that to yourself? Does the increased heart rate make you feel alive? Do you pulsate with excitement as you swarm among your angry feelings? Do you want to feel like this?

Try, instead, to equate the villain with a character in a fictional tale, for the truth is that he or she is no more than that. Your beliefs attracted in the circumstances; therefore, you wrote the script and cast the villain. As you begin to recognize, absorb, and react to this fact, you will understand that the "villain" in your story is no more powerful or permanent than the villain in a book. It happened; it was an interesting story, perhaps even a clever plot, but that is all!

Write off the character in your story. Or better yet, have the evil villain turn into an angel in the plot. The switch could be as intriguing as the initial encounter because the twist was unexpected and out of character.

Decide that your villain is your friend, at least in your thoughts for now. As you learn to equate the antagonists in your personal novel with the insignificant story-line operators that they are, you will then free your pondering time to examine why you added this villain or incident into your plot. You had a very good reason – figure out what it was.

I will outlay a brief description of a typical cause for casting villains into your script. Not all examples fit all humans, but this overview will serve to indicate a reasonably likely chain of events.

For most children, the constant bombardment of the actions precipitated by others' belief systems not only layers the soul, but creates a chaotic system of colliding energy all around them. The layers hide the children's ability to connect with their souls' intent and the chaotic swirl of maligned beliefs and incidents throws them off-balance. The more chaos swirling and the greater amount of time the chaos swirls, the more the "off-balance" feeling will become normal.

[break 2:00 pm – 2:56 pm]

Once a negative feeling becomes "normal" in childhood, the more difficult it is for the person to understand that the "normal" is false. Sadly, their adult antennae will often seek swirling energy that matches the energy that they experienced when young. This feeling is normal. They expect it and their belief system of the newly defined "normal" becomes the reality they will likely create. This explanation is a rudimentary depiction of why some people "want" to be unhappy. They do not actually desire chaos or sadness, but they recreate feelings that became so familiar as to become their "normal."

A child feels alive. Adults want to feel alive. An almost predictable way to feel alive as an adult is to recreate the swirls that surrounded them early in life. As you can see, there is no blame involved. The pattern is common. So common, in fact, that it is predictable. The greatest consequence of understanding the concept of a soul song is that it crystallizes the fact that not only are masks and layers normal, but also that people do not "choose" them; there is no one to blame.

You are the author of your novel. Can you write a happy novel?

123

With the knowledge of the existence of the soul song comes forgiveness. Forgiveness is nothing more than the ability to understand that another is doing the best they can at any given moment with their level of awareness. It is frustrating to many to watch others repeatedly err or repeatedly attract in villains or villainous circumstances, but remember, they are doing the best that they can at their level of awareness. If they repeat the pattern, it is because they did not or were unable to increase their level of awareness as a result. They had an opportunity to learn and grow, but the opportunity eluded them. The intent of books like this one and of Ambassadors of the Mission is to guide an increasing number of people towards awareness, to teach others how to extract the meaning from a challenge, how to remove layers to avoid similar trials, and how to allow one's soul song to shine.

We like to give examples to illustrate points. Think about this scenario. A drunk driver kills a man. The man had children and a wife and parents and friends and siblings and coworkers and neighbors and so on. The aftermath of the drama is catastrophic. Thousands pour out of their homes with support and gifts and sympathy. All reel with shock and complete contempt for the perpetrator. You can imagine the pain experienced by those involved.

Now think for a moment about the driver. He has a wife and parents and friends and siblings and coworkers and neighbors and so on. How do they feel? How does the driver himself feel? Do you think he woke up that day and decided to kill a man? Do you think he is pleased that it happened? Did he learn something?

Now suppose the driver was your nephew. You love him. He's a "good" kid. Suppose he is eighteen years old and this incident was the first time he drove after drinking. How would you feel? How would he feel?

Now picture two choices for the future. Your nephew is given a maximum sentence and is imprisoned throughout the years of his peers' marriages and children being born. He is in prison throughout his college years and career start-up time. The families of the victim cannot forgive him, so their anger adds to his own personal burden of grief.

Now suppose he learned all he needed to know from the accident. He understood why he chose to drink and drive. He understood what belief system he possessed to attract in an incident that resulted in him causing the death of another. He understood the process of grief that the man's family was enduring. What if he dedicated his life to enlightening others about what happened to him and why? He was not imprisoned, but he used his wisdom to teach teenagers how to recognize their layers and their motivation for choices. All the drunk-driving education in the world can't teach that. Do not drink and drive ... do not drink and drive ... do not drink and drive. Yes, the message may prevent some future stupidity, but what would be far more effective would be for those kids to learn about their layers, to learn about their energy, and how they create their reality. They can see themselves in this "normal" kid's life, a teenager with a teenage world. If this young man teaches them "why" the incident happened, he can prevent far more injurious experiences than if he just told them, "Do not drink and drive."

The family listens to his perspective and the contribution he is making and learns about masks and layers. They understand that the purpose of life is to love, create, and learn. They comprehend that soul songs get hidden, *badly*. They learn how to remove their own layers and swirls of chaos. And they forgive the young man.

Now back to the path where the boy is imprisoned. Several of his potential audience members eventually drink and drive and kill. The cycle continues.

I am not commenting on the judicial system. I am not commenting on the rightness or wrong-ness of drinking and driving. I am simply trying to get you to think independently, to look at an all-too-common situation from a different perspective. To examine your beliefs and to recognize how devastating layers can be. To think creatively about how you can help others learn without devastation. What can you do to increase the awareness of others without them needing negative challenges to learn from?

Somehow a young nephew with a bright future evokes feelings of sympathy, but how different is this scenario if the driver was a forty-five-year-old chronic drinker? Isn't his soul layered?

125

Just think about things.

In the immortal words of John Lennon, "Imagine ..."

There can be a better world.

[3:57 pm]

July 5, 2005 11:31 am   (Book Session 31)

Every novel has a plot. There is a beginning and an end. There is action or a story in the middle. Are you at the beginning, end, or middle of your story? Your birth was a miracle, so the plot got off to a great start, and the end is full of excitement; we already know that, but how about the middle? Are the readers enticed? Is the plot worth following? What exactly is it that you are trying to say?

Do you even know what the purpose of your novel is? Is it to scare, excite, enlighten, or bore others? Will your story leave the earth a better place, or extract some good from it and cast it aside? What is your legacy, the plot of your book? Granted you will be elevated a few steps upon death by those you leave behind; your stature increases with your demise. People either see the fun part of the plot, or they feel too guilty to mention how dreary it was; in any case, you will be slightly exalted. False elevations aside, how did your novel read? Was it a passionate book? Passion is what people remember. Was it a ground-breaking book? Or was it a bleak repeat of so many books before yours.

When we talk about the importance of creativity, we are largely talking about the plot of your book. What did you contribute? What makes you unique? What will people remember you by?

Many Greats left a legacy to carve out a physical reminder of their plot long after their separation. Beethoven, Picasso, Thoreau, Shakespeare ... they each left a physical reminder of their plot so that their novel would persist long after they rejoined the energy realm. Their legacy, their craft, their art, their thoughts, represent their creativity in life. The far reaching expanse of the plot, the part of their plot that brought

126

others to a new level of awareness, extending beyond generation after generation, reinforces the creative force that they lived with.

Perhaps your legacy will not reach for generations beyond your physical life, but where does it reach? Where do you want it to reach? You have but one chance in this lifetime to make an eternal difference. How do you want to use that chance? What is the middle of your life all about?

Exploring your creativity is the key to unleashing your potential. Your plot is creatively driven if it is to be far-reaching or impactful. Perhaps yours will extend to one hundred people instead of ten, or maybe it will reach one thousand instead of one hundred. Use your creativity to maximize your impact.

Many are intimidated by the word "creativity" because it connotes to them the ability to create art. Creating art, music, drawings, paintings, songs, lyrics, poetry and the like is only a small area of possible ways to express creativity. To be creative means to discover what you are passionate about and do it without reservation, without worrying what others will think.

Creativity is innovation, thinking outside the box, getting "lost" in a project, imagination, accomplishment, showmanship, show-offish-ness. Creativity is letting the inside out, allowing yourself to be free. True creativity cuts through layers, allows your soul song to sing aloud, makes you feel good and proud. I will give you examples of expressions of creativity to help you think beyond art:

Coming up with a needed solution to a work problem.
Showing others in unique ways that you care about them.
Successfully getting someone to stop gossiping … telling parables to children, baking, dancing, writing, singing, laughing (it takes imagination to see the funny side), telling jokes, gardening, dressing, accessorizing, decorating, building, constructing, naming your children, acting, cooking, counseling, teaching, throwing parties, giving gifts, pressing flowers, producing, directing, sports casting, crafting, inventing, operating a business, running a day-camp, grooming animals, hanging pictures, taking photos, raising children, helping, being a stylist, researching …

The list goes on and on and on. Anytime your passion and your imagination are engaged you are being creative. Note, however, that every one of those tasks can be performed without passion or imagination ... then they just become the flat performance of a dull plot.

Instead of yelling, think of a creative way to turn the negative into positive. That's creativity. Organizing a cohesive, supportive team ... that's creativity.

Find your passion, use your imagination, and spice up the plot to your novel. Do not limit yourself, either. It's just as easy to find ten things that you're happy creating as it is to find one.

Solve a problem. Your plot will gain intrigue. Finger Paint. Your plot will gain intrigue. Make a sand sculpture on the beach ... you know what will happen.

Expect fun. Endorse fun. Have fun.

[2:05 pm]

One thing that physicists got right is that energy never dies. Your soul is energy and, as such, it never dies. It metamorphoses the same way energy on earth changes from one form to another. Knowing that your essence is eternal should help you discover freedom in examining a creative life. You have nothing to lose. It doesn't matter if you are six or sixty. Creativity can begin at any age. If you can't imagine where to begin, pick up a local course catalog from adult education or from any local school. Read through it until you find something, anything intriguing. Try pottery. Try ballroom dancing. Try drawing for dummies. Try home design. What is the worst that could possibly happen if you don't like it?

Go to the library or your local bookstore and search for books that intrigue your imagination. Find books about cooking or making paper. Find a book about marketing and stimulate your business creativity. An active life, an active mind, and a good plot all demand creativity. Pursue it gladly.

[2:28 pm]

July 7, 2005 7:04 pm   (Book Session 32)

Tough times call for tough measures. Your nation is amidst tough times right now. Think about it, though. Has there ever been a time when things were not tough in one way or another? How can you, as a nation, surpass the choices made that created such problems in the first place? Once war ceases, how long will it be until another is active? If poverty is overcome, what other ill will replace it? The questions themselves imply that your nation is to blame for its own limitations and that is true to a certain extent, but not in the way that you imagine. It is not necessarily the decisions made in government or the inadequate social response that is the cause. The cause of all problems is the way people think [and feel]. We have examined how your beliefs affect your reality; likewise, the collective beliefs of a region or a nation will create a reality for all involved.

The decision to enter war is not the decision of a few politicians in Washington. The direction the nation takes is a direct consequence of the collective beliefs of those in the nation. And those beliefs are affected by the collective beliefs of those in other nations.

To be more specific, the sad fact is that the collective beliefs of terrorists that effected dramatic events on your soil changed the populace's beliefs about the "elusive" group known as terrorists. Other nations and people are categorized unknowingly en masse: good/bad, mean/nice, unthreatening/harmful. Individuals can intellectualize the reality that no one nation is comprised of all bad, but the general consensus in mass beliefs among American citizens is that certain regions of the world are "bad." This collective belief creates a massive energy, let's call it "hatred," which seeks events for normalization. The energy seeks to return to its familiar state and the only way that it can achieve that state is through an energy shift. The shift in energy can be catalyzed by a positive event or a negative event, but the most common catalyst for normalization of a collective energy is through a like energy; therefore, the easiest path to restore the collective energy of the Americans is through reciprocal "hatred."

This concept is so advanced that few people on the planet can fully comprehend it, but many will act according to the principle by

129

expending positive energy in response to negative. Unknowingly, they return the negative energy state back to its normal state through only positive actions.

Let's return to our example with specific details to illustrate the point. After 9/11, millions of Americans began to solidify their abstract beliefs that the Mid East region is "evil" or "barbaric" or "not-to-be-trusted." The odd component of the power of beliefs is that they affect reality without most people even knowing what their beliefs are. To continue, these millions believe, without recognizing their beliefs or "wanting" their beliefs to be acted upon, that their world and the future world for their descendents would be safer and happier if those regions no longer existed.

Does this mean that Americans want the systematic annihilation of all the people of the region? Absolutely not. Perhaps a few fanatics may, but the masses would not advocate nor support such an action. The collective belief, however, combined with the feeling of vulnerability and anger, allowed a grand energy to swell, similar to the way a hurricane gains power off the coast as it is fueled by the sea. This energy seeks a release, the same way a hurricane eventually explodes, until the mass energy is displaced differently.

This energy not only fueled the Washington leaders' decision making, but also fueled the extent and severity of the conflict. The whole chicken and egg thing is at play here. The more casualties occur, the more chaos is inflicted, and the further from settlement the forces appear, the more energy is added to this massive boulder. The very conflict that was initiated to dissipate the energy has bound it more strongly.

Let's parallel this situation to the debacle of the Americans' participation in the Vietnam War. The similarities are apparent in that the conflicts resulted in far more loss and devastation than was previously conceived with no clear outcome on the horizon. Yes, there are clear differences as well, but the energy forming and bonding does not differentiate. The energies bound by the beliefs of Americans during both conflicts are similar.

130

As the grotesque losses mounted during the Vietnam conflict, the energy mass could not find a release; it continued to gain momentum. Each parent burying a dead son sobbed more anguished energy into the mass. Every news report gripped the hearts of the compassionate young, whose disillusionment for the future added energy to the mass.

The turning point came. The young, followed by many voices of the nation, grew full of contempt for the situation. They rose through peaceful means to allow another way to be heard and recognized. Ultimately, it was their collective powerful mass of *positive* energy that led to the resolution and the pulling of troops. (As an aside, those who reacted with violence to the war actually fueled the negative mass of energy, resulting in the opposite of their intent).

Luckily, the power of their beliefs was strong enough to defuse the massive negative energy that had formed. The movement was based on love, not hate, and the energy of love was strong enough to dissipate the negative energy.

You may not completely comprehend the mechanisms and systems affecting the energies in this example, but if you are attuned to your intuition, then you KNOW that the only way to dissipate negative energy is through positive energy. Think about any world conflicts that have ensued for hundreds or thousands of years. The conflicts are not reaching a resolution because no opposing force has been applied to neutralize the negative energy. The longer the negative energy mass has existed, the more concrete and snarled and grotesque it becomes. War met by war doubles the hatred as the two hideous energies intertwine. Additional violence adds more fuel. The only weapon that can cut through the energy is positive. Massive amounts of positive energy must be collected to battle the negative.

Now, for the corny portion of this lecture: The strongest of all the positive energies is LOVE. Love is a like an acid on a blubbery fat blob of hate. It eats away at the blob until it dissolves.

Love is expressed through the response to others' soul songs, but love of humanity can be expressed even when individual songs are not heard; the only necessary component is the knowledge that everyone has a soul song.

Perhaps the most clear indication of this power in practice is the through the life's work of Mahatma Gandhi. Gandhi (a Great, of course) understood that the only weapon against hatred, subjugation, cruelty, and injustice was love. His love of truth and love of India allowed him to raise the beliefs of the Indians to emit a positive energy that dissolved the abhorrent negative energy of oppressive rule. His path was vast, as only a vast expenditure of positive energy could neutralize the opposing forces.

In his immortal wisdom, Gandhi understood that sacrifices through love would never equal sacrifices made in hatred. As an entity, the Gandhi personality knows that those who sacrificed for the freedom of India increased their own personal vibrational levels and, more significantly, raised the awareness and vibrational level of humanity. Those who fought against did not.

We reap what we sow. The plantings of love on earth will bear love, the plantings of hatred, hatred.

We, the entities of the mission, are sowing as fast as we can, as much as we can, and as often as we can. Help us harvest love by planting your seedlings along ours.

July 10, 2005 2:30 pm (Book Session 33)

Every now and then, something happens that shakes you around, opens your eyes, causes you to pop out of your self-induced hypnosis. A tree falls, a person dies, an explosion happens. Your eyes fly open and you feel alert and eagerly seek information to explain the occurrence. You submerge yourself in the mystery and collect the details as best you can. A thought may linger long after the happening, but the effect wears off rather quickly.

This rush that occurs after events is addictive. It is why many people feel compelled to watch gruesome details on the news repeatedly. Even the anger, fear, or sadness experienced makes people feel alive. Gossip can also be explained in this fashion. Having juicy stories to hear and to

132

tell can be exhilarating. It can cause the pulse to quicken slightly, again, snapping a person out of rote into a feeling of being alive.

Tranquility does not cause body signals that are as addictive as those responses to stress. The physiology of the human sends dramatic changes through the body in response to stress. Without these chemical changes, many people feel restless or agitated. The exact feeling that stress creates is self-imposed when stress is not present.

The pattern is fairly obvious, but the effect is not. When stressed, the body emits an energy quite contradictory to the energy emitted when one feels tranquil. When subjected to repeated stress, the body can no longer function at its peak when unstressed, thus it seeks to replicate the reaction. The result is that a person who becomes used to stress, or used to being submerged in negative news or gossip, emits a constant "negative" energy. Small escapes or vacations are no longer sufficient to level the negative energy emitted with positive. Humans are correct when they indicate that stress causes illness, but not for the reasons they suppose. The reason is that the energy emitted during stress sends out antennae that look for like antennae, usually more stress or stressful events. In today's culture, busyness has the same effect as stress. Forgoing leisure repeatedly has the unwanted effect, over time, of real crises.

Are you able to be alone in a quiet house for an hour? No radio, no television, or computer or videogame? Can you spend an hour with your family with no electronic entertainment? Can you do either of these activities every day? For most people the answer is "no." Try it and see. Avoid the phone, cell phone, iPod, DVD player and any other form of electronic distraction. First try to pass an hour alone, then try to pass an hour with your family.

It's not easy. Then try to achieve the same goal for two hours. Even the highest functioning families will be challenged.

The feeling that stimulates your desire for television or noise is the same impetus that can propel you towards enjoying your leisure with your mind or your hands. Feel good about listening to the quiet. Let your mind roam uninterrupted. Allow your thinking to bounce around all the fun things you could do with your quiet time ... then do one. With family, pick a family activity. Do something together without electronics. I am not implying that electronics are evil or the precipitous for a downward spiraling America, but I am asking you to take inventory of your dependence on outside stimulation. Relaxed leisure is a dying art. The feelings and antennae emitted during the tranquil moments of your life are among the most successful in attracting a peaceful set of circumstances back into your life. If you daydream about vacation, if you are obsessed with retirement, then you crave this type of leisure. You can have it as a part of your life today. There is no need to postpone the feeling. Enjoy it and savor it. Crave it as strongly as you crave external stimulation.

What happened since you were a child? You used to enjoy blissful days of leisure, playing with neighborhood kids and losing track of the time. Your parents had more leisure than you do yet you have so many timesaving solutions at your fingertips. What are you doing with your time? What have you enslaved yourself to? What is so important?

Think about it. Think about it a lot. What are you doing with your time?

Set a goal to improve your leisure and stick to it. I can't help you. The pressures in your life are of your own choice ... you are the only one that can remedy it. The more free thinking time you allow yourself, the more you can begin to reverse the stress overload. The more you reduce the stress, the more your receptors or antennae will seek non-stressful events, people, and circumstances into your life. By taking the first step, in such a simple way you can help yourself to have a happier life.

[4:02 pm]

July 12, 2005 5:15 pm   (Book Session 34)

Organize the troops. Long live Hitler! Heil, Hitler! The madness was buoyed by the maddest man of all. If you stop to ponder, how did the madness get so out of hand? Why did he have supporters? Why did so many obey and trust his command? Would you argue with the fact that he was a good leader? A good leader creates passion within the ranks,

134

creates a cohesive unit committed to a solitary goal, and inspires others to follow. Doesn't Hitler then qualify as a great leader?

Were not there Independent Thinkers among the ranks? Dissenters? How is it possible that so many people thought that his ideas were good ideas? What went wrong?

The art of thinking independently must be taught and encouraged. It needs to catch fire with increasing intensity until all corners of the globe have the composition of citizens who think independently. The power of reasoning is what will prevent future monarchs and dictators from precipitating actions that are clearly wrong.

I am going to tell you a story. A young Hitler of nineteen loved a girl. She was from a respectable family who encouraged his courtship. Her feelings for him were reciprocal, although they never spoke of their attraction.

Hitler had an opportunity to collect her for an outing. He would be formally introduced to her family and be expected to visit an appropriate length of time. When he arrived at her home, he could not enter. He was paralyzed with fear. Unaccustomed to the emotion that she evoked in him, he felt uneasy with the new feelings. He was drawn yet repelled simultaneously, since control was his mantra. He controlled his thoughts until that moment and relinquishing his control was unacceptable to him. He found himself paralyzed with indecision. His fear of emotion pulled him one way and his passion for the girl pulled him another. His paralysis remained, until the moment was lost. He had remained fixed for so long with fearful thoughts swarming his head that he could no longer move forward. He had only the strength to back away and never turn back.

Shortly afterwards, very shortly afterwards, as his fear subsided, he became angry with himself and from that moment on dedicated himself to never losing control again. To revisit her would mean humiliation, an experience that young Hitler would not endure. He made his choice and proceeded to disallow positive passion to contain or divert or control him again.

Until this point in Hitler's life, his upbringing had been reprehensible, savage, brutal, and unimaginable. At the moment when his hand was on her door, he faced a crossroads. Had he entered, what would have become of him? He did not know a thing of love. He did not know how to form relationships or allow anyone to love him. He had become disconnected at an early age from the nurturing love that every person needs to grow up to become a healthy adult. He was denied the chance to forge loving relationships, to feel the warmth and compassion of another who loved him for who he was.

The moment came; the opportunity to experience love came when he stood on the steps. His innate beliefs, his instincts, told him to call for her, but his fear of the unfamiliar feelings of love kept him away. His instincts told him that he had made a devastating mistake and he punished himself, unknowingly, for the rest of his life for that mistake. He would never again let an outsider or a frivolous emotion direct his behavior.

There is no excuse for his actions in his life, but there is an explanation.

Had Hitler's soul song been heard in infancy and throughout his youth, where would the world be today? He was born with the purity of a glad soul with the ability to love, create, and learn. How strong were the layers thrust upon him? How heavy was the cloak that enshrouded him? A mighty pickaxe could not have released him.

Do you know how many other problems throughout history or presently could have been prevented through love? If you thought, "every one of them," then you are learning from this book. Yes, every single problem known to mankind, presently and in the past, could have been averted through the acknowledgement of others' soul songs. There is no such thing as a "bad seed" or born evil. Every person is born with a pure soul in a state of bliss.

From this moment on, I want you to treat every newborn baby as a pure soul. Listen to or acknowledge every child's soul song. Give your love freely to those who are young. You may not be able, single-handedly, to repair the damage already done to the adults around you, so start in the easiest place – with the children. Leave your ego behind and hear the child's soul song when it is singing most clearly. There is no such thing as a bad child, only children whose songs have not been heard.

If everyone starts to listen now, then eventually all new people born will have fewer layers burdening them and hiding their true purpose.

Love.

[7:14 pm]

July 15, 2005 11:01 am   (Book Session 35)

Once established, a concept, unfounded, takes on a life of its own. Although untrue to begin with, it becomes true as more and more people grant it significance and believe it. This is not always the case, but sometimes it occurs. For example, there are some people on earth who are in the beginning stages of "cancer" which will eventually be "proven" to be caused by cellular technology. Of course, this technology does not cause cancer, but the fear that lies latent in some individuals, the fear of new, the fear of change, will actually cause cells to mutate in response to their belief system. Cancer will stop progress for the individuals involved. Either they will succumb to the illness and perish, or they will reject all non-wired electronic sources in the future. By eliminating the supposed source of their illness, they are halting progress within their own control, thus "simplifying" life, slowing it down, and allowing the nostalgia of a better time to take root.

These individuals will be verbal about the evils of wireless technology. They will attempt, passionately and vehemently, to halt progress, or even reverse it.

For those survivors who partake in this campaign, the cancer has served an additional useful purpose which is congruent with their latent beliefs. As they campaign, and solicit Congress, they are passionately alive with vigor and purpose. The episode actually *gave* them life! The thing that threatened to take it away, gave it to them. Part of the lack or wayward believing prior to the cancer was a lack of purpose. A feeling of being invisible and unheard made them languish. Now, their lives are filled with purpose, filled with vitality, and filled with the romance of saving the world.

This demonstration is not intended to point out right or wrong. It is not intended to convince you that cellular technology is or is not harmful. The essay simply points out the possible course of a life resulting from a faulty belief system. There is likely a condition in your life that is a direct result of faulty beliefs, beliefs that were buoyed by others with equally faulty beliefs. If you have a negative condition, primarily a chronic negative condition, as most do, it is necessary to examine your beliefs to determine the root. Even without understanding the exact cause, analyzing your beliefs will allow you to determine the root of your consequences, step one in redirecting your path towards the positive.

I will give you additional simplistic examples of how a person's life can be negatively affected by faulty beliefs in order to exercise your thinking about how events transpire. The goal, of course, is not to blame yourself for the messes in your life, but to allow you to take control towards a happier future from this point forward.

Let's talk about GUILT, one of the most fascinating of all human emotions. Guilt is an obsessive form of "conscience," as you understand it. Interestingly, some of the most offensive wrongdoers experience no guilt. Isn't that interesting? Doesn't that fact alone mean that guilt is not an accurate indicator of the "rightness" or "wrongness" of your behavior?

Wouldn't you agree that compulsive behavior of any sort limits a person's ability to maximize enjoyment in life? GUILT is a compulsive form of listening to one's conscience. (By the way "con" and "science" are the root words of this ethereal idea, meaning "contrary to science.") To continue, your conscience, your ability to detect right from wrong, guides you towards appropriate behavior. The problem with allowing your conscience to govern your action is that it may be as faulty as your beliefs are. Then, compound that flaw with a compulsive twist and you have conditions for chaos.

You KNOW right from wrong. You innately know right from wrong. A simple assessment of each action you take, or don't take, will reveal to you whether it is inherently right or wrong. On issues that confuse you, think independently for a bit to determine whether or not your conscience has been corrupted by another's teachings. If you experience guilt, ask yourself "why." Why do you feel guilty for not going to church on Sunday? Why do you feel guilty for not returning the ten-dollar excess change you were given by the clerk? Why do you feel guilty for not exercising? Which of these actions (or inactions, actually) are a legitimate push from your innate sense of right and wrong, and which are an acquired response to the thinking and beliefs of others?

A momentary flicker of discomfort is not guilt. Guilt is an invasive feeling that saps your feeling of self-worth. You can briefly consider that you *should have* gone running, but if your thoughts compel you back, repeatedly, to your inaction, then that is guilt. Train yourself to eliminate guilt by thinking about its cause. Think earnestly and diligently about whether your action or inaction merits self-loathing.

The detrimental consequence of guilt is that you cannot change what you imagine you did wrong. You cannot go back and choose to act or not act differently. Let your innate sense of right and wrong be your guide, but eliminate guilt. If previous actions or inactions gnaw at you, then "right" them. Apologize, exercise, do whatever you need to do to right your perceived wrong. Then move on. If you imagine you wronged one now deceased, then remember … they DON'T care. They understand your actions and reasons. They understand your guilt. They want you to be happy, not paralyzed, locked in a pattern of thought that is non-productive.

A college student is putting herself through college. Getting to her house of worship every Sunday is challenging, but according to her upbringing and belief system, it is a sin to not attend. She is poor, very poor. A gourmet meal is having canned tuna with Raman noodles, yet each time she visits her house of worship, she puts ten dollars in the basket.

The money alleviates her guilt. She metaphorically "pays off" her sin of not attending regularly. Do you suppose that an all-loving God appreciates her restitution? Do you suppose that the Almighty "forgives" her "sin" and spends the money wisely? What do you think really happens here? The Loving Source of Life is, first of all, unaware of this tiny event. Secondly, if the Almighty were aware, the reaction would be one of disappointment (meaning vibrating on a slightly less euphoric scale). Would an all-loving, all-knowing being want her to place those ten dollars in the basket, or perhaps would the Almighty prefer she buy a robust meal and continue to live a life filled with beneficial intent?

The truth is that ALL THAT IS, as many understand the GOD concept, wants humans to live their lives in accordance with the true purpose: to love, to create, and to learn. How do your actions or non-actions stack up to those criteria? Answer the question, over and over and over again, to uncover your truest sense of "right" and "wrong."

The trickiest area to determine if your actions meet the criteria is matters that are health-related. Begin your questioning in areas that are less complex and eventually you will master the process enough to analyze areas related to your physicality. For example, "Should I attend my daughter's concert?" is easier to assess than, "Should I eat this ice cream?"

Beware, however. There is a natural tendency to assess your actions according to your faulty conscience. Watch. What was your reaction to whether or not you should attend your daughter's concert? Naturally, I assume, you said "yes." "Yes" is the answer that seems to show love, correct?

You do not have enough facts to answer that question in this example. More questions should naturally ensue. Does she want you there? Or is she indifferent? Is she passionate about her participation or is she fulfilling an obligation that has no meaning? Have you attended six out of the last six concerts? How old is she? Who will attend in your stead if you don't go? Does she feel loved and valued? If not, will your attendance "pay off" your guilt for otherwise faulty parenting?

As you can see, right and wrong are not as easy to determine as they first seem on the surface. Like all great progress I am asking you make in this book, this one takes a little work as well. I am asking you to retrain your random, unproductive way of thinking. I am asking you to harness the power of your gift of reason. I am asking you to think independently. I am asking you to take responsibility for your life and your happiness. I am asking of you to do the nearly impossible, to take your life's outcomes into your own hands, to understand the power you possess in these outcomes, and most importantly, to respect and value the purpose of life ... you know ... to love, to create, and to learn, in that order. There are no exceptions.

Let's talk about guilt, conscience, and health-related matters. Throughout this book, you may have noticed that I have not been giving you all the answers. I am compelling you to tune into your intuition to find the answers for yourself. However, I will make an exception and boldly give you the answers to questions which seem to elude the wisest among the masses.

What is health? Health is merely a balance. A balance of thoughts and beliefs. A balance of food and exercise. A balance of life and death. A balance of white and black. A balance of yin and yang. A balance of right and wrong. A balance of sorrow and laughter.

Every health-related question that you have about what is "right" or "wrong" related to your health can by answered through the thorough understanding and absorption of this statement:

Health is merely a balance.

Before I turn every limiting belief known to mankind on its head, please read and understand that statement. Allow your mind to wander for a bit about what it means. Pause from reading and conjure up your own ideas of what that statement means. If you were a student, could you write an essay about what it means? Could you write a paragraph, a few hundred words, perhaps?

I could write a book, a long book, about the phrase. Perhaps I will one day, but for now, I will give a brief definition of what it means in practical applications.

You are born healthy. For the purpose of this illustration [and this book], I will not yet address congenital defects. Let's assume you were born healthy. Your guiding principles, your innate senses, your intuition, your intention will all act together in unity to keep you healthy until you decide that it is your time to pass to the next realm.

Your health is as simple as that! But, obviously, something comes along and murkies up the possibilities. I hope that you are thinking, "Ahhhhh! The same factors that corrupt my belief system also destroy my relationship with optimal health." If your thinking is along those lines, then you have learned a great deal from this book so far! The same factors that cloak your true intent also camouflage your relationship with optimal health. You learn with each sneeze, with each fever, with each passing day, to absorb the misbeliefs of others regarding your health. If you are fortunate, the corruption to your optimal path to good health has been minimal, but most people have had much corruption.

The human body is designed to be innately respected and cared for. The uncorrupted sense allows for humans to choose life patterns that honor the physical vehicle. Honoring the physical vehicle is as simple as making balanced choices. Has a vegan ever had cancer? Has a person with 3% body fat ever had a heart attack? You cannot avoid ill health by embracing any extreme, just as you cannot embrace optimal health by ignoring the innate sense of self-preservation. If your belief system is in balance, you will experience harmony in your body. If your belief system begins to embrace extremes, you will experience dis-ease.

All humans experience minor passing illnesses. What your reaction and the reaction of those around you do with that illness will affect your developing belief system. An extremely over-protective caregiver will severely corrupt the innate sense of maintaining optimal health. Likewise, a punishing personality or one with complete disregard for any discomfort you may experience will severely corrupt your relationship with optimal health. The greater the bombardment of excesses in either extreme, the more profound the corruption. It is likely that such an individual will develop a life-long relationship with poor health.

Caregivers are not alone responsible for corruption. Virtually everyone has an opinion about health-related matters that they eagerly share or inflict others with. Newspapers, teachers, health care workers, government representatives, virtually everyone and every forum have opinions they eagerly share. The result is a kind of hypnotic state that humans exist in. The idea that poor health is the norm becomes physical truth. The idea that you are "susceptible" becomes the prevailing belief. The idea that optimal health is for the lucky few pervades thinking.

As you can see, the thoughts and beliefs that result from this bombardment of ill-health messages are that balance is lost. The harmonious balance of healthful beliefs is systematically destroyed. And, sadder still, is the fact that this destruction accelerates as you age! I defy you to find an individual who does not believe that his or her health will deteriorate as the body ages. The deterioration of human cells as the physical body progresses in time is often a direct, predictable consequence of this belief. Some, many actually, use this pervasive belief to accelerate or exaggerate their own ill state in order to fulfill some need: a need for love, a need for attention, a need to feel relevant, a need to pass the burden of caring for others, a need to be self-indulgent, a need to be in control.

[1:49 pm]

July 16, 2005 3:40 pm   (Book Session 36)
(This material is a continuation of the previous essay)

False ideas about the causes of ill health are so persuasive that it is almost impossible to disallow all the faulty thinking you possess. As a matter of fact, so persuasive is the thinking, that attempts to go "cold turkey," that is to instantaneously disregard all of the misguided beliefs you have, may actually do you harm. Let me give you an example. Please remember that the information here is to help you think independently; it is not to scare you - it is to empower you. You must continue to decide for yourself which elements of this book you hold true and which you doubt or question. By all means, please live your life according to your level of comfort.

To continue, suppose you are convinced that it is necessary to obtain a full epidermal body scan by a dermatologist each year to check for any skin abnormalities. After reading this book, you decide that the logic behind this annual exam may be faulty, so you stop going. If you do **not** *believe*, in your deepest core, that it is safe to discontinue this practice, you can actually cause the condition which you are fearfully attempting to avoid. Your subconscious may allow the mutation of epithelial cells in response to your vulnerable frame of mind. The fact that you do not *feel* safe even though you logically embrace these new ideas about health can contribute to causing what you fear. I am not stating that you will erupt in a spontaneous full fledged case of cancer, but I am saying that a slight abnormality may develop. After consulting a dermatologist who recommends removal, you will confirm your deeply-seeded belief that the exam is necessary. Further, you will continue to believe that matters of your health are not within your control.

To avoid situations like this, proceed as you normally do with medical intervention and prevention as you know it. To examine your beliefs before attempting any alterations in your patterns, ask yourself questions such as, "Do I *believe* that the annual dermatological exam is necessary to insure good health?" Your answer should be respected. Do not try to change your relationship with medical and health care in areas where your beliefs have not changed. Begin with smaller experiments until you are confident that you have regained your innate ability to maintain optimal health. For example, next time you get a pesky little virus such as a cold, decide why you got it. Did you need a break from stress? Did you need a little extra TLC? Did you need time off to do nothing? Did you need someone to focus on your needs? Did you need *you* to focus on your needs?

As quickly as you can determine the benefit of your minor illness, you will see symptoms subside. Simply by understanding the reason for the occurrence and *honoring* that reason, you can compress a ten-day illness into two or three days. The key here is that you have to honor the reason once discovered and give to yourself what it was you needed instead of allowing the virus to obtain it for you. If you needed time off, take it and ENJOY it!

Start small and allow evidence of the power of your belief system to accumulate before you embark on larger experiments. Unless, of course, you have availed yourself to all medical intervention with no positive outcome, then *smash* your faulty belief system, read up on spontaneous healing, figure out why you needed your dis-ease, eliminate the cause, and rebuild a healthy relationship with optimal health, one which honors your innate but hidden ability to be healthy. What challenge is your ill-health offering you that you could not have obtained otherwise?

I am going to take a brief detour here for those individuals that are facing life-threatening disorders. Continue along your path of medical intervention as you see fit, but simultaneously, I implore you to examine the very, very challenging factors surrounding your illness. You do not have the luxury of time to wait for physical evidence that what I say in this book is true. Do you want to live? I am serious. Do you want to live? If the answer is "yes," you want to enjoy the richness and magic of the beauty of physical life, you want to give and receive love, you want to take risks, you want to learn … then examine your belief system wholeheartedly until you reveal the truth. What is your illness giving to you that you can obtain on your own without it? What aspect of living are you afraid of, if any? Go on the Internet and seek others who have recovered from the same illness and find out why. What do they believe? You will learn about major transformations in their way of thinking and viewing life. You will discover that, knowingly or unknowingly, they altered major beliefs that they held. Life is not random. You are not a victim. You control your thoughts and attitudes and, from now on, your life.

Remember, also, that the purpose of life is to love, create, and learn with the intent of increasing your personal awareness or the awareness of others. Some individuals unknowingly choose death as a way to help others increase in their awareness and their vibrational level. This method is risky because there is no guarantee that the others will learn and integrate the lessons intended. Further, a fact that I will continue to repeat, growth of the soul can occur through joyous and positive events. Negative events are not necessary to enable growth and increases in vibrational levels. You can recover now and increase others' awareness in a profound way, thus increasing your and others' vibrational levels.

I highly recommend, again, you research the topic of spontaneous healing. Get in touch with those who recovered. Talk to them about their lives and about the positive change in circumstances that occurred or were manufactured that supported recovery. Usually change involved some sort of taking control. Perhaps an area or several areas in an individual's life felt out of their sphere of control such as domination by another in a relationship, fear of illness itself, or fear that environmental or genetic factors held power.

You are never powerless. If you have the power to think then you have an amazing well of power, profound, deep, everlasting power. You can tap into it.

Now, back to the issue of maintaining optimal health. You likely understand the importance of balance in nature. Rain and sun, heat and cold … any extreme is not conducive for long-term life bearing. Certain species adapt to extremes under certain conditions, but extremes limit the probability of an abundant propagation in nature.

Likewise, you probably recognize the harmony in the balance of opposites. Throughout nature and physical life as you know it, opposites exist and co-exist in harmony: lightness and darkness, male and female, up and down. To maximize your potential for a long, healthy life, you, too, should coexist in a balance of extremes. Do not become too sedentary. Do not eat an extreme quantity of one food at the exclusion of all others. Do not overindulge in alcohol consumption. Do not partake in a diet that does not make you feel healthy, alert, and full of energy. If you are tired, consider your diet and exercise patterns. Move your body. Like all machines, your physical body will atrophy if it is not used; that includes your brain.

Get your kids off the video games once-in-awhile. Get a little sun. Run around, jump, play. LAUGH! Do not be extremely serious!

Balance your life and your physical body will support longevity. Work and play. Sit and run. Eat vegetables and protein and fat and carbs, but not too much of any and more of some. Find balance. Seek balance.

One question that may come to your mind is that if you create your own reality through your thoughts, can't you eat anything you want if you think it's not harmful? Creating your reality through your belief system involves obeying certain physical "laws" that have been collectively agreed upon. There are physical parameters or laws accepted en masse that are adhered to. For example, the physical property of the calorie as a unit of energy is founded. If you consume more calories than you burn, you will gain weight. This principle is pretty widely accepted, so

146

much so that it has become "law." Yet even this law has exceptions or loopholes. For example, conditions of the thyroid have developed as a window of escape from this parameter.

You can train yourself through vigorous intensive studies to change the chemical interaction between food and your body … meaning that through an extreme state of mind self-control, you can cause what may be known as harmful food choices to react positively with your physical composition. However, this ability to master the mind-body connection to that level is rare. I suspect that the capability will be rather common place in a few million years, possibly sooner if human awareness continues to grow at its recent pace. I also suspect that when humans can eat whatever they want, whenever they want, with no adverse effects, then more entities will choose physical life!

(Side note to those gullible: that last statement is entity humor. All-you-can-eat is not a big goal of ours!) Speaking of entity humor, did you hear that Ponce de Leon discovered the eternal fountain of youth? …

He died!

[5:49 pm]

July 18, 2005 1:54 pm   (Book Session 37)

The reflection pool mirrors what it sees. You cannot create a new image in the reflection. Your life is a reflection as well, mirroring back in physical matter the quality of your thoughts and your beliefs. The pool can only reflect back what is there. It cannot manufacture new images.

Look in your mirror. What are you reflecting? What beliefs are you casting into the pool? The mirror reflects the truth. Your life mirrors the truth of your beliefs, transparently so. As you master the understanding of these concepts, you will see others' beliefs reflected in their actions, their circumstances, and the character of their lives. The reflection will be so obvious that others will appear to stand before you naked and you will be tempted to avert your eyes.

As you understand your craft of choice, others understand the essence of the nature of human reality. If you studied a profession and practice it, it seems common-sensical to you. A brain surgeon cannot remember not understanding her craft and often struggles to communicate with those who are ignorant of the workings of the brain about the workings of the brain. Many workers wear the language of their craft and can hardly understand one who does not understand.

In essence, one who understands the nature of the creation of human reality understands the language ... a language which is not easily defined. There is a knowingness that surrounds their encounters with others. Others suspect something different, odd, or unexplainable. A power or a strength. A knowingness in their eyes. Those with powerful vibrational energy can engage in meaningful relationships with the knowing ones, but others become uneasy and limit their encounters with one who knows.

Have you ever locked eyes with someone and felt that (s)he read your soul? I do not mean in a creepy way, I mean in a comforting, knowing way. If you struggle to apply the material in this book on your own, nurture these encounters. You can learn a lot from others. Those who "know" do not need to proclaim to know.

There are many on earth who "know."

Dysfunctional behaviors, unhealthy habits, compulsions, and self-sabotage are symptoms of misguided beliefs. Most of these external manifestations of faulty beliefs are not visible to the average person; they are secretive. People often go to extreme lengths to mask their symptoms and live in a manner that is socially acceptable. Their "mirror" may not be visible to any other than those who are close or to the "knowing" ones.

There is an exception which I will use to explain the mirror. Obesity is a reflection of faulty beliefs and one of the rare symptoms which is visible to others. My discussion in this area is tricky because many Americans believe that it is politically incorrect to indicate that obesity is a problem. The current myth is that at any weight, a person can be truly happy and content with him or herself. There is a distinct difference between "acceptance" and "happiness" with one's weight. Yes, those

148

obese are best feeling content whatever their weight, but obesity is a symptom of misguided beliefs in 99.9999% of all cases.

Now, to compound the challenge of having faulty beliefs unknowingly, the person also experiences external ridicule, overt and subtle, because of the symptom. Ridicule can come from disparate sources such as the media's obsession with ultra-thin, to the more obvious of condescending looks and attitudes of others.

If the majority of people have symptoms of faulty beliefs that sap their ability to maximize their happiness, how unfair is it to have their symptom visible for others to judge and comment on? Most enjoy the privacy of their symptoms remaining hidden, that is unless or until it surfaces.

Just as I can write a book about the essentialness of balance, so can I write a book about the causes of the symptom of obesity; however, for the purpose of this essay, please accept my premise that it is a symptom.

With her permission, I will use Mama Cass Elliot as an example. Mama Cass experienced encounters during her childhood which layered her intent with cloaks. I will not specify, but I will tell you that she was a profoundly caring and loving person who was harmed, unwittingly, by those who could not hear her soul song. The strength and power of her love shined through all that she did and to all that she encountered. Her one visible symptom, her obesity, served a meaningful purpose in her life, a layer of protection against those who might hurt her tender heart. Many assume that obesity is subconsciously desired to keep others away, but in many cases it is quite the opposite. It is to filter the deep from the shallow. In Mama Cass' case, her weight acted as a prescreening mechanism to keep the disingenuous away. Those shallow who could not love openly to her degree were warded off because they would not see past her weight.

Those who tread closely were those who had at least the capacity to love greatly. The result was that the people who Cass shared her life with loved deeply and profoundly. She developed relationships that were magnificent and spiritual and rewarding and satisfying. Yes, she hurt sometimes as a direct result of her weight, but all the more, she valued her trustful relationships.

149

Cass' weight mirrored her misguided beliefs, in her case, visibly for all the world to see, but it was the power of her love that allowed her to be a commercial mega-success in an industry that rewarded thinness. Cass had a high vibrational energy which she selflessly dedicated towards teaching love. Today she is an integral part of the mission, still working tirelessly towards enlightening others about love, soul songs, and the importance of knowing love to know happiness.

[4:07 pm]

July 19, 2005 2:57 pm   (Book Session 38)

There is no excuse to be unhappy. Look back on the past decade of your life. Another one zoomed by. How many of those days could you have been happy instead of indifferent or worse? How many dreams could you have achieved? What got in the way? Let's assume that you're not in the 2% of all people who could have had the worst imaginable things occur in the past ten years. You're an ordinary person with an ordinary life. How could it have been better? Extraordinary even? What's holding you back?

Make a plan. Please don't let the next ten years zoom past you while you're busy doing. Mark this date on your calendar. Ten years from now you will look back and say, "That was the best decade of my life … SO FAR! And the next one will get even better! I can't wait!"

There are no age barriers unless you allow them. There are no health restrictions unless you allow them. There is no sadness that can't be blasted away with joy.

You know now that your present plight was not your fault. You know now that you were in no way responsible for negative events in your life. But now you have the information to BE responsible. Now you have no excuses. You are in control of your life. YOU. Not your mother. Not your boss. Not your child. Not even your GOD. YOU are in control of your life. Seek support and guidance where you choose, but you direct your course. You are the Master of your Ship. You are the creator of your own autobiography. It is you.

You are precious. You are smart. You are self-reliant and wise. You know things that amaze you. How do you explain the mysteries in your life? It's because there are unseen forces and energies and senses all around you that you, occasionally, tune in to. You would not know what "déjà vu" was unless your innate senses worked. You would not be able to think of a distant friend who suddenly calls unless your primal intuition was working correctly. You would not recognize "coincidence" as something grander if it weren't for your ability to attune to your inner wisdom.

I have mentioned this great man's work previously, but now I would like you to examine it further. Edgar Cayce demonstrated the most prolifically documented example of the ability to tap into universal awareness. His gift leaves little question about the veracity of there existing a source of universal truth. Perhaps I cannot teach you to tap into your power to the extent that Cayce was able, but your knowledge of his ability should erase doubt about the existence of a source greater than your physical carriage. Your physical matter contains a billionth of the power that your soul and intuition hold. Just being aware of its existence will open doors to your ability to discover truth. If I told you that seeing a silver Volkswagen Bug was a sign that God loved you, wouldn't you then see every silver Bug on the road? They would jump into your awareness. Likewise, by being aware of the power of your intuition, the power of coincidence as a guide, the power of your dreams, the proof of these facts through the works the like of Cayce, you will now "see" evidence. The little silver Beetles of your intuition will begin to pop up all over the place … at the craziest times, in the most unusual circumstances.

Karen's "coincidences" happen so often now that they are commonplace and expected. Because her awareness enabled her to focus on what was already happening, her focus allowed her to recognize more. Try jotting down the little oddities that occur. Don't make a chore of it; just record the events and dates briefly as they occur. If you have a little extra time, jot down some "unexplainable" happenings that have passed.

You will see that you, too, have a talent for extruding your latent capabilities. You are more than mere ligaments and vessels and organs

151

and imagination and thought. You are the powerful center of your personal universe. You were born with the power to love, create, and learn. You were born to *know* more than you have been taught. Take the first step towards enjoying your other gifts and allow them to work for you. Your unseen senses are there to guide you, to free you of encumbrances, to help you help yourself towards happiness. Take the first step by enjoying these free presents: ever present presents to help you maximize your life.

You were not born into agony. You were not born into permanent poverty. You were not born into twisted beliefs and resultant discord. You were born to be happy and healthy.

Take back your life, DAMMIT!

The next ten years are yours.

[4:55 pm]

July 20, 2005 12:05 pm   (Book Session 39)

Greed is when you take from the earth more than you will use or enjoy. Stockpiling, hoarding ... those are signs of greed. Wanting, attaining, and using with pleasure that which you obtain are not signs of greed. If you want a big screen TV and you obtain it and you use it ... that is not greed. That is fulfilling the quest of your intent. You are entitled to obtain as long as you appreciate what you have. And you can have much. It is a faulty myth that there is a moral limit on the amount you procure. The only limit is that the accumulations should bring you pleasure.

If you collect antique cars and garage several without driving them, is that greed or pleasure? If owning the cars is a burden, it is greed. If owning the cars brings you satisfaction, it is not.

If you add another emerald to your collection, is that greed or pleasure? If you have so many emeralds that an additional one is only bringing you a brief moment of joy upon purchase, then that is greed. If it is burdensome to insure and store the jewels safely, then it is greed. If

152

having the largest emerald collection on earth is your goal, then it is your pleasure because you are working towards a satisfying goal. You will act creatively and passionately to meet your goal. If you purchase emeralds to enjoy wearing them, that is not greed.

When owning or obtaining is not a burden, then the attainment is not likely induced by greed.

Is greed a negative? The use of the word "burden" in connection with the word "greed" indicates that the process can be detrimental. Anytime you "burden" yourself with ownership, you are depleting your natural ability to be happy. If you own emeralds because they appreciate and you consider them a worthy investment, is that greed or a pleasure? Again ... is ownership a burden that is outweighing the pleasure you have in owning? If it is, greed mixed with fear is operating. You are afraid of selling your collection for fear of the market advancing after the sale. Therefore, you hold them burdensomely. On the other hand, if watching the ups and downs occurring in the emerald market is fun to you ... then ownership is a pleasure.

Why is it necessary to think about greed verses pleasure when it comes to ownership? Quite simply, burdensome ownership depletes your ability to maximize your pleasure. Spend some time thinking about what you own and what you want to own. Material possessions should enhance the pleasure of your life, not deplete it.

Let's begin by looking at what you own. Are you a pack rat? A minimalist? A hoarder? A giver? Focus on one closet in your home. What do you really want to own in that closet? Is the rest a burden? Could some of the burdensome items be pleasures for another? Are you saving for a rainy day? Are you saving for the purpose of capturing memories? I am asking you to assess, honestly, your possessions. Why do you have them? If they are in the closet, they are certainly not to impress others. Why do you keep them? Why does every closet and cabinet get filled to capacity (if you're like most)?

I recently discussed balance as it relates to health. Balance, however, is far more important than just its useful guidance as a tool in matters of physical well-being. Balance is the natural state that supports the maximum capacity for happiness in humans in every area. If you are a pack rat, ask yourself why. What are the possessions giving you that you would be uncomfortable without and why? Is it laziness? Is it fear?

Laziness as an excuse to hoard burdensome possessions is actually not the answer to the problem, since laziness is a symptom of other faulty beliefs. Hoarding because of laziness is layering maligned beliefs through physical manifestation. If you want to free yourself of the burden of over-ownership, you must first assess your beliefs to determine the cause of your laziness. Laziness is a form of control, as are a wide variety of symptoms of maligned beliefs. Laziness can be worn as a badge, keeping people from bugging you or nagging you to do what they want you to do, when they want you to do it. It often manifests in childhood as a mechanism to gain control when parents hyper-influence their children's every move. Laziness also is a tool used to mask confusion or feelings of inadequacy. If a person feels insecure in their ability to succeed in tasks of their choosing, laziness protects from the anguish of trying and failing. Laziness insulates a person from not meeting the expectation of others.

With an elementary understanding of laziness, can you assess why your laziness led to the compounding symptom of hoarding? Do piles of unnecessary possessions affirm your position with others that you cannot be controlled? Do you send a message to others that if you are too lazy to expurgate the mess, then you are certainly not going to take the steps necessary to precipitate a different improvement in your life?

Let's now examine fear as a reason to hoard. I'll offer you generic questions to stimulate your own assessment. Were you "poor" growing up? Are you afraid of having a lack in your life? Do you fear poverty? Are you afraid that the best days or moments of your life are past? Do you fear the future? Do you fear death?

Many hoarders hold onto unnecessary possessions because they are afraid that the best is past. There will not be as happy times in the future as there were in the past; therefore, the objects saved during the happy days are compulsively gripped as a reminder of the good times. The premise is that the objects will make the owner feel the pleasure of the happy days, but in actuality, they will only be a boldfaced reminder of their belief that future days will not be as joy-filled. Such hoarding brings melancholy and grief rather than pleasure and can also prevent the individual from engaging in a happier life or from allowing the future to be happy.

I am not claiming that saving artifacts as memorabilia is detrimental. Remember, we are focusing on balance. Are the items saved balanced with the responsibility of ownership? In other words, is ownership creating chaos by jeopardizing safety or by cluttering to the point of pain? Or, is ownership representing the pleasure of happy trips down memory lane?

[2:22 pm]

July 21, 2005 3:04 pm (Book Session 40)
(This material is a continuation of the previous essay)

Now let's look at possessions you wish to attain. For many, shopping is a form of escape. When checking out all the well-marketed and beautifully packaged items, you briefly escape mundane reality. So many things would be nice to have. They're so pretty and useful and intoxicating. A day of shopping can get the heart pumping with exhilaration.

Do you shop for the sake of shopping? Do you ever regret your purchases or the amount of money you spent? Shopping and consequently experiencing negative results is a form of greed, a greed which masks an underlying problem. If you fall into this category, try to assess why you shop to the point of pain (either the items do not bring you pleasure, or you can ill-afford the money or the space for the new acquisitions). What are your beliefs that contribute to the unnecessary sprees? Do you feel inadequate and believe that you must "keep up with the Joneses" to establish your worth? Are you avoiding more meaningful use of your time, either to build relationships or fulfill a responsibility?

More and more Americans are falling into a negative cycle of shop and spend, shop and spend without thinking about what they are doing or why they are doing it. Pretending you can afford all your purchases will not make it so. Believing that you can or will afford your desires will make it so. Running up debt to acquire possessions that are burdensome will trap you in a cycle of not allowing the abundance, the natural state of abundance, to occur. You must assess your belief system about possessions to reveal the faulty ideas.

Applying the principle of balance to your desires, decide which of the possessions that you wish to obtain will actually bring you pleasure. They do not qualify if you are challenged in paying for them, storing them, or owning them in any way. Once you can narrow down your range of desire by identifying and eliminating choices that would be burdensome, then allow your beliefs to accept and foster the idea that abundance is natural. You were intended to be happy at birth and if the attainment of your new list of desires would make you happy, then you are entitled to those items. As I explained, it is not greed if you acquire or possess items which bring pleasure to you.

How does abundance happen? How can you attract in the abundance that you desire? It is simpler than you imagine, so please, keep it simple and do not overcomplicate it. First, you must exert some effort, once again, to determine what your beliefs about scarcity and abundance are. What is your relationship with money like? Do you believe that it is easy to attain? Or challenging? Do you believe you will never "get ahead"? Or do you believe that you will be wealthy? Do you believe that you will have everything that you want? Or do you believe that you will always lack?

Try examining your family's relationship with abundance, or lack thereof, in your youth. For example, some children watched their parent(s) wield power through their use of money. Others' parents so firmly believed that they were poor and would always struggle with money, that they passed these beliefs on to their children. Did you feel poorer than your peers, richer, or equal?

When you were set on this earth, you were born to experience abundance. You were born to be naturally satiated in external comfort and experiences. As with other beliefs and innate senses, this natural state was likely cloaked by the misguided beliefs of others. Once you reject the misbeliefs and remove the cloaks, you can attract in abundance as a natural state. Focus on what it is you want. Make sure you indicate the objects that will bring you pleasure, not pain, and create a list of your desires. Review the list several times a day and believe that it can all be yours. Gradually, you will witness unusual occurrences happen in your life as your positively charged abundance-antennae magnetize abundant circumstances. Whenever unusual occurrences happen which lead to an increase in abundance, savor the experience and know that you attracted it in. As you accumulate "successes," you will attract in more and more success.

[4:38 pm]

July 22, 2005 12:41 pm   (Book Session 41)

Are you numb or longing? Have you accumulated layers upon layers of thwarted expectations to which you respond with numbness? Or do you "wear your heart on your sleeve," so to speak, longing for deep and meaningful personal encounters? Most people fall into one category or the other, unless, of course, they have been fortunate enough to remain free of masks and cloaks.

Either response to not having your soul song heard jeopardizes your ability to maximize your future happiness, but can you guess which one is more potent? Do you think it is potentially more harmful to show eagerness towards the love of others, or to show indifference? Let me ask it another way. Who do you think has a greater potential for getting hurt?

Before I answer the question, I would like you to assess your own response to this question of extremes. Do you think you hold people at arm's length? Or do you pour your heart out to anyone who is kind to you? Are you one of those people who others judge as "afraid of commitment"? Or do you love and lose and love and lose?

My hope is that you fall somewhere between the two extremes. I hope you have a healthy skepticism about others' ability to be faithful in the quality of their relationship with you balanced by a willingness to let others get close. An extreme in either direction indicates a laceration between you and your intuition, usually instigated by the maligned beliefs of others when you were young. It's not easy to determine if you lean towards an extreme, so take your time in reviewing your relationships of the heart, those with friends and lovers and acquaintances. Do you sense that you are overeager in a new relationship, forcing a depth that did not naturally unfold? Or do you feel strangled by others when they want too much of your attention or companionship?

If you recognize yourself in either extreme, do not feel diminished. There is nothing wrong with developing either trait if you have the ability to recognize it and turn it around into a characteristic that enables you to remove layers. The only wrongness here would be the recognition of the extreme trait within you and giving up the willingness to buffer it with a balancing approach towards relationships in the future. Then you would effectively deny yourself the full potential range of human interaction, thus depleting your ability to achieve full happiness.

Now back to the question: Which extreme is more damaging? The extreme of indifference carries the potential for more damage to one's happiness. I explained to you the "joy" range that humans exist within. By hardening your response to others, you decrease your joy-range. You limit your potential happiness. You give up the opportunity to vibrate on a higher level by cutting off your promise for deep, harmonious, joy-filled relationships.

The extremist who loves openly and freely without wariness has the potential to be wounded more, but (s)he also has the potential for greater highs. It is not necessarily an easy path to "highs," but the moments of "success," that is meaningful relationships which are mutual and joy-filled, allow opportunities to reconnect with one's intuition. By subconsciously assessing what went right with this relationship, the person can tune into his or her intuition more readily, increasing the likelihood of future success. This potential alone makes the extreme of "loving too much" less of a threat to future happiness.

Understanding the extremes in all areas of life often helps you to sort out where you fall in your life. Understanding the extremes introduces you to the potential for harm when your reactions and actions in life are not in balance. Once again, we see the operative of balance at work here, this time in the ability to allow love. How rich are the relationships in your life? With neighbors, lovers, family, and friends? Do your relationships reflect a healthy balance between the extremes of loving too much and too little? Your personal answers are further complicated by the fact that your relationships in different areas may be approached with different responses. For example, your friendships may abound with meaningful, fulfilling relationships, whereas your ability to develop a loving one-on-one relationship with a mate may be troubled.

Are you satisfied with the relationships in your life? I impress upon you the significance of striving for a "yes" answer by reminding you of the purpose of life: to love, to create, and to learn, in that order. Therefore, the most important aspect of fulfilling your intent on earth is to love. As the order of purpose is significant, so is the potential for happiness that you will experience as you master each. The ability to love openly, reciprocally, freely, willingly, and passionately is the greatest path towards total happiness that you have available to you.

What can you do to improve your relationships? The mere act of reading this paragraph indicates that you are already on your way. Simply acknowledging an inadequacy in the depth of your relationship is half-way to resolution. You have at your disposal now the tools that will allow you to improve your relationships. First, assess your beliefs, as you have done repeatedly throughout this book, to determine where and how you donned your cloaks in the matter of love.

Did you feel loved as a child? Were your parents or others demonstrative and consistent in their love of you? Did they withdraw affection when you displeased them? Did they smother you with love to the point of suffocation?

Only you know the answers to these questions. Look for threads of similarities when you were not loved unconditionally by others hearing your soul song. What patterns can you discern? If you recognize inadequacies among your caregivers and those closest to you, can you recall a special relationship with another where someone did love you unconditionally in a healthy way? Perhaps an uncle or a teacher seemed to hear your soul song when no one else could. Use these cognitions to determine what layers you put on in response to inadequacies. Understanding the inception of the layers will allow you to remove them.

159

The second component of developing healthy relationships is to continue to exercise your intuition as you have been taught in this book. The combination of understanding your layers and improving your intuitive abilities will enable you to trust stalwart instincts as guidance in your relationship encounters. Your intuition is the most valuable guide in directing your interactions with others, in assessing the "vibrational" level and intent of another, and in protecting you from becoming involved in a relationship which is unworthy of your trust. Your intuition "feels" whether your vibrational energy is similar to that of those you meet. You instinctively know whether you are compatible in a relationship. If you are one who sees the error of your judgment about someone after a relationship has ended, you would be wise to focus on attuning to your intuition to prevent you from erring again. You know the truth. You may deny it, but you do know it. Wishful thinking does not have to squash wisdom. Let your intuition become your partner and reliable guide in the future.

Further, remember that your antennae will attract in the people who will reaffirm your belief system. As you work towards improving the quality of your beliefs, you will automatically begin to "attract in" the quality of people who match your vibrational level, therefore, those with whom you are most compatible.

[2:37 pm]

July 24, 2005 1:55 pm   (Book Session 42)

How can you, in the simplest way, enjoy your life more? Recognize something that is always there, always has been, available for your pleasure whenever you choose. Walk outside. It matters not what season, what climate, what culture you live in. Walk outside and look around you. Feel the breeze; see the sky. Look for the green around you or the wistful trees aching for their summer clothes. Listen to the moon. Hear the stars call you gently.

Wherever you live, find nature. Nature is one universal constant across the globe that can be counted on to deliver awe and pleasure ... if you just tune into it. Did you ever hear of a Stale Air Program for underprivileged children? No. You know not to bus children to the city for summer camps ... you bring them outside. Fresh Air programs capitalize on the fact that nature is good for you.

Blue skies, rainstorms, gray clouds ... it matters not. Nature will astonish you if you let it.

Sit on a quiet lake. Read a book under a tree. Hike with binoculars and watch the birds. Stand by the ocean and feel its power. Allow the outdoors to mesmerize you with its simplicity and complexities.

Do you think that Native Americans had serial killers? Yes, there were isolated savage tribes whose soul songs were buried in maligned beliefs, but there were not individuals living among nature who murdered their own for pleasure. Nature is harmonizing. Nature is balancing. Nature is soothing and pacifying. Nature is uniting. If you live in China or Alaska, the stars are the same. A bird chirps in Greece; a bird chirps in Montana.

It is not always enough to turn off the electronic devices to hear yourself think. Sometimes you need to stand before something grander than you. Look at a weeping willow and wonder how may years beyond your life it will stand. Hold a newborn kitten. There is majesty and, oddly, predictability in nature. There is chaos, too, but chaos with an explanation. Nature makes sense even in its fiercest power or gentlest breath.

Mend a relationship through nature. If you want to communicate on a deeper level with your mate, go to the sea once a week and talk and listen and say nothing. Your problems will diminish in their significance. Kayak with your daughter. Play volleyball on the beach with your brother, then take time to look and listen peacefully to the world around you.

You were born in a natural state; your world surrounds you with naturalness. Allow the two to coexist in harmony. Allow nature to reduce your blood pressure. Allow the night air to remind you of the simplicity in life. Breathe deeply and take pause to value your physical earth: the stones, the clouds, the rivers, the mountains, the sand, the flowers, the canyons, the rain, the produce, the clay.

If you are one who claims to not like nature, or you have built-in reasons for avoiding the outdoors, then take small steps to get closer. Sit by an open window with no noise inside to distract you. Pick up a leaf on the way to the grocery store and study it. Buy flowers and appreciate them. Sit in your car and watch the clouds go by through your moon-roof. Grab an icicle off the house and lick it.

Humans have bug repellents, sun blocks, net screens, and four season rooms. You can find a suitable way to appreciate nature. Sit in your car by the sea and watch the waves lap the shore. Hang a bird feeder on your window.

Ultimately, nature and everything in it is made up of the same matter as you are. You pulse to the same rhythms and, whether you understand it or not, balance one another. As you have learned, the collective energy of thoughts and beliefs within a region affect the course of nature. As nature harmonizes after an eruption of power, so do humans. As humans' energy amasses to great magnitudes, so does nature until the natural corrections transpire through change, the force of which is determined by the magnitude of the energy built up.

Harmony and balance are the natural states between humans and earth. Humans balance nature and nature balances humans. Together, working in flawless harmony, they allow each other to operate at their peak. As individuals commune with nature, so their thoughts and energy emitted relax to an internal harmonious state. As more and more humans connect with nature, the more the effect balances the state of nature as well.

In summary, the fastest and easiest way for you to increase the pleasure in your life is to allow yourself the peacefulness that surrounding yourself with nature brings. You can improve your health, your relationships, your level of awareness of your purpose, all while improving nature itself just by valuing its gifts.

Continue to work towards assessing your belief system and removing your cloaks, but accelerate your progress by doing so in the presence of nature. You may find the happy feelings you are seeking long before your tasks are accomplished.

[4:04 pm]

162

Once upon a time, there were three little bears. Their names were Mertle, Gertle, and Tertle. Now, unlike another story about bears you may have heard, all three of these bears were little.

Mertle made muffins, Gertle made cheese, and Tertle ate hotdogs. They were all supposed to bring something to the neighborhood picnic, but Tertle had eaten all his hotdogs and went empty-handed. The neighbors were displeased. How dare Tertle siphon off us! Everyone brought something except for him!

The situation was obviously unfair. Tertle regretted not bringing anything, but he had had no choice. The neighbors were annoyed and snubbed him. They did not share their abundant fare with him, and Tertle went home to cry.

Little Portulaca felt her heart leap out to Tertle and hurried to catch up to him. She strolled along side, not saying a word, and Tertle felt comforted by her companionship. When they arrived at his den, something was amuck. The room was far from tidy, with furnishings strewn about. At last Portulaca spoke. Gently she asked, "You are not messy, Tertle. Why is your den so sloppy?"

"They came today," was all the little bear could say.

"Oh!" replied Portulaca sadly, "Why don't you come stay with me?"

The little bear smiled and took her hand. "Thanks," he said, "I think I will."

They left and walked the long distance to Portulaca's hole. She fixed him some tea and asked if he was hungry.

"No," he replied. "I found some hotdogs by the carnival and ate them today."

Once again, she could only say a sad, "Oh."

She knew at once what she must do. Portulaca told Tertle that she would return, and left the hole abruptly. She returned to the picnic and looked sharply at the other animals as they gorged themselves with food.

"Excuse me!" she shouted. "Does anyone here know why Tertle did not bring anything to the picnic?"

They all stared at her in surprise. It had never occurred to them to wonder why. He was just lazy or rude, of course.

"They came today!"

There was a startled gasp among the crowd. Some animals bowed their heads in shame while others gently cried. No one could eat another morsel as they stood quietly trying to think of what to do next.

"I'll tell you what we'll do," Portulaca called out, understanding their thoughts. "We'll march right over to my hole where he is staying. We will bring all the food and music. We will wipe the tears and shame from our faces and we will ask for his forgiveness."

She paused, collecting her thoughts and continued, more gently this time. "And we will ask ourselves why we treated our friend that way. We will think about his sorrow and wonder if it would have been worth alienating him even if he had just forgotten to bring something. If he had been too lazy to cook, couldn't we have looked inside for one of our own flaws and gently reminded him of his responsibility?

"Dahlia, didn't he fix your roof last spring? Armand, what about your strawberries? Who helped you plant them?" She went on for a few minutes reminding the others about why they all loved Tertle so. And as she finished, the animals packed up all the food and marched towards Portulaca's hole.

When they arrived, they hugged Tertle and sang and danced and laughed with their dear friend.

When you were little, others would read you fairytales and fables. They all had a twist or a moral, one which you instinctually knew was correct. You likely had moments of excitement when you figured out the moral without being told because it meant you were smart.

What happened since then? How many of the moral teachings do you presently practice? Are you kind, consistently, to others? Do you litter, cheat, or steal? Do you accept all others as equally important to you or do you judge the worth of those around you? Do you feel some people are more valuable than others because of their intelligence, their address, or their speech? Do you feel prejudice towards any group – Jews, Muslims, women, American Indians, lawyers, janitors, or any class of people? Do you believe that all people on earth are entitled to the same privileges that you are entitled to? Do you believe that all humans are entitled to fulfill their soul's intent: to love, to create, and to learn?

I am using this questioning to help you decide for yourself what your morals are with regard to others. How often do you judge people and feel superior because of some weakness you assign to their actions, race, religion, or sexuality? Do you judge someone because of their clothing or their weight? You are alone in your thoughts now; no one knows what you're thinking or passing judgment about what goes on inside your head, so be honest with yourself. The people on earth who are completely judgment free are so rare that I can count them on one of your hands.

Your discovery of your own beliefs about others is not intended to make you feel shame; it is intended for you to feel truth. The truth is: it is [comparatively] easy to accept that others, ALL others, have a soul song, but it is far more challenging to hear it. When you hear of a terrorist, can you imagine hearing this individual's soul song? When you learn of a drunk driver killing an innocent passenger, can you imagine hearing the driver's soul song?

[7:38 pm]

165

July 26, 2005 11:55 am   (Book Session 44)
(This material is a continuation of the previous essay)

How often you judge others is not the issue here. I am asking you to become aware of the depth of your prejudice for your own sake. Remember as you think about your thoughts towards others that "prejudice" means to "pre-judge." Human nature has become so judgmental that it is nearly impossible to interact with others without passing some sort of judgment about them. Humans "prejudge" others commonly and automatically based on an endless myriad of characteristics or actions. Listen to the voice inside your head all day and think about what you are saying to yourself about others. "Her hair's too short." "He's lazy." "Look at his car." Followed by a quick subconscious, "Mine is better than his."

Humans naturally graze through interactions seeking ways that they can feel superior. If someone arrived at a potluck dinner without a contribution, what would your immediate reaction be? You would likely "prejudge" the reasons why the individual came empty-handed. You would store that little bit of "knowledge" away for future reference and validation of your superiority in that area.

Even by considering the negative attributes that would cause this person to renege on the responsibility of bringing a dish, you are prejudging the acceptability of the reasons. For example, you may believe that if he was recently unemployed and didn't have spare money, then that "excuse" would be more acceptable than if he forgot it in his refrigerator at home. Somehow, being down on his luck is more permissible than being forgetful. You may decide that he is overwrought because his wife just left him, thereby giving him a somewhat valid excuse. But if you assigned "cheapness" as his excuse, then you would judge him more harshly.

Take the time to recognize the way your mind scans situations with judgment. By recognizing the depth of your prejudgment, you can begin to use your ability to judge as an asset in understanding the differences among people and their cloaks and layers.

For example, suppose you do not know why a man came empty-handed to the potluck dinner. It's normal to allow the range of prejudgments to occur, but follow up your thoughts with additional ones such as:

He's so cheap; I just knew he wouldn't bring food. (Hear yourself and think …)

I wonder why he is so cheap. I guess he must not have been brought up with abundance … that's too bad.

(Continue … and here's we separate the men from the boys …)

I hope he gets past his feeling of lack and can enjoy his life and abundance.

(Then for the biggest show of understanding others' soul songs of all …)

Maybe I'll tell the hostess that my dish came from both of us or maybe I'll grab him and take him to the deli by pretending I forgot something. I'll strike up a conversation that will cause him to conclude that he should pick something up as well.

What a difference a few extra thoughts will make, not only in the way you feel towards him, but also in the way you feel about yourself. Even if you take him to the store, he may not increase his awareness about how he can improve his ability to be happy, but inadvertently his day will be better and that is the first step towards removing a cloak. By acting contrarily to the conditioning that the cloak has produced, he will be one step closer to removing the layer.

The result? You are happier. You are more aware. You are vibrating on a higher level. Others around you pick up on your higher vibrational level, not because you tell them of your kind deed, but simply because all people can intuitively sense a higher vibrational level. And, furthermore, as if one small deed could have any more rewards, the man may be closer to removing a cloak, thus closer to increasing his level of awareness and strength of vibrational energy. To continue, you know what happens when his vibrational level improves … yes! So does the vibrational level of those around him.

It seems silly now to prejudge, for even if their "misstep" was worth judging, no good comes from your conclusion of one's inferiority.

The same premise holds true for viewing people by the way they look or speak. Or by the way they worship or don't. Or by the country they or their ancestors are from. Or by the gender of their mate. Or by the car they drive or the company they keep. Or by the amount of education they have or the house they live in. Or by the job they hold or the color of their skin.

Prejudice, that is prejudging others, is normal. Take this normal trait and turn it to your advantage in reaching higher levels of personal satisfaction. Would you have gone home from the potluck dinner happier had you simply concluded he was cheap, or would you leave happier had you opted for the trip to the store?

At a minimum, I am asking you to make an effort. It is unrealistic to assume that you can, at this point, creatively conjure up helpful scenarios like going to the store every time you encounter your own prejudgment, but I can ask you to think. I can expect you to demonstrate curiosity about why a person acts the way s(he) does. I can expect you to understand that every person on earth has a soul song.

If you cannot hear all others' soul songs, I can expect you to practice tolerance.

Think what you want, but demonstrate tolerance – at a minimum. And remember, if your thoughts and beliefs are harsh, so is your ability to maximize your happiness. For your own sake, watch your thoughts. You have the power to control, correct, or change them. They belong to you and no one else. They also indicate your beliefs, the mastering of which is the surest path to lifelong happiness.

[1:13 pm – Yesterday's essay is now completed and a long pause preceded what follows.]

One of the greatest love stories of all times was the story of the love between two friends, two men. Set in a period of racial unrest, the story of Brian's Song depicted a bond so strong that it transcended common ideas about racial differences. At the apex of dramatic change in the beliefs of whites and blacks in America, the story crosses the boundaries of prejudice to demonstrate that all people are worthy. Further compounding the beauty of this tale, the love that was shared was between two men, lambasting another grotesque distortion of imposed limits.

Perhaps you do not practice prejudicial actions, but your thoughts collect with like thoughts to create an environment of prejudice. Just as feelings of angst or despair in a region collectively force a change in nature, so do shared thoughts against a group grow in collective force.

One of the most profoundly predictable outcomes, from the entities perspective, is the different effect that collective prejudice has compared to collective despair or anxiety. This concept will be challenging to understand for all but the most enlightened minds, but I will attempt to describe this phenomenon simply.

When a region grows in despair due to a suppressed economy or increasing crime rates, the collective energy amasses and, upon reaching adequate strength, may bring about a crisis in nature, such as a flood, earthquake, fire, or tornado. We have explained this happening, although the concept may still be beyond most people's grasp.

When the negative energy amassed is based upon prejudice, however, the eruption or correction of the force occurs man against man, not nature against man. (Obviously, the term "man" is used to represent humankind, an unfortunate limitation in the English language.) Prejudicial energy vibrates on a different plane than the energy of despair. The energy produced, or hatred emitted, collects, charged with a specific "direction," if you will, the direction of the hatred. The result is that the energy, when it gains enough strength, will erupt in violence, not in a natural disaster.

Hatred brings war: war in neighborhoods, war between nations, and war between religions. The thread of intolerance among people grows to become a collective prejudice. The energy emitted by the collective prejudice grows into violence or war. The depth, length, and scope of the war depend upon the depth, length, and scope of the prejudice. Sadly, while the war is underway, the strength of the negative energy

169

emitted on each side usually increases dramatically, exacerbating an already merciless situation.

I carefully used the word "usually" in the previous situation. Greats have had the awesome power and insight to prevent the emissions from compounding. Greats such as Lincoln and Gandhi minimized the growth of the prejudice against the perceived enemies through their acute intuition and practical application of compassion. Even though they clearly stood upon one "side" of the conflict, their capacity to practice reason, empathy, and tolerance prevented the conflict from continuing to grow towards the ultimate destruction: the destruction of a group or a nation.

In the absence of Greats, wars escalate in time and destruction until one side is defeated, spiritually, emotionally, and financially. For fear of reminding anyone about which side in conflict emitted the harshest forms of prejudice, suffice it to say that every war was precipitated by collective prejudice; sometimes the prejudice was largely one-sided, but often it was a two-way street.

Although I mentioned that your prejudicial thoughts are private, you can now see that they can be far more detrimental than merely sapping your ability to maximize your happiness. If your prejudice grows into hatred and others share your detest, then ultimately, after continued emissions, war in some magnitude will ensue.

You have heard of the "Power of One." The Power of One can make a difference as demonstrated in historical elections, through great advances in technology, and in the eternal works of great artists. You are misguided if you do not practice tolerance for not only do you lose, but others do as well. Use your Power of One to improve the collective awareness and vibrational level of humankind by exercising your ability to free yourself of prejudice. If you can't hear everyone else's soul song, at least be respectful that they exist.

[2:17 pm]

170

August 2, 2005 12:56 pm   (Book Session 45)

If you want to change your opinion, it's easy to do. The question is - do you want to change your opinion? Negative opinions, or opinions which you hold that decrease the quality of your life, are like deeply rooted weeds: left alone they flourish, choking out all the splendid growth around them, but attacking them takes desire and focus. Eliminating weeds means first becoming aware of their existence. From a distance, a lush lawn may seem impeccable, but at closer glance, the weeds are visible. How can you snap yourself out of complacency long enough to see the weeds in your thinking?

First, as we said, it takes desire. If your own thinking is sabotaging your happiness and the happiness of those around you – change it! There is a little voice inside your head that tells you right from wrong. Heed the voice. Listening may be challenging because of years of ignoring the helpful hints, so clear your head and try to focus on that voice. It is the greatest guide. For example, if you say, "You're stupid!" to someone, what is the voice saying? Do you feel good about yourself? Are you proud?

Try to determine the thinking and then the beliefs behind the words. Assuming the victim of your meanness was not a perceived enemy, what caused you to think like that, let alone say it? Perhaps you were ridiculed when you were young. You imitate the behavior as an adult as a way to disprove the accuracy of the harsh insults said to you. Perhaps your cloaks are hiding your innate self-esteem and criticizing others makes you feel a little more powerful.

Do you want to be the one in the room that no one cares to be around? Or would you prefer to be the one that others feel good near? The way that you think, as an expression of the way that you believe, is what others sense through their "antennae." Actions speak loudly, but thoughts can also be "heard" or sensed by others. You may sit with a smile on your face at a gathering, thinking all kinds of insulting thoughts about the people around you and, although you believe your thoughts are private, the energy that they emit can be readily picked up by other people. Individuals with the highest development of their intuition will perceive the attitude behind your thoughts more readily than those less

171

attuned, who will base their reactions to you slightly more on your actions.

The point is that your belittling thoughts about others can cause the potential relationships you seek to repel you. The quality of the relationships that you attract in will reflect the quality of your thoughts and beliefs. It sounds like a huge responsibility, attracting and repelling people based on your thoughts, but until now it was not. As your ignorance allowed you to give your thinking free reign without cause for consequence, you were largely free of responsibility for the relationships that you attracted. That freedom is now gone. If you are unsatisfied in your loving relationships, then you have the responsibility to change them for the better through your own thinking and believing.

You have likely heard that you are responsible for you own happiness. You have likely heard about the power of positive thinking. Now I am here to confirm the accuracy of these schools of thought with the caveat that it is your *beliefs* that determine your happiness. Your thoughts reflect your beliefs; therefore, changing your thoughts alone will not improve the quality of your life unless you improve the beliefs behind the thoughts.

You have walked through a door that you cannot pass back through. You now know that you are responsible if your relationships are dour, lifeless, or agitating. The responsibility becomes greater as you realize that all others who have read this book understand that your relationships are a direct reflection of your belief system. Your mate is a neon sign for what your beliefs are. The quality of your encounters with friends, family, coworkers, neighbors, and acquaintances is a direct reflection on your belief system.

One of the most remarkable observations that entities make about human life is the bizarre ability of people to hide the transparency of who they are. Highly developed individuals in terms of intuition can see through the camouflage, but most people make superficial conclusions about the essence of others without checking with their inner guidance. So powerful is the inner guidance, in fact, that when humans collectively develop it to even a fraction of its capacity, crime will be eliminated. Humans will "sense" the wrongdoers and ostracize them. (Or ideally, hear their soul songs and guide them towards removing their layers.)

Eventually, they will die off as new humans are born with their innate intuition intact, creating an environment similar to what we experience in the energy realm: cooperative, peaceful, and supportive unity.

The leap in quality of human existence is not as far-fetched as it seems. Let me summarize the process as has been explained to you throughout this book. Forgive the redundancy, but reinforcement is an effective tool for learning … and you certainly know how important learning is.

You are born with the intent of increasing your self-awareness and life knowledge, thereby increasing your vibrational level. As your vibrational level increases, so does your level of joy. Now, the more you are able to increase your awareness on earth, the more you are able to increase the awareness of others around you, thus improving their vibrational level and happiness. The fortunate, beautiful quality of the soul is that the growth cannot be undone. You cannot become "unaware" or decrease your vibrational level.

The result is an exponential improvement in the vibrational levels of humans. As souls are born again and again, their vibrational level increases each time. As you know, "lessons" not learned on earth are integrated after death; therefore, each physical lifetime results in an increase in the soul's vibrational level. When and if these souls choose a new physical life, their next lifetime will naturally be more happy. Further, their ability to improve the awareness of others on earth also increases. Can you see the positive domino effect?

Now for some new information that may be challenging to absorb: new souls are born every day. Not old souls with a new physical life, but brand new, never before existing, virgin souls. The creation of these souls is too complicated to explain in human terms, but conditions occur in the energy realm that allow for the combustion of a new soul. A new soul is as pure as a new human on earth, uncorrupted and undamaged. You may assume that, without accumulating lifetimes of awareness, these souls are darker or meaner than "enlightened" souls, however, this assumption is incorrect. A new soul's awareness is fresh and uncomplicated, but it is not mean. What occurs to a new soul born on earth is that its weaker vibrational strength does not offer as much protection against corruption as an older soul with a stronger vibrational level. Therefore, the new soul has the greatest potential to be damaged,

173

to collect harmful cloaks that limit its ability to enjoy life and experience happiness.

And the good news? The collective increase in awareness that developing souls have experienced, or are experiencing, increases the probability that the new soul will have fewer cloaks thrust upon them than previous new souls had. The family of the new soul is likely to be better equipped to allow the new soul to remain pure and happy. By definition, the higher the vibrational level of those around a new soul, the greater their ability to parent and to interact beneficially.

As you can see, the positive domino effect continues. At the moment of this writing, August 2, 2005, humans are on the precipice of taking leaps in human awareness, thus accelerating the process of humans becoming increasingly happy, less violent, and more tolerant. Although you can detect a swelling of unrest, violence, terrorism, and lack of regard for humanity, these conditions will peak, then dissipate … as long as humans on earth are willing to do their part. That means to take responsibility for their beliefs and to act in accordance with their intent: to love, to create, and to learn, in that order.

I will in no way condone the ill behaviors of certain individuals on earth, but I will indicate the silver lining. As the ill behaviors crescendo or gain in magnitude, those souls less cloaked will increase in their collective repulsion of the ills. The increase in repulsion will force humanity to approach old problems in clever new ways and, with the collective increase in awareness of humans, these new ways will be based upon positive attributes and consequences.

Humans by nature tend to remain complacent until shoved. As they are shoved out of their comfort zone or selective ignorance, they will tap their passion, their intuition, and their creativity in finding solutions. I would like to point out an example and the example can then be applied to more global problems such as improper governmental leadership and terrorism. After the debacles of fallen corporate giants due to greed, extortion, and abuse of power, Americans are growing increasingly intolerant of corporate fraud. In this environment of mistrust, true leaders presently shine. Corporations whose leaders are on a high vibrational level are capable of competing through creativity and passion, rather than defaulting to the loathsome practices of some

174

competitors. America is ripe for the massive successes of honorable institutions. To compound the benefit of the supposed increase in corruption, those who behaved corruptly are pulling in the reigns, covering their illegal tracks for fear of prosecution, and unexpectedly discovering ways to do business honorably.

What this situation demonstrates is that, for humans, the pendulum often swings to the extreme before it effects change. The highly publicized downfalls of major corporations, local governments, and area public and private businesses, serve to increase the good practices of other organizations. As you can see, sometimes things need to get worse before they get better … and this I tell you to help you understand the unrest that you witness. To further stimulate your thinking in this area, think about the women's movement and racial disparity in the United States. How bad did unjust situations become before shoving people towards the path of correction?

And today I will leave you with a final thought. (In case you have not yet realized, I "dictate" essay-length passages almost daily to Karen.) So, the final thought of today's essay is: You are responsible for not only your own happiness through the quality of your belief system, but also, on some level, you are responsible for the happiness of humanity!

[4:00 pm]

August 3, 2005 12:20 pm   (Book Session 46)

We have discussed the importance of balance with respect to your health and your life choices. Let's now look at excesses in society and view them from the perspective of balance. First, allow me to point out that many, if not *most*, excesses today have existed for years, decades, centuries, even millenniums. They may seem rampant or rising because you, or your generation, are viewing them from a fresh perspective.

Opium, prostitution, gluttony, murder, genocide, terrorism, alcohol abuse, child abuse, oppression, racism … virtually any excess you can conceive of has been around long before this physical life of yours. Parents remarked about the liberal-mindedness of youth back in the 1950's and back in the 1440's. Nearly every generation of adults has had a strong percentage of the population believing that the next generation is ill-mannered, disrespectful, lazy, unimaginative, and heading towards the destruction of society.

Excess has always existed.

When your Founding Fathers created the Constitution, they wisely foresaw the need for balance and provided for it through a brilliantly constructed document designed to prohibit excess ... to promote balance. The intent was for the government to act as a guide, a first line of defense, and to provide services which could not be individually obtained. Do not add a liberal interpretation to my use of the words "could not." Americans *cannot* obtain a position of national defense individually. Americans *cannot* obtain parity in interstate commerce individually. Americans *can* operate in a fair market system profitably individually. Americans *can* obtain wealth and provide for their economic and physical well being individually.

The burgeoning government is an example of unbalanced excess. You can likely cite numerous examples of the excess, from duplication of services to redundant taxation; however, the significance of the excess is not the moral, financial, or legal implications, but rather the transference of power from the individual to the government.

The stifling controls and "services" provided by the government have contributed to the deterioration of humans' self-sufficiency. This predicament is virtually global, not merely limited to the American form of government. The moment a person seeks dependence on a source outside his or her own personhood is the moment when a measure of power is transferred. With the exception of seeking assistance in areas outside the parameters of the individual, people who turn to the government for answers diminish their reliance on the intuitive, knowledge-rich source of guidance that they were born with. The governments' willingness to provide excessive services fuels the people's hunger for more assistance.

The mindset that exists is that the government has unlimited resources, power, and money. Any shortcoming on an individual or regional basis *should* be compensated by the government. If in the 1800's farmers faced a drought, the planning for, the response to, and the solution

176

during and afterwards were the responsibility of the farmer. The individuals relied on their intellect, their intuition, their creativity, and their previous learning to manage the crisis. Their passion for survival fueled creative solutions and, as a result, the individuals' vibrational level increased. (And you understand by now that surrounding persons' vibrational levels were increased as well).

One development that transpired from drought conditions was modern irrigation technology. Had the government come in with "drought-relief payments," what would the incentive have been to find long-term solutions to the waxing and waning rainfall? Further, a handout may have bridged the farmers' income gap, but what was the effect on the town that lost the produce? What is the ripple effect of the farmers not having enough incentive to solve the issue in a self-reliant manner?

Each governmental agency, every governmental official, and every act in legislation should be viewed from the perspective of how do they compromise the self-reliance of the constituents? How do they disable citizens' natural reliance on innate senses?

As the present growth in enlightenment continues, the excesses in governmental imposition will decline. It's a matter of supply and demand. Currently there is an insatiable demand for governmental services, but as more and more individuals create their own positive reality, the demand will decrease. As the demand deceases, the supply will need to contract. The contraction will not take place naturally as it does in the free enterprise system, since the government is virtually exempt from the economic laws of free enterprise. However, the contraction will be prodded by those who are aware of declining demand.

[1:36 pm]

Excess can be analyzed in areas other than government. For every excess there is an equivalent loss. In order to "balance" the excess, something must be sacrificed, similar to the principle that energy never dies, it simply mutates.

Since before the days of Shakespeare, lovers of language have complained that its correct usage is a dying art. Lincoln was widely

177

criticized for his infernal abuse of prose. Later generations exalted Lincoln's command of language and lashed out at modern displays of vernacular. Then there was the lingo of the "Valley Girls" and "Ebonics." The excess in question is actually a lack, an *excessive* lack of use of the riches of a splendid language. Statistically, the percentage of the population that can conceptually grasp the writings in *The New York Times* is steadily declining. The loss balancing the excess is the loss of vocabulary which, generationally, is not being replaced. Words are becoming extinct because, like animals facing the same plight, they do not have an environment in which to flourish. What is being sacrificed is the ability for Americans to communicate in prolific, descriptive, accurate, or intensive expressions.

Why do we want to eliminate or limit excess? The same factors that individually deplete one's ability to maximize one's happiness also deplete society's. A lack of balance in individuals' lives diminishes their capacity to maximize their vibrational level, and the lack of balance in society diminishes the capacity of the society, collectively, to maximize their vibrational level. Excessive noise can lessen one's hearing capacity and lead to irritability. Excessive drug use in a region can lead to increased crime. Excessive pollution can lead to a deadening of nature.

(I need to postscript this passage with an important side note intended to clarify confusion among those readers in a high state of awareness. The consequences of the excess occur because people collectively *believe* that they will occur. And to take this concept one step further, the manifestation of the excess appears because people collectively *believe* that it will appear.)

At this point in the collective awareness of humans, it is sufficient to state that excesses of any sort are contraindicative to individual or societal happiness. As important as it is for individuals to seek balance, it is equally important for society to seek the same.

[2:31 pm]

August 6, 2005 7:46 am   (Book Session 47)

The responsibility for your happiness is yours. You get that. Now how do you prevent yourself from compounding difficult circumstances with guilt that you brought them on yourself? The biggest challenge in knowing your participation in your own life story is: what do you do with the information to improve your life?

Every skill on earth takes some measure of practice. Walking, talking, drawing, singing, cooking … a little practice, or in some cases, a lot of practice, helps people grow in their ability. Many skills are mastered until the point that they become second nature. Do you ever think about walking anymore? Unless you lose the capability or need to rebuild it, you will not likely think about it anymore. As you watch a young one take his first steps, do you consider how talented you are for walking effortlessly?

Creating the life path that you choose will occur as effortlessly once you master the skills. Consider people you know whose lives seem easy and happy. Wouldn't you observe that that state remains fairly consistent over time? Wouldn't you say that year in, year out, these people seem rooted in a stable happiness? Unknowingly, these individuals have mastered the skill of creating the life they desire.

As with mastering any skill, observing a person talented at the task helps you to grow in yours. Try to notice people who smile and who seem nonplussed. Seek the company of people who are crisis-free in their own lives – not necessarily crisis-free from the events of those around them, but individually crisis-free and seemingly impervious to the effects of those crisis-bound. You can learn from them. They already "know" what they're doing. Observe them. Observe their reactions. Listen when they speak. Your innate senses will uncover remarkable traits that such people have in common. They *under* react. They do not get caught up in other people's dramas. They do not gossip – not out of a Pollyanna attitude, but simply because it doesn't interest them. They'll converse about people, but not in a gossipy way – there's a difference.

If you set goals to lose weight or get your college degree, you wouldn't hesitate to seek the advice of knowledgeable people. Now you are setting the most important goal of your life … the goal to be happy.

There are people around you who know how to do it. At a minimum, observe them, but it's more beneficial to ask them questions. There's nothing wrong with saying, "I notice that you seem happier than most people and I'm just curious how you do it." Most people will be happy to share their secrets and may even look at themselves in new terms.

One roadblock in helping people obtain happy role-models is the media's focus on the crisis-bound. Most people are interesting to the news media because of a problem they are in the midst of. When was the last time you read an article about someone who was consistently happy and how they obtained that state? They exist and others could learn volumes from their beliefs and actions.

You can turn the lack of "happy people" stories around to your advantage. Read the stories about the crisis-entrenched people and determine why they are *not* able to live contentedly. Provided the writer is skilled enough to elicit meaningful information from the subject, you can recognize trends and observe commonalities among the unhappy. Be cautious to observe and not entrench yourself emotionally in the stories, however, which proves counter-productive.

Consciously seeking information about what makes people happy, or what happy people believe, will open your ability to obtain the same satisfaction in your life. What you focus on becomes attracted into your life. You change the energy you emit through seeking happiness ideals. The energy becomes one of attracting in that which you observe. This phenomenon will assist your success, will hasten your path towards happiness. Therefore, not only will you learn intellectually how to attain happiness, but the sheer act of seeking evidence and witnessing joyful lives will attract some happiness-building skills into your own life.

In addition to helping you understand the process of happiness, observing others' levels of achievement will also bring into focus the appalling lack of contentment that exists in general. Not intending to make you pessimistic about the state of humanity, I ask you to observe the state to make you realize that you are normal. If you haven't achieved the level of happiness you desire, you are normal. And it is highly likely that as you observe others, you will notice that most others' state of happiness is far worse than yours. What is the benefit of acknowledging this fact? Until now, until reading this book, none of you knew much about the process of creating your own life stage. Without this knowledge, how could you possibly create the life you want without knowing how? Without knowing that the power lies within your belief system? Without knowing that your belief system was likely contaminated by others before the age of reason and self-reliance? How could you possibly feel guilty about the undesired conditions that exist in your life prior to this knowledge? You can't.

If a person next to you had an aneurysm and required immediate life-saving brain surgery, would you feel guilty if you couldn't provide it? Would you even comprehend that with the proper education and training you could improvise life-saving actions? No, you would not feel guilty. You did not have the awareness or skill to assist. So you did what you could do. You called 911. You kept that person safe and calm. You did what you could do with the level of knowledge and awareness you had. And for that, you should be proud. Others will likely appreciate your efforts and commend you for your actions. And you will be proud.

Likewise, the conditions of your life are based on the knowledge and information that you have at any given moment. You should be proud of what you achieved with your limited understanding. There should be no feelings of guilt or remorse because you did the best you could at any given moment. Yes, you would likely choose different actions for many moments or periods of your life, but you learned and grew in awareness with each mistake and now, with the knowledge and awareness you have gained, you can stop making unwise choices and begin to create the happy life that you want.

The path to happiness is simple and it is not. Unfortunately, humans tend to lose interest in a project if results are not immediate. Your ability to write your own life story to match your desire takes focus and commitment. You have to remain focused to achieve your goal and not let yourself drift back into old nonproductive patterns. The effort is worthwhile though because, like walking, once the skill is learned it becomes automatic.

No one can force you to focus – not even me. You have the tools at your disposal to create the life you desire if you choose to focus and commit. There are a million excuses to falter on the simple assignments in this book, but then the results belong to you. Ignorance about the way to manifest your happiness is no longer a reason to not obtain it. You are now a brain surgeon with a patient's life in your care. The operating room is set up; your skills and awareness are in place ... you have no option but to perform the surgery. The life you save is your own. Apply your knowledge about beliefs and antennae and happiness to your life and save it from unnecessary unhappiness.

August 9, 2005 1:46 pm   (Book Session 48)

Formulate a specific goal plan before you begin. As in all course of study, learning how to maximize your ability to be happy takes structure. This task is not one that can be undertaken haphazardly, as though reading one book will guarantee your joy through some osmosis-like exchange. You must work a little. Be forewarned, however, that a good number of people are so complacent and comfortable in their present state of discontent that they will not extend the effort to release themselves. Imagine that? Some people will actually make a subconscious choice to remain unhappy ... because the familiarity with that state is less intimidating than a state of joy.

If you are joyful, what will you complain about? What excuse will you have to be lazy or late or rude or unforgiving? Think honestly about how many negative cloaks you don and the reasons why. Think about what those cloaks are preventing you from having to do or protecting you from. For example, perpetual lateness protects you from having to obey others' schedules or demands. It puts you in control of where and when you go. Being happy and losing your cloaks will cause you to remove a protective layer that may have served you comfortably.

I do not mean to make happiness sound like a negative state; I am merely pointing out that change, even for the good, is not always easy. Please recognize and appreciate the fact that the changes described in this book are worth the effort. The exchange of old counter-productive habits for new life-building choices is complex and unfamiliar at first, but you will adjust quickly and I guarantee you will love the results. Think about a person who is progressing through a twelve-step program. As the days of exercised willpower accumulate, do you think that the individual experiences any regrets about overcoming the

182

addiction? Regrets for improving are not likely. One may experience moments or challenges when the temptation to slip back into old habits is great, but regrets for improving one's quality of life are rare. The point is that you may find it difficult at times to remain focused on your worthy goal, but stick with it. The rewards are amazing and often permanent.

Formulate your plan. The exercises in this book are intentionally few and manageable. If you have not yet done so, go through the book and complete the exercises. You cannot discover the layers, cloaks, and beliefs that you hold without taking the time to complete the assignments.

Paper and pen (or electronic notebooks – I keep up with progress) are essential to the successful implementation of the ideas in this book. There is a process that occurs when the brain and hand connect to record ideas that greatly enhances the learning and understanding that will take place. Put it down in words. Likewise, your dream log cannot benefit you if it is recorded in your head. You cannot possibly remember the significant occurrences without recording them and referring back.

Time is on your side. You can decide now to become happier or choose to postpone the effort and stay in your current state longer. My guess is that if you fail to complete the minimal exercises detailed in this book, you will kick yourself in thirty days. And if the difficult challenge of figuring out exactly how to kick yourself isn't great enough to make you stop and exert some effort towards your own happiness, then you will likely kick yourself even harder in another thirty days. Imagine, instead, that in just thirty days you will see a change in the quality of people and events that you attract into your life.

Imagine all your dreams coming true. It may sound corny, but it is a doable goal. You can make all your dreams come true by getting to know your belief system and by removing your cloaks and layers. By understanding the purpose of life, to love, to create, and to learn, in that order, you will be able to fulfill your soul's intent. You will increase your vibrational level, increase your state of happiness, and also increase the vibrational state of those around you.

Nobody expects you to be perfect. As with any new skill, your ability to attract in your own circumstances and people for a better life takes practice. Give yourself some understanding and patience. You will never have to return to square one – the state you were in when you began to read this book; you will always make progress just by remaining aware of your goal. The act of reading and understanding this book has already pivoted you in the right direction towards being happier. Keep building on your new healthy foundation and you will be stunned by the positive results.

[Pause … start a new essay]

A good way to begin the formulation of your plan is to list your desires. It sounds so simple that you can easily convince yourself that it is unnecessary. It *is* necessary! Give yourself twenty uninterrupted minutes and follow the standard writing "rules," meaning that there are no rules. No editing. No grammar checks. No punctuation unless it comes automatically. No attention to spelling. No cares. Just write.

Try to keep your five well-known senses in your thoughts as you write your desires and try to be as specific as possible.

> Good:
> I want to vacation at the beach

> Better:
> I want to vacation near the ocean and feel cool, salty water lap at my feet as I drink my morning coffee. I want to smell the fresh sea as I awaken each day and rest each night …

> Best:
> I want to vacation in Cozumel for one week during the next year with my husband and two children. I want to feel the cool salty water lap at my …

You get the idea. Try to be specific. Knowing exactly what you want helps charge your antennae with the correct inscription before going forth seeking like antennae. Reread your list often. Try to keep your desires in your thoughts positively without saddling them with burdensome negatives such as, "This is a waste of time," or "I know this will never happen." Try to believe that you are entitled to your desires. You *are* entitled to your desires. Contrary to all previous myths, humans are intended to create the life they desire to the extent that the "law of accumulation" is not exceeded. If you recall, your possessions and accumulations should not exceed your ability to use or enjoy them. You do not have to "sacrifice" your desires in order to prove your worthiness. It is only noble to struggle for financial survival if you *believe* that it is noble to struggle for financial survival.

To help dispel the myth that poverty is a necessary component of being qualified as a "good person," let me explain how the myth began. By choice, Jesus Christ was willing to forego unnecessary material possessions because during the period that he walked the earth, he understood that the collective belief system of humankind prescribed to the notion that goodness and charity required selflessness and sacrifice. Jesus, a Great, was willing to deliver his message in the manner in which he felt humankind was capable of accepting it. After his life, the Church taught individuals that sacrifice was a necessary component of a life deemed worthy for acceptance into Heaven, thus the myth began.

Being humbly poor or middle-class does not make one a better person than one with great wealth. As a matter of fact, one's wealth has absolutely no predictive value in measuring or commenting on a person's goodness. There are wealthy people on an extremely high vibrational level who love, create, and learn beautifully, and there are wealthy people on a lower vibrational level that are clueless as to the purpose of life.

Other Greats have metamorphosed their lifestyle into the period of their existence as well as Jesus Christ did. Gandhi, for example, intuitively understood his need for piety and poverty to affect the masses of the people he wished to enlighten. His notions of sacrifice and poverty were necessary in his region during his period on earth and the inclusion of these ideas in his work had the desired result.

The more prolific tool which he used to enlighten humanity still remains a necessity: non-violence. Non-violence respects and honors all three essential components of humanity's purpose: to love, to create, and to learn. Non-violence shows love of others by refusing to harm another; it demonstrates creation by using a creative solution and rejecting the

185

principles of war to solve an age-old problem; and it demonstrates learning by millions upon millions of people who learned, during his lifetime and afterwards, the value, credence, and successfulness of resolving conflicts without violence.

As you complete your list, remember that you can modify it or fine-tune it at a later date. After completing the other exercises in this book, the items on your desire-list that are the most clearly defined and believable to you are the ones that will be achieved first.

To give you a hint of what you have to look forward to at a later date: as more and more people successfully meet the goals of this book, then more and more people will be ready to set a "desire list" for groups larger than just the individuals involved. For example, a group of highly-aware people can create a list of desires for their ideal community, neighborhood, region, state, country, and world. The more people that join forces in creating such a list and remain focused on it and believe that it can and will happen, the more quickly the larger desires will be achieved.

The concepts that lead to individual awareness can be applied to small groups or areas and then to increasingly larger regions. Individual antennae collect to produce the outcome of the charges. If more individuals are emitting positively charged antennae, then the region will change for the better. This phenomenon explains why a region growing in poverty or despair will frequently continue to spiral downwards until an infusion of positive energy takes place. The Tsunami of 2004, for example, attracted in great amounts of positively charged antennae after the devastation.

You as an individual may not yet be ready to try to change your belief system towards outside events and people en masse. Don't worry … take one step at a time and improve your present state first. When you see great results, then apply the concepts to your loved ones and help to improve the relationships among you.

Just take one step at a time. You will be very happy with the results.

[4:11 pm]

August 13, 2005 11:57 am   (Book Session 49)

Squeeze the life out of your life. Don't die with all the rich juices bottled up inside this life that is yours ... squeeze every last drip of sweet nectar out and enjoy it. If you are like most people, your senses are extremely underutilized. Your sense of smell and taste and hearing and sight and touch are taken for granted and under-appreciated. Feel textures. See the rich colors of your world. Hear the music. Taste the sweet and bitter fruits of the earth. Dazzle your senses every day.

Don't live in grayscale. Live in rich living color. Throw away your black shirts – wear lime and orange and purple and fuchsia and aqua. Let others know you are alive by acting alive! How many people around you are dull or pasty in their thoughts and actions? Don't be grayscale. Tell a joke. Belly laugh. Skip. Blow bubbles. Whistle. Smile. Curl your toes in the sea. Feel the wind on your cheek. Catch the autumn leaves as they fall. Suck an icicle. Walk. Run. Hop. Play. Laugh. Laugh some more. Make others laugh. Take a deep relaxing breath. Stand under a waterfall. Watch a biplane. Watch the clouds. Read a great book. Learn a magic trick. Drink fresh squeezed apple cider. Listen to the heat-bugs.

If you claim that you don't have time, then your belief system needs reworking. Get diagnosed with a terminal illness today and see how much free time you suddenly have. Lose a loved one and realize all the things you would have liked to do with that person – then do it without losing anyone!

Don't think grayscale. Don't deaden your own life. Even though your senses and pleasures are not as great as ours, you are very likely not taking advantage of them. Why not enjoy your life? What problem is so great that you cannot enjoy some fun? Some color? Some music? Some popcorn? Some scissors and craft paper? Why not just enjoy your life? What is preventing you? No excuses. What is honestly preventing you from living in living color?

Think about some of your happiest memories. Were they at work? Did they occur while you were nagging or cleaning or running errands? And why shouldn't some of your next best memories be while cleaning?

Dance and sing and make a game of it with your family. Why so dull? It has to be done anyway – why make it so dull?

Cinder blocks make a fine sturdy foundation for a house, but they are dull and gray. Build your foundation with some fieldstone that has coral ripples etched into the rock. Let nature's charcoal specks and sienna layers glisten in the sun on your foundation.

I can't say you only live once, but I can say that you only have one opportunity at this life as you know it. Make it orange. Make it bold. Make it count. Stop being afraid to live life. Stop being afraid to enjoy.

Try the old reliable getting-to-know-yourself trick and ask yourself, "If I could have dinner with any one person no longer alive (in this physical life), who would it be?" Think about it for a moment. When you have your answer you will discover a person who was passionate. It is the passion within that individual's life that you want to get to know. Live your life with passion.

When you're angry, smile. When you're sad, dance. When you're frustrated, sing. When you're bored, finger-paint. When you're lethargic, skip. When you're annoying, snap out of it and tell a joke. Stargaze at midnight. Linger in the meadow. Be fun. Be nice. Be able to be loved. Let your soul song soar. Let others hear you dance when you are still. If you're eighty or you're eighteen … today is a fun day and tomorrow is, too.

You don't have to be bored or boring or dull or mean or complaining or cranky or fearful or angry or judgmental or rude or plain or invisible. Decide now that forever more you will live a colorful life, one that embraces joy and fun, one that does not conjure up reasons to be drab. Listen to the music that makes your heart glad. Look at the art that makes your insides dance.

All the magic in this book can be yours if you surround yourself with joy instead of worry or anger or boredom. The freedom that you have which is greater than any other is the freedom to enjoy your life. Enjoy your life. Surround yourself with things and people and colors that you love. In this setting, complete the exercises in this book and let the magic unfold. Within a happy setting your ability to create a life of passion and love can flourish. You can attract in a happy life faster among the rich stimuli that you enjoy than you can in a gray room with black clothing on from head to toe.

Remember this: Your life is meant to be passionately enjoyed!

[1:38 pm]

August 15, 2005 2:08 pm   (Book Session 50)
(Received personal information for about an hour)

Let's go fly a kite. What happens? On a still day the kite never ascends; it just hangs in the air like a leaden weight. And then, a breeze picks up and gently tugs the kite into the sky. The kite's tail dances. The colors spin and glisten, magic from a few scraps of material.

One day the kite is magic and fun and excitement; the next, it is merely a non-functional piece of fabric. What makes the difference from one day to the next? You can define it, yet you can't. You know that the air pushes one day and sets still the next. You name it "wind," but how do you define "wind"? Can you describe it without using its own word or synonyms? Can you see it? Can you hear it? Can you smell it? Can you taste it? No, you can only sense wind by touch. You *feel* wind. If you claim to see it, you are being fooled by watching the effect wind has on its surroundings. If you claim to smell it, you are only being fooled by the essence it carries to you from your surroundings. If you think you hear wind, you are being fooled again. You are listening to the air pushing against or across objects in your surroundings. Wind is tasteless, odorless, and silent, yet it is one of the most powerful forces on earth. It cools you on a summer day, carries seeds for planting in its midst, and gently pries the spent leaves from the trees. It twirls and spins and rushes. It knocks things down and picks things up. It uproots and tears down. It erodes shores and builds up banks. Yet you don't even know what it is except by its own definition.

You can measure it, but you cannot capture it. You can harness it, yet you cannot hold it. What a mysterious power. The only clue you have to its existence is the effect it has on your surroundings.

189

If you contemplate the awesomeness of the wind, do you think that other like forces may exist which do not enable even the sense of touch to detect it? The truth is that such forces or energies do exist; science is simply not ready to detect them. On a windy day, turn an open jar into the wind then quickly shut the jar. Take your captured wind into the house and release it. What happens? Does it swirl about? Can you measure it or smell it or feel it?

In essence, that defines the problem in scientists' inability to detect other forces that surround you. Looking for or at the energies changes them. Trying to study them deems them inoperable. It is an act of faith to accept the nuances and characteristics of the wind. Humans do not try to change the force, they merely try to predict it for protection or harness it for power. They readily accept that wind has its own course undeterred by humans' existence or needs or wants or objects.

Accept on faith, as well, the existence of other forces, some more powerful than the wind. The existence of these forces will eventually be proven similarly to the way "waves" were detected in the atmosphere. Who now can remember life without the unleashing of the power of radio frequencies? Can you exist as comfortably without cellular and wireless technology? Was the existence of either a suspicion a century ago?

Accept on faith that there are still forces in your world that you cannot see. These energies make radio and satellite seem primitive, in fact. Although empirical data about these forces cannot yet be collected, you can bolster your faith through the findings and credible reports that surround you. Do not dismiss the precepts of Edgar Cayce. Do not dismiss the "medium" who assists police in uncovering clues. Heed the possibility of life-after-physical-death. Stay open to the concepts of intuition, ESP, channeling, out-of-body experiences, and time travel.

Just as you explain "wind" by defining its effect on the surroundings, you likewise describe instincts by their effect on animal behavior. You do not "know" scientifically what "instincts" are. You cannot measure them, hear them, hold them, taste them, or see them. Yet you accept that instincts are real because of the otherwise unexplainable actions of animals. Is this act of faith any different than accepting, for now, that

190

Karen is "receiving" through automatic writing a book of knowledge from Ayn Rand?

Humans will one day "prove" these energies. For now, accept their existence based on the effects they have on your surroundings. With or without your consent, the wind will blow, animals will survive with an inner knowing, and people will create their own life stories through their vibrational energy, beliefs, and the antennae that they release.

If you do not evacuate before a deadly windstorm, the wind cares not. If you do not harness the power of your beliefs to create a reality of your choosing, your antennae care not. They will bring back to you what you unwittingly tell them to bring back. You are welcome to wait for scientific evidence proving the existence of your vibrational energy and the charges of your antennae. The choice is yours, but remember that the evidence is not likely to be viable in this lifetime of yours, so make your choice wisely!

[4:09 pm]

August 16, 2005 3:00 pm   (Book Session 51)

Are you ready? To take matters into your own hands? This book has given you an overview of the true meaning of your life. Perhaps you have been exposed to some concepts previously, such as "coincidence" as a powerful indicator of attraction. Perhaps this read is your first exposure to the awesome ability you hold in creating the future of your desire. Perhaps you believe in an almighty deity that intervenes at your command. You may even believe in destiny.

Whatever framework of ideas you brought to this book, we are hopeful that we have dispelled myths that are counterproductive to your ability to achieve happiness. We hope that you are left feeling more in control of your "destiny" than ever before. We hope that you understand the new concepts that we laid forth such as "soul song," "vibrational energy," and "attraction." But more important than anything else, we hope that you embrace the purpose of your life as it was intended: to love, to create, and to learn, in that order. There are *truly* no exceptions.

This book is the beginning, not the end. Your awareness has been expanded and it will continue to grow as you "attract in" material to continue your learning. Take a good look at what you are drawn to. Allow yourself to focus on the object or material that catches your attention. There are no coincidences and your mysterious focus offers clues as to the quality of life you are able to create.

We, Ayn and my fellow "mission" entities, are aware that your culture is rapidly accepting and endorsing ethereal ideas that were previously ridiculed or condemned. This cultural change indicates a growing increase in the collective vibrational level of your people. Holistic medicine, crossing-over communications, the abundance theory, and the surge in popularity of "intuitive" pursuits all show the slow transformation of collective thinking. As we have specified, the increase in vibrational energy of one person increases that of others. The increase of vibrational energy of an area increases the prosperity and happiness of the region.

The more people who accept the true ideas as true and begin to reject false myths, the more the collective awareness will increase. Everyone benefits as additional people shed misbeliefs. We see this trend continuing and gaining in strength over time. We see, over the next few decades, the institutions that are founded upon maligned beliefs faltering at their own hands. Attempts to compel others to agree to false premises will lead to a kind of internal combustion where the institutions self-destruct from within.

Americans' tolerance of what is and is not acceptable from institutions is influencing the future course of the establishments. Even the oldest groups will soon be unable to continue as always without validating their truthfulness, integrity, and meaningfulness. They will have to prove their worth, their value, and their credibility to the masses. If not, they will become extinct.

Your world is in a period of passages. The percentage of earth beings that have high expectations of themselves and their fellow neighbors is increasing at the greatest rate ever in the history of humankind. For those of you young enough to enjoy, you will witness a major transformation in the collective awareness of your nation and like nations. You will see worldwide improvements in the way people live.

You will witness peacefulness as never known before. For those of you a little older – fear not. You, too, will witness the transformation, simply from a different plane or a different lifetime.

We do have one request, however. As these magical transformations are underway, there will be some setbacks. As institutions rooted in maligned beliefs scratch and claw in their attempts to survive, they will accentuate their flaws and failings. We ask that you do not panic at their destruction. Instead, know that the extremes that you are witnessing are necessary to bring many individuals into a new state of awareness. Sometimes people only see the truth when the untruthfulness is grotesquely exaggerated.

Do not fall for manipulations. Do not let others convince you that their way is right and yours is wrong if you intuitively know that their way of thinking or controlling has passed. If you recognize a truth that they do not, honor it. And let them be. Do not be angered, for you fuel their fire. Turn your attention to the good and the honorable. Live your life the way you know you should and let the organizations based on falsehoods die.

You will see overall strides towards betterment. The setbacks will be less than the progressions. Focus on the progressions for they will nourish your soul. As they grow, you grow. As you grow, they grow. Support the establishments and individuals that you *know* are aligned with life's intended purpose.

And, most of all, enjoy the transformation. Enjoy your life and enjoy your passion!

[4:57 pm]

August 17, 2005 6:08 pm   (Book Session 52)

Often people celebrate birth and mourn death. There is really no such thing as either. The soul passes through realms but never dies. When a person is born, the soul is simply completing the passage from the energy realm into the physical realm. When a person dies, a soul is merely releasing the physical carrier and rejoining the energy realm. As humankind advances in its intuitive capabilities, it will become common practice to access and assess previous existences. Initially, the study will be limited to the comprehension of previous physical lives, but the practice will eventually advance to include the study of the energy realm and other realms with which you are not yet familiar.

Existential means the extension of existence and properly terms the process of physical life. Physical life is the extension of the existence of the soul. The soul willingly extends itself into the physical realm for a variety of reasons, but fundamentally with the intent to increase its and others' vibrational levels. The soul never dies.

I will explain to you one way, however, that a soul can alter its state of energy to the point that the individual soul can no longer be detected. Some souls choose as their life path to continue their growth and climb towards higher and higher vibrational levels until the vibrational energy is a near match to the energy radiated by ALL THAT IS. At this point, the soul may choose a type of fusion with ALL THAT IS. Overly simplified, this means that the soul's energy joins that of ALL THAT IS and does not continue an individual existence. The force of the energy of the soul still exists, but it becomes a part of a stronger energy. This process is an option for all souls, yet not many select it. The learning and joy that we experience is so great and the options available so vast, that most of us choose different realms in lieu of fusion. Since I personally have not reached that vibrational level, I cannot describe it completely, but I understand that the state is one of pure bliss, pure ecstasy, pure love, and pure peacefulness. For me, it is hard to imagine such a state, because our state in the energy realm seems to fit that description. It is nearly unimaginable to me that my state could be improved upon!

I want you to think for a moment about a great university. Now imagine taking every course of study that is offered and learning all the material in each course. Now imagine continuing this process at every university until all new knowledge has been exhausted. Could you possibly learn all the information available for absorption? Not in one physical lifetime and not in a hundred physical lifetimes. Now imagine, if you will, that our realm contains more knowledge to be discovered than yours does. Imagine that knowledge on earth is just a small speck in comparison to universal knowledge. How many life-years do you think it would take to uncover all of that material let alone learn it?

Now imagine trying to explain to a creature from another planet all of the knowledge available on earth in his native language or form of communication. If this book leaves you with many unanswered questions, that is because we are attempting to communicate universal knowledge in one short book within the confines of your language. Many decisions were made as to which information is the most critical to be disseminated at this point in the existence of humanity. Decisions were made as to how to simplify the material to make it meaningful and useful to you. Even though you now know such a vast amount more about the purpose of physical life and the place a soul plays in the history of existence, you have only been to one course in one university, in one town, in one country, in one world, in one realm. Yes. You will have questions and we will do our best to provide answers as readily as we can, but you now have a working knowledge of the fundamentals of living a happier existence in your present physical vehicle. That is the purpose of this book.

I know you have questions and doubts. We want you to have doubts. Doubt is the signal from a healthy mind that independent thinking is your guiding source. Independent thinking is your protector and your mentor. Those who are unable to think independently are unable to create the life of their choosing.

What should you do with your doubts? You can bury them, you can analyze them, or you can seek proof. Burying them is stupid; analyzing them is a good start in the right direction, but seeking proof is the best way to proceed. We have presented you with numerous opportunities to seek evidence such as the teachings of Edgar Cayce or Seth. This information is available for you to absorb. We encourage you to seek the information. We encourage you to bear an open mind. We encourage you for *your* sake. We want you to succeed at increasing your vibrational level on earth. We want you to be joyful. All entities want the best for you and for humanity; ALL THAT IS wants the best for you and for humanity. We have noble intentions for a noble purpose, and a purpose that is self-serving as well. Because, as you know, when the collective vibrational energy of earthlings increases, the collective vibrational level of entities and ALL THAT IS increases as well. Even we are not sacrificing. We provide you with information of value so that you may help yourself and help others, which ultimately helps us!

Try something new. If your old way of living was not gaining you the results you desire, then try something new. Try to determine your belief system and understand the way it influences the quality of your life. Try to make a real effort to follow what makes you feel *passionate*. Try out your creativity. Use the tools that you were born with to carve out a happier path for yourself and others. Let your vibrancy show. Allow your intuition to flourish. Take a reputable course in past life regression just for the fun of it. Isn't this one physical life of yours too short to not enjoy the fun of exploring and learning? Why not see for yourself what is real and what is not?

Question everything you encounter. Question old ideas, new ideas, young ideas, "proven" ideas. Let your brain work for you. Exercise the ol' thing to keep it in top shape. If you intentionally don't use your leg muscles for a year and then they don't work the way you want, only you are to blame. Don't let others exercise for you. Do your own exercise. Think for yourself; don't let others think for you. You were born with vast amounts of universal knowledge that has gotten buried – but it is there for the asking if you remove your cloaks and exercise your power of independent thinking.

As this book unfolded, we intended to reveal to you the truthfulness or fictitiousness of many ideas. We wanted to dispel myths with the intent of freeing your energy for pursuits that would prove productive. We have done so in many cases, such as shedding light on life-after-death, reincarnation, and the power to create your own happiness. There are many concepts which remain still shrouded in mystery such as angels, Satan, extraterrestrial beings, ghosts, heaven, hell, Jesus Christ as The Son of God, Mohammed as a Prophet, UFOs, time travel, telepathy, and the list goes on.

We will cast some light on some of these notions to help ease some fears and allow you to redirect your energy towards the gainful pursuit of happiness. There is no such thing as evil [spirits]. There is ignorance on earth. There are susceptible imaginations. There are wrongdoers and wrong deeds, but there is no such thing as evil spirits. It simply does not exist. What is classified as evil and attributed to evil spirits is all manmade in action and in occurrence and is completely fabricated by physical beings. There is no such thing as Satan or the devil. The only "spirit" that exists is the spirit of good intent in varying degrees, from being reprehensibly covered to the point of being completely unseen, to the compassionate, loving spirit that is visible through kind deeds. ALL THAT IS radiates the purest spirit and every person on earth was born with the capacity to radiate similar energy.

People who behave evilly differ from those who don't in one simple way. They have more profound layers and cloaks. Their essence and spirit of good intent has become grotesquely hidden. They feel not love because they did not receive it. They know not compassion because it was not known to them as children. They care not for others because they were never taught how. They value not life because theirs was never valued.

There is not one person on earth who was properly loved according to the true definition as we previously set forth who has ever become a doer of evil. It is not possible. Among "doers of evil," there is an absolute cause and effect between what a developing physical being lives with and what he or she becomes. There is an absolute, irrefutable connection between childhood love and adult functionality. You are bombarded with contrary information in your society, but the contradictions are stated out of ignorance. When a person states, "Oh what a shock; he came from such a good home," the truth is that they have no idea what happened along that person's life path. They could not possibly know unless their intuition was so finely attuned as to enable a knowingness rarely found on earth. And if this sense was so highly developed in such a person, then he or she would *know* that the culprit was not privy to an upbringing according to the proper definition.

What did happen was that the surrounding people in this person's upbringing were also cloaked and knew not how to provide love according to the definition. They may have created the illusion of being a "good family," but what is a "good family," after all? Perhaps the children are well mannered and the house is tidy. Perhaps they attend church or volunteer at the local soup kitchen. Maybe they are friendly towards others. Who knows? But what you do not know is what goes on inside the house. What you do not know is how the members of this family unit charge their antennae and what they attract back as a result. What you don't know is how capable this family is at expressing love and respectfulness towards each other's soul songs.

What do you know? What the family wants you to know.

Be careful here, however. I caution you against judging those associated with an evil-doer. Remember, every person on earth has a soul song with good intent; they are simply cloaked to varying degrees. If this family was unable to provide love according to the definition, it is because their own cloaks unknowingly prevented them from doing so. The goal is not to judge others; the goal is to understand that everyone has a soul song – some are just far more hidden than others.

There are no evil spirits. If you heard fancy tales of evil coming through a Ouija board, they are false. The only evil-like thing that can happen during a Ouija session is that the overactive imaginations of some players can cause chaos. If you have heard warnings of caution in experimenting with séances or visiting "psychics" because you may unleash evil spirits, heed not. If a medium demonstrates any evilness during the communications it is because he or she is a fraud.

I recently "read" a story about a criminal that was facing a sentence of seven-to-twenty-five-years for committing a stupid act that accidentally severely hurt another. You have seen these stories or similar episodes. The victim met the convict at the sentencing. After a grueling recovery, she wanted to meet the man. At the sentencing, he apologized. He cried and told her how glad he was that she was alright. He was genuine and she intuitively knew it. She embraced him and he kissed her hand. They sobbed and hugged; she stroked his face. She told him that she forgave him and let him know that she would watch his life because she felt certain that it would be a good one. As a result of her forgiveness, actions, and recommendation, the boy was sentenced to a prison term of six months.

A rare woman. She relied on her strong intuition to recognize that imprisoning this man would not serve justice. She knew that he was a changed man because of what happened and he would make a good life from this point forward. Unknowingly, she expressed love for his soul song and he felt it. The connection will forever positively change his life as well as hers.

She increased her vibrational level and that of the boy's tremendously. She increased the vibrational level of every person who read the story and felt overcome with positive emotions. She increased the vibrational energy of those who saw the pictures of their genuine embrace. Yes, the initial events seemed tragic, but who on earth can explain the mystery of the outcome? Who can assess why these two people's paths crossed and for what purpose? Who can decide what it all means in the overall scheme of things? We can't give you all the answers, but we can tell you that she fulfilled her soul's intent to love, to create, and to learn. That does not mean she's finished; we suspect she will increase many more human's vibrational levels in her lifetime.

Please look at events with a new eye. See doers-of-evil through a new lens. I am not making any recommendations as to the validity or effectiveness of your judicial system. I am simply imploring you to recognize that everyone has a soul song, that all events have a purpose even if you do not understand it, and that people create their own realities through the antennae they emit. Antennae can only be charged to the best capacity of the emitter. A person cloaked will emit antennae reflective of their cloaks, no better and no worse.

I'll leave you with a final thought. There is no such thing as destiny. Possible events change every second based on the antennae people emit. You will not die when you are sixty just because you think you will. You can change your future by changing your beliefs. You can improve your course at any given moment by improving your beliefs. You are no longer ignorant as to the process and significance of determining your beliefs – you now have an obligation to do so if you want to improve your life and the lives of others.

[9:03 pm]

August 19, 2005 2:40 pm   (Book Session 53)

Perhaps one of the most misunderstood and overlooked "valuables" on earth is children. The present concept of what children are, and what their role is, is distorted. Happily, there have been great improvements in the awareness of the understanding of children in the past thirty to forty years, primarily in developed nations, but overall, and especially worldwide, children are undervalued and misunderstood.

I am going to change your view of people under the age of eighteen by explaining factually what they are all about. A person's age in chronological years is nearly irrelevant except for the matter of the aging of the physical body. The soul is ageless in your terms and since a person is a container for the soul, he or she is "ageless" as well.

This may all sound confusing at first, but bear with me. You have been told that a soul is "born" spontaneously through a process that you cannot understand in your terms. A type of combustion occurs through the right alignment of energy and conditions far too advanced to explain. The soul is born in the energy realm and may or may not choose a physical life. Whatever path is chosen, however, the soul will grow in learning and in vibrational strength as it advances on its road. The "age" of a soul, therefore, in your terms, is the chronological time that has passed between the combustion and this moment. We do not tag souls in terms of age. Age is irrelevant. What we observe, which represents the passage since combustion, is the soul's vibrational energy.

Although we explain vibrational energy to you very simplistically, it is actually complex. It is not linear like a two-dimensional bar graph or line chart. It is actually beyond three-dimensional. Suffice it to say that vibrational energy is more analogous to a star than to a line. The variations among stars are more similar to the variations among souls than lines are. For example, two different stars have different size diameters. They radiate in strengths, emitting more or less power than one another. Their outwardly expanding rays project in different lengths and widths and numbers. As I hope you can visualize, the soul's vibrational energy is multidimensional. Just as no two humans have the same fingerprint, no two souls have the same vibrational energy.

When a soul fuses with a physical carrier, the vibrational energy is the closest element that can compare to a person's age. When we observe a person, we see that person in terms of their soul's vibrational energy rather than in terms of his or her physical age. Yes, we recognize the different stages that the person passes through as a physical being, but we also know that the far more significant measurement is the vibrational level of the person's soul, or the "age" of the person's soul.

Two three-month-old babies are about as alike as a princess and a pea. Yet for simplicity, humans categorize them as being alike and treat them as so. They should, perhaps, be treated similarly with regards to nurturing and nourishment and other care, but don't assume that they are alike. Humans' talent in recognizing the differences among people becomes greater as the people grow older, but the ability to recognize those differences among babies is lacking.

The purpose of childhood is to allow the soul to adjust to the extremely complex change that takes place from the energy realm to the physical realm. Ideally, children should be guided, protected, stimulated, taught, loved, nurtured, and nourished during the formative years to enable the maximum possibility for the soul's intent to shine through. Children are not possessions. Children do not fall under ownership of parents, guardians, or the law. Many adults get lost in their "responsibility" or false notion of what is best for the children and assume a role of authoritative power which actually harms the children's souls' intent. Children need to be respected and to be treated individually. There are not blanket solutions or uniform methods for child-rearing. Children are simply developing physical carriers that house souls of vastly different "ages." What works in methodology for one child will not necessarily work for another. Different vibrational strengths of different children cause them to have very different abilities to successfully navigate the world around them and to successfully protect themselves from cloaks and layers.

A child that is repeatedly hit will develop different layers in regards to thickness and strength depending upon his or her vibrational strength. For example, a newer soul may experience a much thicker layer covering the soul's intent than an older soul might. Striking either one is damaging, but the pervasiveness of the damage is determined by the strength of the child's vibrational energy.

Likewise, some souls require far more expressions of love to develop to their maximum capacity, whereas others may need less demonstration to maximize their potential. All children need lots of love, but the optimal amount required varies greatly. What does this fact mean to humans? It means that you need to rely on your sense of intuition to respond to individual children's requirements. Eventually, children grow and can fulfill their own needs, but until then, the responsibility for "hearing" and responding to their needs is tremendous.

Properly cared for children will develop with the fewest cloaks possible, meaning that they will best be able to fulfill their souls' intent and increase their and others' vibrational levels. A child who is raised with love and respect and loving guidance and limitations will not only be happier as an adult, but will help to make others happier as well.

Children's physical dependence on adults makes the responsibility of child-rearing significant. Groups of children living in regions which are not attuned to their needs will develop problems in increasing magnitude in order to attract a correction to their plight. The souls of children have as much ability to charge their antennae as adults do. Collectively, they can be quite powerful, moving oceans and the emotions of nations.

The purpose for understanding how the age of the soul differs from the age of the person is to learn to respect that a person's vibrational energy is more accurate in indicating similarities among people than physical age is. An old soul in a two-year-old physical carrier has more in common with a 40-year-old with a similar energy. The repelling and attracting energies that adults recognize occur in children as well, but the children are more attune and responsive to this law. A child with few cloaks is less likely to be deceived or harmed than an adult with a greater number of cloaks; and the children with the higher vibrational strength are more protected from cloaks.

Although many, many Americans parent their children quite beautifully, for the future of the world we hope that more start to do so. Children should be respected. Their physical and emotional boundaries should be regarded as equally important and they should be loved according to the definition that we established:

What does a child need? Love beyond all else. Unconditional love and acceptance combined with gentle and consistent discipline and guidance. They need a balanced diet. They need to have their minds and their bodies engaged and stimulated. They need quiet and security. They need respect. They need their soul songs heard so that their individual beauty can be honored.

With those final thoughts, I would like to remind you that children's antennae are working as hard as yours are, creating a life that is attracted in by their antennae's charges. Help your children to charge their antennae positively to allow them to attract in positive events and people. They will be happier and you will, too!

[5:55 pm]

August 20, 2005 4:08 pm   (Book Session 54)

Who in your society should be lauded? Who should be revered? Who should be respected or admired? And should those individuals be infallible?

These are interesting questions and it's fascinating how different societies have different norms. Some revere the old; some revere the religious leaders; some revere the political leaders, and others, the scientists, doctors, and professors. Some societies revere the actors, others the musicians and artists, and others the athletes.

Who do you admire? And why? It's fun to talk about this question with others. You can learn a lot about yourself and others by the way they answer this question. Do you think your answer now is different than when you began reading this book?

We have a collective answer about who we think should be admired. You can probably guess the answer. Any person who consistently helps others to grow in awareness about love, creativity, or learning, one who increases the vibrational level of those around him or her – that is a person who should be admired. It matters not whether the person is a doctor, lawyer, air traffic controller, comedian, pastor, teacher, hair stylist, shop owner, baker, factory worker, millionaire, talk show host, runner, dog groomer, or a neighbor.

If you list the people you personally admire, what do they have in common? Assuming you are wise and have a good working knowledge of the purpose of human existence, you will probably recognize that the people on your list have these traits – the ability to increase others' awareness in love, creativity, or learning, in one way or another. Don't mistake increasing others' learning to mean that every teacher qualifies. They do not. A teacher who also happens to increase others' awareness qualifies. A teacher who increases the vibrational level of others qualifies. Likewise, there are doctors who qualify and those who don't. There are sanitation workers that qualify and those who don't. There are parents that qualify and those who don't.

Identifying those individuals worthy of our admiration is valuable to enable you to learn from their character. Having worthy role models or mentors can help you to set your sights on your personal goals and recognize that they can be reached. Having a role model can help you strengthen your character and standards of acceptability.

Don't hesitate to ask questions of those you respect. People with vibrational strength that can help you are generally not boastful. They can understand the point of your questions and reveal to you the information that will help you to grow. The encounters don't necessarily have to be personal, either. You can learn a lot by reading about someone you admire or by writing him a letter. If the person exists only in history, read up on her.

Remember, however, that all people are fallible. Don't be unreasonable in your expectations about others' "greatness." Even people with extraordinarily high vibrational levels make mistakes or lack awareness in certain areas. Don't rely on those you admire or who mentor you to be perfect or you will set yourself up for a grave disappointment. Everyone is flawed in one way or another. The question is, does such a person have traits or qualities that you can learn from regardless of their flaws? Also, if they made notable mistakes, what was their reaction? Did they address their mistakes with dignity, learn valuable lessons from their errors, and grow in their awareness as a result?

I'd rather spend a lifetime with a flawed person who integrates life's lessons over someone seemingly perfect any day! Frankly, someone who seems perfect is quite dull – but more importantly is quite deceitful. They have mastered the art of allowing others to see only what they want them to see. Sadly, perfectionism masks insecurities that began as layers in their younger days. They have learned that the way to extract "love" or at least kindness from others is to be "perfect."

The point? Everybody is flawed. Learn forgiveness. Learn to understand the root cause of someone's flaws, or at least that a viable root exists. A person who makes a mistake can still be admired. A person you know who makes a mistake can still be loved. Are you to judge the extent of flaws that are acceptable or forgivable? Can you decide on a line that can't be crossed? What is that line? What is your definition of character and actions that you deem worthy? What is your definition of mistakes or traits that are no longer acceptable? Is the entire mistake-maker then disposable? Should you cast a person's worth aside at the point the line is crossed?

Think not only about the people you admire in terms of acceptable behavior. Think about the people you love. How big of a mistake are you willing to accept? More from your child and less from your mate? More from a stranger and less from a neighbor?

Assess your own character. How many flaws do you have that others deem unacceptable? Have you made any unforgivable mistakes? The answers to these questions are based upon your belief system and do not reflect an actual gauge as to your worth. Some feel horrible guilt over missing a lunch date while others feel no remorse after verbally attacking another.

The point is that everyone is flawed and everyone was born with the same intent of the soul. The mistakes people make are a direct consequence of their faulty belief systems and the cloaks that they wear. They did not intentionally choose the layers. They did not intentionally choose to be flawed. They did not intentionally choose to lose some measure of sight of their soul's intent. People make mistakes in proportion to the thickness and quantity of their layers. It is that simple – which is one more incentive to assess your own belief system and layers.

A firm understanding of the causes for human flaws helps your capacity for forgiveness. Forgiveness is desirable because it helps to increase your vibrational level as well as that of those you forgive. Forgiveness cannot be forced. It comes as a natural extension of understanding that there are causes behind the deed done or the deed not done. You are not perfect. Your mistakes are in proportion to the cloaks that you bore in childhood and had not released by the time the mistake occurred. Other people's mistakes are in proportion to the cloaks they bear. If someone makes more mistakes than you, shouldn't you exercise some compassion knowing that the beauty of their soul's intent has been more buried than yours? Perhaps it's time to value your greater capacity to assess your soul's intent than other people can. Maybe this skill will help you to forgive and move on – for real, not just for show.

And if enough people acquire this skill, then more and more will forgive your past mistakes as well.

[5:51 pm]

August 28, 2005 12:04 pm (Book Session 55)

Whenever you think about communications with the "great beyond," you think of ghosts and crystal balls and fraud and evil. There will always be a number of people on earth trying to capitalize on your fears or curiosity, who will pretend to communicate with us – when they plainly can't. The truth is that you have to be pretty gullible not to tell the difference between the authentic and the showmen. Most communicators allow you to tape your sessions with them. Listen back and discern whether or not you "fed" information to the supposed source. Feeding information is an easy mistake to make out of eagerness and a naïve desire to believe. Charlatans aside, don't let the foolhardy make you a fool. It's better to recognize the con artists for what they are rather than let them convince you that authentic communications can't exist.

The best reason to open your mind to your own communication possibilities is that entities can and want to guide you. There is no real benefit in "going it" alone. This life of yours is not a test that you are forbidden to cheat on. On the contrary, this life of yours is meant to be enjoyed by any means and utilizing any resources that you have the capability of tapping. If you can discover a way to communicate with your guides, then your chances for sustained happiness improve.

If you experiment with the Ouija board or automatic writing, you are not likely to communicate with entities such as myself, but instead you will communicate with entities that have *your* personal happiness and best interests as their goal. Your guides "know" you. The only hesitation we have in advertising the fact that we are available to help is that we do not want to create a land of dependents. It is your life! Just as we don't encourage you to depend on another too greatly, we also do not want you to depend on us too greatly either.

Let's talk about dependence. You were born an independent soul connected to all else through a common energy. The common energy exists in all things and is a part of you regardless of whether you are a physical or a non-physical being. ALL THAT IS is the extender of the energy and you are an extension of that energy. Beyond the commonality of your source, you are an independent being.

As a young human, you relied on others to fulfill your emotional and physical needs. You developed your independence gradually until the point that you could become self-sufficient. At some point you could walk, communicate with others, and obtain your own food. It is natural for you to gain independence. It is natural for all humans to gain independence and self-reliance. You cannot explore your human potential under the constant supervision of an interdependent relationship. You need, to be quite frank and quite colloquial, to try your wings.

What is more often the case, however, is that the cloaks developed by your caregivers and guardians, as well as by you, distort the possibility of maximizing your self-sufficiency. You've heard the terms "enabling," "stifling," "smothering," "over-protective," "controlling," etc. These patterns develop in response to the layers that others wear. They need you or need to be needed or need to be given a great deal of attention. Regardless of how those layers are worn, the effect is universal. Most people do not reach a level of true independence that maximizes their potential for growth and self-exploration.

The pattern is not limited to parent-child. The pattern of distortion is echoed in education, the workplace, and the government. The pattern is so prevalent, in fact, that few people are completely self-sufficient.

There is a difference – a very big difference – between dependence and cooperation, between dependence and guidance. Humans, at their potential best, work together cooperatively to create communities and families and nations and organizations that accentuate the strengths of the individuals in the group. All flourish. This mutual collaboration results in an organization that excels beyond the capabilities of the individuals involved.

In any group, no one person can have all the knowledge. Dependence and guidance differ in that an autocrat will dictate action, whereas a guide or master or teacher will share beneficial knowledge. The sharing of knowledge or wisdom is necessary for all to flourish and the sharing is circular, not linear. The guides teach and learn. The students learn and teach. No one is the master of all ideas or knowledge, not even me. I am still learning while I teach. I guide and I willingly accept guidance. I do not feel superior to those that I teach nor do I feel inferior to those that I learn from. I even learn from Karen.

Mutual cooperation and circular sharing benefits all in any group. You can almost predict the successfulness of an organization by observing the level of autocracy or mutual cooperation that exists within. A group comprised of self-sufficient individuals will exceed the capabilities of a group in which autocracy dominates.

Can a twenty-year old teach a sixty-year-old? Yes, as long as both parties are capable of hearing each other's soul songs. Can a veteran of a firm learn from a new hiree? Yes, as long as both parties are capable of hearing each other's soul songs.

Some of life's greatest lessons are learned contrarily to the assumed guide/student relationship. A grandfather can learn to love by enduring his grandchild's illness. A teacher can learn to hear soul songs by the student who simply would not go unheard. The physician can learn the priorities of life by an against-all-odds recovery. A close-minded, firm-

208

footed person can teach others about the ethereal after a near-death experience.

(As a brief side note, please recall that life's lessons can be learned without tragedy. Life can and should be happy and meaningful without great challenge. Great challenge is a response magnetized in by antennae.)

Stifling dependence is not limited to obvious relationships. Dependence that thwarts one's ability to maximize one's potential can be found in any group. Blind dependence is responsible for most horrors recorded in human history. For example, cults, gangs, Nazism, communism, and terrorist cells are all founded upon an acute inability of the members to think independently. They follow, unquestioning, even when the acts requested are contrary to their desires. The reasons for the grotesquely distorted dependence are depicted in this book – a mere gross exaggeration of cloaks worn and the maligned beliefs that result.

A limiting dependence can be seen as well in areas where the interaction is assumed to be beneficial. Some examples where the reliance may hinder independent thinking are in fraternities and sororities, between a physician and patient, and between a believer and his religion. Widely reported tales of religious "brainwashing" exist among churches that are not based upon the mainstream faiths. Scientology, the new Kabbalism, and the Church of the Latter Day Saints, as examples, are sometimes viewed as comprising only fanatical followers. Unconventional faiths are no more likely to contain fanatics than any other religion. Religious organizations, by nature, discourage independent thinking by professing to have all the answers and assuming an air of superiority to all other organized beliefs. If a Christian has the belief that his faith is more accurate in its account of truth, doesn't that allow him to feel superior to a Muslim or a Jew? If an extremist believes that his faith is the "right" one, then doesn't he have the obligation to educate the ignorant?

Giving up your right to think independently to anyone or any group will limit your ability to be happy. It is possible to embrace ideas and still think independently, but the risk of using others' ideas or organizations as a crutch is great. Evaluate all others' ideas through your innate knowledge and accept only those you intuitively know to be truth.

If you are excessively dependent on another person or any group, then I caution you against using your communications with entities improperly. We are here to guide you towards your own knowledge. We are here to help you discover hidden universal truths. We are here to enlighten you, not to decide for you. It is your life. You decide how it will play out. Turn to us for guidance, but not as a crutch. Turn to mediums for their ability to attune to guides if you are unable, but do not allow yourself to become dependent upon them to make decisions for you. It is your responsibility to live your life and make your own decisions.

[3:00 pm]

August 31, 2005 2:13 pm   (Book Session 56)

Service

Successful organizations have one thing in common – they understand and apply the concept of service. Service goes beyond the predictable concept of having a good customer service policy in retail; it has to do with the treatment of others. "Service" as a predictor of success is not limited to retail or the standard service industries; it applies to families, governments, hospitals, organized religions, not-for-profit organizations, clubs, fraternities, educational institutions, the legal system, and so on.

In every relationship or encounter between two or more people, service is necessary. Each party has needs which must be recognized for the encounter to be successful, for the encounter to maximize its potential. What service means is that each person in a transaction or in a situation or family has a soul song. If the existence of the other's soul song is ignored, the transaction will not be completely successful. Suppose, for example, you are in a hurry at the grocery store and your cashier is tattooed and sports a few facial piercings. On top of the notable appearance, she is also slow and not very competent.

You can react in two ways. You can judge her based on her appearance and incompetence as inferior and discharge energy, or actually "act" in accordance. (You can be polite but still transmit your disapproving energy just as readily as you can transmit your disapproving energy

210

through rudeness.) Or you can accept that she has a soul song and is doing the very best she can at the moment. Perhaps your kindness is the impetus she needs to allow her confidence to shine through, thus allowing her competence to improve. Perhaps she just needs someone to accept her or realize she is valuable. Perhaps her parents have told her for the millionth time that she is stupid and looks like a freak. How could you possibly know what circumstances and cloaks have brought her to this moment and this encounter with you? How can you judge her?

You are in service during this encounter. You are serving another by being respectful. You are serving others by understanding that they have soul songs.

In every encounter, in every organization, in every mission, in every interaction, figure out what is being serviced. How are you in a position to be of service to another? What do they need from you in this encounter? The value of discovery in this arena serves you as much as it serves those you interact with because, by servicing their needs, you will improve the transaction.

Let me give you another example. The passport agent is gruff, overweight, and a bit of a know-it-all. His people skills are minimal and he immediately antagonizes Tom with his arrogance. Tom thinks, "What a @#!&%" and proceeds to treat him as such. Tom's wife, on the other hand (please note that my gender choices here are purely random), knows that the beastly man has a soul song. She suspects his self-esteem is not high and he compensates by overpowering others. A show of strength makes the passport man feel more powerful. She treats him kindly, respectfully, and allows him to feel important. The encounter changes from a gnarly, acidic transaction, to a smooth pleasant one. Since this is a true story, let me add that when the couple returned with their children a month later, the man greeted them with a smile and was kind and hospitable throughout.

Could he have made the process irksome? Most definitely. Did he? No, because he felt valued. It is that simple. It is that simple in every interaction you have with others.

There are masters at the art of service. Then there are masters at the art of service in business who don't know a darn thing about it at home. Can you challenge yourself to be consistently of service to others? Not a doormat, not a push-over, just someone who recognizes that everyone has needs, expectations, rights, and a soul song?

Think about the business man who is earning fistfuls of money, working late, late hours, enjoying respect, promotions and accolades at work, then comes home exhausted or indifferent to his family. We, the entities and I, do not rate the importance of your encounters, but we can say that, universally, the service element for family is far greater than the service element for business. It is greater in difficulty and it is greater in importance.

Be a success at work, but if you do not treat your family with equal or more respect then you have failed at one aspect of primary importance in your life. If your home relationships are poor, now is an opportunity for you to blame and excuse yourself from civility and respectfulness, but you are an equal contributor, even if unwittingly, through your belief system and cloaks.

We are not suggesting that you remain in a physically or mentally abusive situation. If that is your case, you face the challenge of assessing your belief system that brought you to this point. But most relationships are not overtly abusive. They are undernourished, therefore, not satisfying through a lack of mutual service and respectfulness.

Let's continue examining interactions and the role of service beyond family-life and simple daily encounters. Why do many governmental agencies have a poor reputation in service? Why do some stores fail while others succeed? Why do some not-for-profit organizations raise funds readily while others struggle for the simplest donations, for the most basic funding?

Interestingly, the term "service" is actually a composite of the three important facets of human existence: to love, to create, and to learn. When these three actions are successfully applied, service in any arena is maximized. As an example, think back to the company Montgomery Ward & Co., a highly successful catalog company throughout the mid-part of the last century. Although they no longer operate as a mainstream retail outlet, their initial success and longevity can be attributed to the founder and executives' ability to love, to create, and to learn. They created a brand-new concept, a mailed catalog where people could purchase a wide variety of products that were previously only available to city-dwellers or locally at huge mark-ups. Montgomery Ward served the suburban and rural classes by circumventing a group of notoriously greedy middlemen who had previously grossly overcharged them. He demonstrated love, not only by making life a little better for his customers, but by being impeccably kind and respectful to his employees. And throughout his life, he continually learned and applied what it meant to value and be of value to others. His community outreach programs and give-backs were unprecedented at the time.

Montgomery Ward is a friend of mine whose contribution to the increased vibrational level of humanity is largely overlooked. He does not seek accolades, but it is my wish that other humans can successfully model his attributes. To exemplify, let me tell you briefly about the author of *Rudolph the Red-nosed Reindeer*, Robert L. May, an employee at Montgomery Ward. May's responsibility was to create coloring books as popular giveaways during the holidays. Since the poem was created during his employment, the work became the contractual property of Montgomery Ward.

As you know, the story gained in popularity and was eventually immortalized through the Gene Autry song version. At that time, the creator had endured the emotional and financial battering of his wife's fight with cancer and he was desolate. Despite Montgomery Ward Company's legal entitlement to the copyright, the company turned the rights over to May, whose financial security was then assured. Ward set a tone of people above greed that carried throughout his lifetime.

What does this mean for you? It means that in every encounter you have with another human being, with or without the exchange of goods or services, service is involved. Service, properly executed, applies the successful implementation of loving, creating, and learning. As a student, a customer, an agent, a clown, a guest, a daughter, and every other conceivable interaction, all parties are servers. Successful service demands that at least one party be able to hear the others' soul songs. If you're the only one doing it, then your responsibility is all the more great. Let other's learn from your example.

IMAGINE …

[3:47 pm]

September 2, 2005 1:13 pm (Book Session 57)

The John Lennon Dream

Why is it that some people who show great passion for bringing people together, people like Martin Luther King, Jr., Abraham Lincoln, John Lennon, and Jesus Christ, die young, tragic deaths? The answer is going to be hard to grasp. When an individual vibrates at a strong level and feels almost unprecedented passion, they may "choose" to die a martyr to prolong the depth and duration of their impact. That does not mean that Lincoln chose, consciously or outright, to be assassinated. What it means is that the purpose of his life was served at the point of his death and was better served by his death than with his continued life.

They made a soulful decision, of which they were not aware in life, to die for the purpose of increasing the vibrational level of humanity to a greater level than they could alive.

This fact is going to cause a lot of confusion. I will do my best to clarify the point. You are born with an intent. Your ability to fulfill your intent depends, as you know, on the strength of your vibrational level (or the age of your soul) and on the number and thickness of the cloaks you've accumulated along the way. That much you probably understand by now.

At the time of their deaths, these people had achieved their soul's intent. The recording of their intent and achievements in minds and in textbooks was intensified by their young deaths. The passion that others felt for these men's selfless attempt to help humanity became more powerful. The result is that their achievements carried more weight and had a broader impact.

214

These men emitted energy that allowed their passage. Do not mistake this terminology to mean they wanted it. They did not "choose" their passing. They did, however, pass in peace as their soul's intent had been achieved.

Nobody dies before their soul's intent has been achieved, whether the physical vehicle is nine days old or ninety years old; the life had and fulfilled its purpose – even if you do not understand what the purpose was. Will this knowledge free people to harm each other more, knowing that the victim released "antennae" which enabled their circumstances? No. There are two reasons. One, most people choose their actions based on the consequences on earth. If they fear punishment for harming another, they will be less willing to harm. If they don't fear punishment, they will be more likely to harm. Therefore, the circumstances of their victims are irrelevant. They only care about the consequence to themselves when "deciding" to harm or not.

Second, since all people have access to universal knowledge, everybody, on some level, knows when they've done something "wrong." Our definition of wrong is "an act that decreases one's vibrational level or that of many." People simply do not feel good or proud when they harm another. They may get a rush or an adrenaline pump, but that surge is a substitute for the love that they seek and did not receive. No moment of rush will replace the inner happiness and peacefulness that the feeling of being loved gives.

Back to the dreamers who shared a vision for the unity of humanity. Although these men's lives were more influential because of their early passages, today's passionate visionaries do not need to die tragically to improve their impact. Today's environment of increasing awareness and spirituality will allow the Greats on earth to flourish and reach the masses. Their messages and ability to increase the vibrational energy on earth can grow and take root during their lives.

Interestingly, even after these men's departure from their physical carriers, they continued to work towards achieving their goal, the unity of humanity, in the energy realm. Their work is difficult to explain, but they still desire the increased vibrational energy of earth beings and thus, the increased vibrational level of entities. One former Triple Great walks the earth today, believing that another physical life would be the best vehicle for achieving the dream.

Another, John Lennon, has opted to remain an entity. His work here is powerful, complex, intriguing, meaningful, vast, and quite extraordinary. He is as unique in our realm as he was in yours, and maybe even more passionate.

As new generations of youth discover his life's work, awareness increases. The young stumbling across impassioned pieces such as *Imagine* are feeling his passion and understanding his dream. They are being introduced to a better way of life. These individuals will sow the seeds of Lennon's dream on earth, firmly understanding that life is intended to be more meaningful than what they have been exposed to. They are awakening to the possibility that life is bigger than themselves. John Lennon's impact will be greater with today's youth than it was in his lifetime.

Today's older generations will begin to change their perceptions about the purpose of life, and individually many will change their course for the better; but it is today's youth that will absorb and nourish the new non-religion based spirituality movement that will change the world for the better. They, through an increase in collective awareness, will tap their universal knowledge more readily. They will be the first generation in thousands and thousands of years to apply their intuition in a purposeful and helpful way. They will implement John Lennon's dream. And their children, further removed from the heavily cloaked elders, will impact humanity even more.

When Martin Luther King, Jr. said, "I have a dream," he did not mean a dream that one prejudice would be replaced by another. He meant that he saw tolerance among all races, religions, and life circumstances. His dream is a world without borders.

His dream is still the same. People on earth have the responsibility to make it happen.

My advice to you is to rise above the crises you witness. "Know" beyond intolerance and injustice that there is a better way and with every opportunity to be better or do better or think better, do it. You will increase your vibrational level. You will increase your happiness. You will increase the vibrational level of those around you. Do what you can, from simply hearing your child's soul song to understanding the presence of cloaks on those around you.

Do it for selfish reasons. As your vibrational level increases, your antennae will be charged with a greater ability to get you what you want. Why not get what you want while helping humanity? Sounds like the ultimate win/win situation if ever I heard one.

[2:58 pm]

September 7, 2005 1:15 pm (Book Session 58)

In the guise of friendship, people often tell others what is wrong with them. They are brutally honest to "help" them. Yet how many people do you know who can receive criticism and not take it personally? It *is* personal! You are talking about them or their actions or their appearance or their personality or their ideas. It is personal.

How can it not hurt on some level? Even if the advice is worthy, it still hurts. There are liberties that humans take with one another when they are in a close relationship that they would not likely take with others, nor would they likely enjoy [receiving] themselves. A bully is merely an exaggeration of a truth-be-told person. Both individuals empower themselves at the expense of another. Having the ability to see an improvement a person can make makes you smarter, even if just for the moment.

People who worry in advance about telling their friends something and fret over how to present it are not exempt. They ultimately will feel superior when they point out the flaw. Think about this: a woman knows her friend's boyfriend is cheating on her. Her friend takes it upon herself to let her know so that she doesn't get hurt. She agonizes about how, when, and where to tell her. Ultimately, she spends time alone with her, explains how difficult this conversation is and how she wishes she didn't have to tell her, then spills the beans. Perhaps you think that because she feels sorry for her friend that she was kind. Maybe she was kind, but the emotion of pity automatically implies that she feels superior in some way. You can not feel pity for someone without thinking you are better off.

There are obvious dangers that you must tell. The stove is hot. The train signal is broken. Most perceived dangers, however, must be evaluated very carefully before you reveal your perception. The person whom you want to help is doing the best that s(he) can at any given moment based on the soul's vibrational energy and cloaks. What is also true is that people innately know the dangers that they face and choose, subconsciously, to ignore them because the circumstance has been magnetized in to assist with learning. Therefore, at the moment, the person is ready for the problem or his or her antennae do not know another way to magnetize in the awareness that they are seeking.

To analyze the situation between friends one step further, you magnetized in the friend. The people in your life, and all their baggage and flaws, have been brought to you by you. Why do you need a friend whose boyfriend cheats on her? There are many answers to this imaginary scenario, but the most prevalent is that you need to be needed. Other people's problems make you feel valuable and loved when you assist or intervene. Of course this answer is simplistic, but most of the situations and people you attract are to assist you in learning about your worth, to assist you in learning how lovable you are or aren't. By telling the others the "truth," you are simultaneously testing them to see if their love for you is strong enough to withstand the painful message. Are you worthy of being loved after revealing your friend's flaw?

As you evaluate your evaluation of others that are close to you, remember that they serve a meaningful purpose in your life and, instead of taking the easy path running around telling the "truth," use the opportunity to evaluate why these people and their imperfections are in your life. Others' imperfections are not a bad thing any more than yours are. They are aids in helping humans' reach new levels of awareness. You have flaws; your friends have flaws. Are yours less annoying or damaging to yourself or others? If you're like most people, you are challenged in evaluating yourself in an unbiased way.

You may be inferring that you should never tell others the "truth" about their imperfections or flawed circumstances. That assumption is false.

There are times when revealing your knowledge is the most loving thing that you can do for another. The key word is "loving." How can you determine if your planned revelation is loving? Certainly, if you can prevent someone from physical danger, then of course you are acting out of love; however – and there is a "however" – you must simultaneously determine why this person and the danger has been attracted into your life.

I will cite an example to clarify this point. If your friend uses drugs and is jeopardizing his welfare or that of others, intervention may be a loving act, but ask yourself, "What do I have to learn from having a friend whose life is in peril because of drugs?" There may be numerous answers, so try to continue questioning your involvement until you can reveal to yourself all the reasons. For example, you may have been criticized as a child for being a "know-it-all." By helping this friend, you are proving to yourself that you are not a "know-it-all." You actually do know enough of value to help save someone's life! Perhaps you were often made to feel unlovable as a child. Successfully helping someone can assure you that you are lovable, that you are valuable. Maybe seeing others in crisis is the impetus you need to appreciate the calmness of your life. The list goes on, but only you can successfully interpret the purpose of your participation.

Evaluating your participation helps you to strengthen your compassion when revealing your truth. As soon as you discover that there is a reason, beneficial to you, that you magnetized this situation into your life, you can better appreciate the strength that antennae have in attracting in what is needed. Imagine the cloaks surrounding your friend that allowed this situation to transpire.

Now let's investigate how to participate when a person's safety is not at risk. This simulation is trickier. First, determine why you attracted in the situation. What benefit or learning is there to you by being involved in this scenario? Let's go back to the cheating boyfriend. Why do you have a friend who is challenged in attracting in a reciprocally loving relationship? Is she insecure? Does her insecurity attract in relationships which prove her unworthy of being completely lovable, thus confirming her right to her insecurity? By having a friend facing this challenge, does it confirm your "lovableness" since you are in a mutually rewarding relationship? Or if you are not in a relationship, does this situation give you an excuse to dislike men, thus "blaming" your aloneness on the fact that men are not worthy? Perhaps by telling her, she will break up and have more time to spend with you?

The possibilities are endless. You are the only one who knows what value this problem has for you. By determining the reason, you will answer the question of whether or not to intervene. You will also better predict how your revelation may affect your friendship. For example, if you decide that her situation proves that you are lovable because you are in a committed relationship, then her reaction to end your friendship as a result of your "truth" may cause you to doubt your "lovableness" again. Perhaps you attracted in an opportunity to discover how lovable you are: will she love you despite your hurtful revelation?

If you decide to be "truthful," do so with integrity and compassion. Do not take with you an attitude of superiority – your attitude can be detected. Your *true* attitude can be detected. For example, if you are subconsciously a bit happy about telling her because you were jealous of their relationship, then feigning concern will be transparent to her intuition and the result will not likely be favorable to you.

Yes, the scenarios are complex. Every situation you are involved in has a reason. You will increase your awareness, thus your vibrational level, by determining what the reason is. Just as you have cloaks, your friends do, too, and neither of you can or should decide whose flaws are worse. Do not judge your friends. If you try to help, do so with a clear idea of why you are involved. Determine why your antennae attracted in the situation.

If you choose to reveal "truths" to others, do so with kindness and love. There are options available; choose the option that is the least hurtful. The wisest choice is to help others discover the truth on their own, such as asking where the boyfriend is when you know he's with another. Gently bring a friend to the truth. By doing so, you spare the friend the humiliation of having you be momentarily superior and you spare yourself the risk of being spurned.

A primary responsibility of all humans is not to hurt each other. Your words can hurt even if they are truthful. Think in advance how to approach a person in the most beneficial way, in a way that is loving.

You cannot increase your vibrational level or your happiness by hurting others … even if it's for "their own good."

[3:11 pm]

September 8, 2005 11:51 pm (Book Session 59)

Where shall we begin?

In the beginning of earth time, life was simple. Life was good. Life was simply good. The complexities that you know today are an exaggeration of minor disconnects that the earliest beings experienced from their souls' intent and from their life force. Each time a minor break from an authentic self occurred, the person would focus on it and study it. This reaction was normal. Humans are programmed to naturally focus on changes. For example, you notice a spider on the wall. It can be small and perfectly still, but you still notice it. The reason is that your brain recognizes change and focuses on it. If everything in the room remained the same, the spider is what you would notice. If your neighbor buys a new car, you will notice it quickly. You notice what is different.

Getting back to the earliest beings, it was natural for them to focus on the change. Usually, the change had negative results and over thousands and thousands of years, humans began to equate unplanned change with a negative response. The reason that the change, or the disconnect from the soul's intent, was usually negative is that the change resulted in one less useful tool that helped the individual maximize his or her happiness. Disconnecting meant losing a part of an innate sense. If you suddenly lost partial sight in one eye, even mildly, it would annoy you.

When civilization began, humans and nature were one. They cohabitated in harmony, knowingly providing for the needs of the other. The molecules that comprised a tree were in tune with the molecules that comprised the man. You could almost say, as an analogy, that man and nature breathed together.

With each disconnect that humans' experienced, they became removed from their oneness with nature. They became self-contained units, relying on their own resources and defenses to serve their needs. The oneness gradually faded for the majority of civilizations, especially "advanced" civilizations.

Simultaneously, as I mentioned, the people also spent much time focusing on the undesired change. The lesson to learn was that they should refocus their thoughts and beliefs on what they innately knew to be true and not allow themselves to focus on the loss. Had they believed that the change was temporary, it would have reverted back quickly to a restored connection with intent and nature. However, their focus changed their beliefs. They panicked, in a sense, as the disconnection from nature and the souls' intent increased. Over time, the loss could neither be regained nor remembered. Now, it would take a long reversal of disconnect for civilizations to convene with nature once again.

Perhaps a trivial example, but the Disney movie *Pocahontas* best described the original communion that humans had with nature. Maybe the creators innately understood the connection that once existed and could exist once again.

As more time passed, people began to become more and more specialized in their tasks and their life pursuits. Progress was often necessary and beneficial, but an unfortunate result is that humans became externally dependent to satisfy their needs. Whereas the first earthlings relied on themselves and the earth to plentifully satisfy their quests, humans now rely on other humans.

This change alone may not have contributed to the disharmony that is often witnessed among humans today, but the change coincided with the belief that unplanned change was negative. Man began to resent their inability to provide for all their families' needs and jealousy of those more plentiful was born. In the earliest civilizations, jealousy was not an emotion experienced; every individual innately knew that his or her needs would be met. The harmony that they experienced with nature and with each other provided all they needed in abundance.

From jealousy was born hatred. Hatred is a direct result of humans disconnecting from nature and the innate intent of their souls. From hatred was born war. As man began to hoard and to depend on others for meeting their needs, they began to fight for each other's possessions. From hatred and war was born a feeling of superiority. From this new feeling, compassion was lessened and people began to hoard not only objects and food, but also ideas. Mankind began to battle over the superiority of ideas. Whose notion of God was right? Which religion was superior? Whose method of controlling or guiding the masses was better?

And so began modern day complexities, all because humans disconnected from their souls' intent and from nature.

In answer to the questions of whose ideas are better, the truth comes from correctly interpreting and applying the purpose of life principles. Each idea, religion, or government can be viewed through the lens of its ability to promote love, creativity, and learning. The better any philosophy or school of thought is at providing an environment in which the three flourish, the better it is. This topic is one that I can communicate endlessly about; however, I will give you a brief primer from which to base your personal assessment. To promote an environment in which love flourishes, an environment for independent thinking must be encouraged. As such, forms of government based upon autocracy must be eliminated from consideration as the best forms of rule.

Interestingly, in the name of God (and therefore in the name of love), some religious leaders have condoned murder. One cannot comprehend the concept of the soul song and commit or approve acts of murder. Regardless of any other teaching of such a religion, an Independent Thinker would use extreme skepticism in following any tenets of such a group.

Furthermore, the exclusion of others from any form of religion or political organization also indicates an inability to comprehend the value of each human. To disregard, at the core of the groups' ideas, the meaningfulness of any human life certainly suggests that the foundation is cracked. A cracked foundation makes for a weak structure and an Independent Thinker cannot rely on any other teachings of such a group as being truthful. In a democracy, the gender of the leaders is decided upon by the people and reflects cultural attitudes. In a non-democratic institution, if one gender is excluded from positions of power, what statement does this make about the value of the other gender? Is this attitude one of reflecting an understanding of the soul song? Can other teachings from such an institution be valid if a basic premise is false? And if universal love is not expressed at the institution's core, then can other messages of love from this group be authentic?

Questioning through the premise of life's purpose is endless. With creativity as the second most important life quest in expressing the soul's intent, do you imagine that an institution that forbids dancing, singing, or art is an enlightened one? Allow yourself to look at old groups and old ideas in new ways. Your intuition will guide you towards successfully determining which teachings and which groups are founded upon truth.

The present day increase in human awareness is the first step in restoring humanity to their natural selves, in harmony with their intent and with nature. As more and more humans begin to honor the concept of the soul song, the process of disconnection that occurred throughout history will lessen and gradually restore. You may expect that the renewal will take as long as the disconnect took, but if you consider the rapidity of change in America between the twentieth and twenty-first centuries, you can see that the speed of change among humans is increasing. Improved communications and transportation contribute to this process and will continue to fuel change.

Globalization is also a factor that will improve humans' capacity to change quickly. One basic universal desire of most humans is that they want the world to be a better place. As more people travel and connect culturally in different regions, they will become exposed to different qualities of life. It is human nature to study the qualities that seem to bring certain people more happiness than others and to imitate the success. It is rare that a person will witness circumstances worse than their own and imitate that state. As positive qualities are imitated, additional people will be exposed to a more harmonious existence.

Your tasks for today ... respect others' soul songs, watch *Pocahontas*, and do one good deed for humanity. And I command you to enjoy it all!

[1:21 pm]

September 9, 2005 12:26 pm (Book Session 60)

Often beliefs that are held are not questioned out of fear. There is a security that comes from believing in *something*. If you disprove your beliefs, what will direct your life? Will you flounder? Will you become depressed? Will you be sinful? By understanding universal truth, you will understand that there is a purpose to your life regardless of what or any groups you belong to. When a devil worshipper dies, s(he) will face the same truths that every other soul faces upon separation from the physical body. There is no devil. There is no evil. There is no hell. There is no sin in not attending meetings inside a specific building on specific days.

What gives people faith or hope in challenging times is valid. People turn, almost universally, to a higher source for guidance and strength. That higher source exists: ALL THAT IS. You and all else are connected to ALL THAT IS through universal energy. When you turn to your higher source, you are calling upon universal energy and are open to universal knowledge.

ALL THAT IS has no more power over your life than you do. That fact may sound scary, but it is not. You were born with the power; you merely disconnected from your source. ALL THAT IS cannot replace your lost connection, only you can. By wanting truth, by understanding the purpose of life, you can reconnect with the power with which you were born. You can peel away the layers and cloaks. You can regain your innate sense of well being and happiness. You can know that your belief system can magnetize in the life of your dreams if you allow the positive, truthful, and loving beliefs to flourish. Your life source is not based upon greed, jealousy, hatred, or anger. Those emotions indicate cloaks which bury your authentic ability to feel good. Remove the layers and reconnect with love, creativity, and learning. As you successfully reconnect with your authentic self or with your life force, the positive emotions will become more prevalent. You will even begin to feel less sadness at times when you expect your grief to be profound. Some humans even worry that they are "dead" inside when they emote fewer negative emotions, yet sensing the growth of the more positive ones will

225

reassure you that you are not dead inside ... you are more alive than ever.

Remove the cloaks. Know that life is good and meant to be fun, filled with abundance and happy moments. Accept that premise as the basis for all you do and you will shine!

If this information "rings true" for you, then might I make a suggestion to increase your awareness further? Tap into your guides. There are loving guides available to every human; their presence remains unknown only as long as you want it to remain hidden. By stating aloud that you seek guidance or give permission for assistance, you can expand your intuitive sense. Some people may find automatic writing as a viable means for communicating, whereas others may prefer the use of a GUIDE BOARD or Ouija. Again, I will reiterate that the Ouija has a proliferation of false beliefs surrounding its usage. There is no such thing as evil spirits. There is no such thing as a spirit that will try to misdirect you. All spirits have reconnected with their life force and cannot harm another intentionally or otherwise. You may connect with a spirit that has less awareness than another spirit, but their awareness about love is still greater than yours. They know, regardless of their vibrational level, universal love and truth.

Further, the guides which have the capability of connecting with you will match or exceed your vibrational level. For reasons far too complicated to describe, you cannot communicate effectively with entities that have a lower vibrational energy.

The previous paragraph may cause some confusion. Let me clarify. If your father, for example, has a lower vibrational level than you, he may, after separation, connect with you on a limited basis to ease your sorrow, fears, or guilt. He cannot, however, guide you to a new level of awareness. Other entities whose vibrational energy matches or exceeds yours can act as your guides. Your father, in this case, is an entity with whom you can converse, but he will not act as your guide.

All entities will try to ease your pain regarding their passing. Their understanding of the purpose of their life and of their death makes it easy for them to see the futility in you holding onto negative emotions. They also understand that loving bonds on earth will reconnect and, since your element of time has no relevance for us, "missing" someone as a painful obstacle is unnecessary. Further, they know that they can reconnect with you across the physical/non-physical realms anytime you are ready and willing.

Regarding the use of a GUIDE BOARD, the present day Ouija used in America is limiting. The layout and design make it difficult for entities to communicate effectively. Once Karen and her husband created a redesigned GUIDE BOARD, communications improved dramatically. Some of the false ideas about the Ouija experience stem from the difficulty in communicating with that particular layout.

Just as you should examine your beliefs in other areas, I recommend that you examine your beliefs about communicating with entities before you proceed. If you are scared, I recommend that you begin with a reputable channel or spiritual intuitive. Get a personal recommendation about the validity of the person's capabilities, if at all possible, and proceed with an open and questioning mind.

We will not focus on minutia about you and your life without your permission. In general, guides are attune to changes in emotion that their loved ones are experiencing, whether extremely positive or negative, or abrupt shifts in emotion. Emotions open the conduit of contact between our realms. Your emotions trigger guides to pay attention, and perhaps to act on your behalf.

If you want to communicate with entities and your guides, then ask. If you call for a specific deceased person known by you, he or she will [likely] hear. If you call non-specifically to your higher guides, those guides will hear. If you ask for guidance, they will attempt to provide you with assistance in the manner in which you are best suited. If you get a positive idea that seems to pop into your head out of nowhere, give it credence. It is probably one of your guides trying to help.

Once recognizable communications begin, permission must be granted each day that you wish to have contact. Granting permission can be as simple as thinking about the guide you wish to contact. This allegiance to your best interests allows you to control your level, pace, and frequency of communications. We never want you to feel anxious, afraid, or uncomfortable in communicating with us or as a result of

227

communicating with us. What we do want is for you to feel relaxed, joyful, and filled with a sense of well being in your life. That's all we want.

[1:29 pm]

September 10, 2005 4:33 pm   (Book Session 61)

To climb a mountain and reach the pinnacle has well-earned rewards. The peak offers vistas and clarity rarely seen by humankind. The offering soothes the soul and makes one feel part of nature and insignificant all at once. Breathtaking, the view and the experience.

Once you reach the top, you long for the encounter again. You long for the majesty of witnessing your own insignificance in the vastness of the universe, but you also long for the sense of belonging, a paradoxical melding of experiencing your smallness and your connection all at once.

Many people experience the same euphoria when standing at the ocean's shoreline or staring into a starry night. The feelings of rightness and peacefulness envelop you. Your personal issues succumb to the larger truths and you join the earth's breath. You can feel your oneness with the universe and rise above your daily distractions and complications. I recommend that everyone find their place of peace and connectedness and visit regularly. There is a valid reason you feel lighter when you commune with nature; it is because you are temporarily removing your cloaks and touching upon your authentic self.

There are people who are energized by the pace and anonymity of the city, yet even they need to experience nature to stay in balance with the world and with themselves. The true connection between earth, animals, plants, people, and objects is difficult to explain, but understanding the synergy is not as important as feeling it. Go to places that make you feel like you are in harmony. Fill your senses with the sensations of being there and if you can't return often, then return in your imagination. Many people find music that gives them that same joyful feeling. Find yours.

The fluidity of life is found in a waterfall. A volcano breathes the earth's sigh. Heavenly bodies echo heavenly feelings. Nature matters and living in harmony with your earth matters.

[5:13 pm]

September 19, 2005 1:26 pm (Book Session 62)

Friday is Sunday. The day is another in the days of the universe. You can be as happy on Friday as you can be on Sunday or Wednesday. All days are joyful and full of meaning.

Joking around can be great or grim. How do you distinguish between beneficial humor and mockery that stifles the soul? The process of enjoying humor is similar to the process of enjoying art or music. All creations that are born of good intent will likely cause you to feel satisfied, whereas creation born of ill will, angst, or anger will likely leave you feeling depleted.

The cultural trend in America is that "anything goes." Humor crosses boundaries that were previously taboo and continues to experiment in how far people are willing to be pushed. "Shock" is in and wholesome is out; however, what is far more important than the content or delivery is how it makes you feel. Do you feel better after hearing a certain joke or brand of humor or do the deepest recesses of your being cringe a bit? Can humor at the expense of another be uplifting? Or is there a reason that the Bob Hopes and Johnny Carsons of the world are remembered endearingly.

A talented humorist makes people laugh without resorting to derogatory means to gain an audience. As a lover of language, I understand that vulgarities often reflect an underutilized mind, and likewise, using the lewd and the raunchy as a crutch in humor also reflects the pattern of a lazy mind. Peppering comedy with meanness is the mask of an insecure person hiding a layered soul. A person with few layers, a person with an awareness, even if just subconsciously, will not need to demean others to be funny.

Your five senses are assaulted every day by a bombardment of stimulations and messages that must be sorted and filtered. Only a small percentage do you actively engage with and "decide" whether you agree or disagree. The human brain has an unfathomable capacity to decipher the information received and choose which messages are worthy and which should be rejected. One way to assist the quality of the stimulation that travels to your long-term storage or affects your being is to do just that: choose the stimulation. Decide how certain people, events, places, and creative expressions make you feel and actively choose more positive and fewer negative. On a small scale, you can help elevate your mood by choosing people, music, adventures, places, and media that uplift you and, eventually, as you cross a threshold into positive stimulation, you will actually attract more positive stimuli into your life – be it jobs, relationships, or living spaces. One of the simplest and most basic steps that you can take to expand your awareness and your happiness is to expose yourself to more positive stimulation. Would you rather listen to a reporter babbling on about the latest murder or hear your favorite uplifting music caressing you in the background?

Even your living space affects your level of happiness. It doesn't take a lot of money to keep your home full of positive stimulation. A can of paint in a color that makes you feel happy can be enough to change your interior to one that can enhance your vibrational level.

Let's talk about color. Can you think about different periods of your life when you were drawn to particular colors? Perhaps for a period, you wore only black or royal was your favorite. Then you changed your focus and allowed yourself to experiment with new choices. How did the different colors in your wardrobe and in your home make you feel? Sure, many choices were an automated response to trends and availability (who could forget the avocado and mustard decade?), but the world offers more choices today. You can find clothes and home accessories to fit any choice. When choosing, does the color make you feel bored, invisible, nondescript, or dull? Or does the color make you feel powerful, happy, and full of joy? Perhaps the trend now is olive throughout the interior, but is olive making you feel alive? What colors work for you? Decide and surround yourself with the uplifting choices.

The point in choosing your entertainment, your wardrobe, and your home setting is to choose *while thinking*. Don't make haphazard picks – think about how and why you make the choices you do and then choose what makes you sing inside. The proliferation of home and cooking shows indicates that people are increasing their awareness of what stimulates their senses and responding to those that bring pleasure. Your physical life is meant to be enjoyed. Increase your enjoyment by choosing your stimulation wisely.

[2:49 pm]

[Note: I took a break from receiving mid-September, 2005, and resumed receiving book material July, 2006.]

July 3, 2006   (Book Session 63)

A portion of the proceeds of this book will go towards continually correcting and improving the reality of others. Humanity, only, benefits … -Ayn

---

Often we see others with our "dream" lives. They have it all: ideal relationships, big house, vacations, good looks, no worries. The envy that we feel is sometimes solitary and fleeting, sometimes hard and screaming. We make assumptions about what we view – they are lucky, they were born into it, they had advantages … but the truth is, had we interviewed and analyzed them at length, we may still be unclear about how they "achieved" the dream life … nor would we know if they were really happy.

Suppose you could read in a book, once and for all, how to have the reality you desire and it was surefire? No more guessing, no more endless ruts and escapes and confusion. What would you give for such a book? I know that most would offer quite a handsome sum for that privilege.

And here you are, blessed to be holding THE ANSWERS in your hand. Now what will you do with it? Read it, nod, approve, and say things in your head like, "Oh, yes." Or will you change your life? The power lies within your hands, and shortly within your mind. What you do with it is entirely up to you.

Creating the reality of your dreams is not that different than succeeding at anything that comes easy to you. Is there something, anything, that you do well? Think about it. Are you a good friend? A whiz with numbers? An excellent driver? Perhaps you garden well or organize things nicely. Maybe you know you're a great parent or perhaps an ideal employee.

At that one thing, how hard is it to succeed? Do you focus daily on being a good driver? Do you consciously remind yourself that you have a knack for working with numbers? No, it is unconscious. What you do well comes easily. What you do best comes naturally.

Your reality also comes easily and naturally – you are just unaware of it. What is in your unconscious or subconscious mind creates your reality just as you expect it. Years of analysis would reveal the truth about every root cause of every external difficulty that you presently see, but this book is not about looking back and heavily over-analyzing all the "whys," "hows," and "whens." It's about letting you succeed with your life right now from this moment on.

Don't look back. If you are not happy – it wasn't working. Look at now – right now. Another quick rule – if you look at absolutes, such as exact dates and precise expectations, you will be sorely disappointed. Recall your present age and remember that it took that many years of living in the real world with a bombardment of misinformation and a gross accumulation of layers to bring you to the point where you are unhappy with at least some area in your life. Had you learned the corrective ideas at the age of nineteen, you'd be further along now – unless you're younger than nineteen, then of course you have the whole of your future in your hands right now.

So, why don't we simplify what it takes to be happy in each and every area of your life?

It is quite simple ... it is simply untaught. Please take the next few pages seriously enough to allow them to take root and be naturally applied in your life.

Being happy is a natural state. As mentioned previously, you are frequently bombarded with misinformation that changes your course as you adopt those miscues into your belief system. Frequent misinformation includes the idea that good health is unnatural – that you will succumb to some illness or many. The thought that money is hard to earn or that you will never be athletic, all of these ideas have taken root supplanting truth because of the belief systems of others around you – your parents, your school, your media, your friends, etc. It is up to you to clear these false, contrary-to-happiness beliefs from your layers, your conscious and your deeper unseen layers.

July 5, 2006   (Book Session 64)

When you imagine the life that you want, does it seem at all feasible or is it a misty "what-if" kind of feeling? Do you believe that it can happen? Or is it a wish? Do you know the difference between a belief and a wish? The answer is important because wishes can't change your reality until they become possibilities. Believing in the possibility is what makes a wish turn into reality.

How do you distinguish between a wish and a possibility? This exercise is essential. Even if you think you can do it in your head, please take the time to write it out. Number your paper from one to ten. Fold the paper in half so that you have a crease for two columns. (For computer and high altitude instructions, please refer to the side panel for directions.) For those of you who actually own paper and a pencil, get yourself ready. Don't read ahead ... just fold the paper.

In column one, list the ten reality changes that you most desire. Don't censor yourself; just enjoy using your imagination. Be free.

If you have finished this list, review it. Make sure you are optimistic and really wrote your desires even if they seem impudent.

233

Next, in column two, take a few minutes to record the likelihood of it happening. Suppose you use a scale from one to ten, ten being the most likely for the change to occur and one being the least. Rate the possibility of each change. Write a few words, also, about the possibility, such as why it may or may not happen.

You're finished? Wait to turn the page until you have finished or the results may be influenced by what you read next.

It's quite easy now to determine which of your desired changes are possible because you believe they *may* happen and which are presently unreachable because you simply wish it – but don't believe that it *can* happen.

A "one," "two," "three," or "four" means that your desire is simply a wish. Until you can convert the wish into a possibility, it is not very likely to occur. If you assigned a value of "six," "seven," "eight," "nine," or "ten," your desires are already possibilities because you believe that they can happen. The tricky number is five. Although there are more digits from six-to-ten than one-to-four, the number "five" is psychologically used to show neutrality, therefore cannot be grouped with one-to-four. Items that you assigned a "five" to are the ones that could go either way. In your deep layer, you have not yet decided if the desire is reachable or merely hopeful thinking.

The objective now is to raise the likelihood of the desires coming true. Let's start with those you assigned the number "five." Is this something that you really want? Does it get you excited to imagine it being a part of your existence or do you feel at all burdened by the possibility. For example, if the item is that you want a million dollars, do your religious beliefs dictate poverty or the abstinence of greed? If you had this money, could you reconcile your belief about greediness or otherwise and enjoy it? If you become wealthy, do you fear others coveting what you have. Do you fear a lack of genuineness among your acquaintances?

After reviewing your thoughts about each item marked "five," decide for sure that you want it or cross it off the list. A free line offers the opportunity for a new desire, which may be more reachable for you, to fill the space.

Next, let's look at the items assigned a value of one-to-four. Are any of those items completely unattainable for a physical, biological, or scientifically known reason? For example, if you are missing a finger and want it back, is it presently feasible for this to occur? If you have any completely undoable items, cross them off because you need the free space in which a more suitable desire can prosper.

(I understand that scientifically-proven ideas may be false. You thought you caught me in an inconsistency? For the purpose of this exercise only, let's make the narrow-minded assumption that certain physical laws exist such as the inability to regenerate a digit or to have crumbled metal reorganize itself molecularly to become once again smooth.)

Now let's peek at the items you labeled "six" through "ten." These items are the desires that you already believe are possible. We will later discuss how to turn them from possibilities into reality.

Take a few moments to fill in the blank spaces for any lines that you had crossed out through this process. Then assign them values so you are working with ten possibilities again.

Let's raise the probability that your desires will come true. Look at your items valued one-to-four. Separately write these items on a piece of paper. Record your ideas about why they are unlikely to occur. Now, brainstorm reasons why you were wrong. Record the reasons that they are LIKELY to occur. Keep coming up with new ideas. Let your optimism flow. Isn't anything possible? Don't stop until you believe that it's possible for these wishes to actually happen in your lifetime!

Re-rate the likelihood of these desires coming true. Unless they are rated above a "five," go back to the last paragraph and rework them again. If you absolutely, undeniably are unable to bring those ratings above a level "five," then cross the item off for today. Try the entire exercise again on a fresh day when your outlook may be more conducive towards optimism. By rethinking these desires until the possibility of their occurrence becomes well … possible, you are moving a wish into the realm of possibility. You are taking a "hope" and making it a "belief."

Spend some time rethinking your desires that you rated "five." On paper, get excited about the possibility that they can happen. Allow yourself to believe that these desires are attainable.

By the end of the exercise, which I hope you engaged in wholeheartedly, you should have a list of ten very doable possibilities. From these possibilities, you will see how you can change them into your actual reality.

July 7, 2006 (Book Session 65)

Do you understand the difference between a wish and a possibility? The [aforementioned] exercise should make the contrast stand out. Now that you have achieved a fine list of ten possibilities, what do you need to do to bring those possibilities into the realm of existence? How do you make them real instead of just images on a piece of paper or in your imagination?

Suppose you imagine your wildest fantasies coming true. When you picture these images, do you believe that they are just a dream or that they may actually happen? Most people have some wild ideas tucked away that they play with occasionally, like a daydream. These fantasies, however, have the feeling of being just that, play and only play. You do not imagine that they will come true. It's just fun to spend a bit of time trying it out.

These fantasies are NOT the possibilities that are presently on your list. This list is real and this list is doable. Reflect upon your list for a moment and see if there's a running theme of achievements that you would like to accomplish. Do your items primarily concern relationships, money, or health as these are the three primary sectors in which we typically imagine an ideal life? If your list contains elements of all three sectors, try to categorize them into three separate lists and choose which one you would like to focus on primarily. There'll be plenty of time later to address the others, but for now let's make the range narrower.

You're probably wondering how to create this working list of wants into reality. Naturally, that's what I would be thinking if I were you. I would

236

also be prejudging what I was about to read and assuming that it would be fluff that would not really help me to change my reality. That is most certainly how Ayn Rand thought during her lifetime. It's rather odd, now, to be presuming to know the answers and, better yet, to actually KNOW them!

Close your eyes for a minute. Wait! You can't very well do what I ask of you with your eyes closed yet. Read on a little, *then* close your eyes and try it out.

I ask of you to picture your stage. Fill up the whole of your vision with images of what your life is presently like. Think about who you are involved with, who you share your life with. Think about your physical condition, your diet, your exercise regime, your overall healthfulness. Think about your wealth or lack thereof.

Now close your eyes and picture.

There are some areas that you are satisfied with. Close your eyes again and picture those areas in full joy … focus on your senses and how these areas of your life make you feel. For example, picture holding your child and feeling overwhelmed with love. Picture having your mate on your arm and the pride that wells up in you as you walk into a room. Is it your health that is wonderful? Picture your body slightly aglow, radiating from within, bounding with energy and harmony. Close your eyes.

When you visualize these successes, all you are doing is watching the play that you created on your own stage. These successes were not handed to you. You are not lucky … you brought these rewards into your life. You attracted them in by the state of your mind. You expected things, good things; from a place deep within yourself, you expected these things.

You may not even know that you expected them.

Think about your health for a moment. If you are in good health without any chronic illnesses, understand that you expect good health. Perhaps you expect it because you take care of your body. Perhaps you expect it because you exercise, because you believe that people of your

237

chronological age are generally healthy, or perhaps you believe that you have good genes. It doesn't matter why you expect it … you just do. Now imagine that you are watching TV and one of those hundreds of pharmaceutical ads comes on bleating out the latest statistics for some scary disease or for a minor physical annoyance. You are besieged with the message to report to your doctor and it is suggested that you take such and such medication.

What goes through your mind? "Do I have this ailment?" "Should I go to the doctor?" Or do you briefly suppose that the commercial is intended for others and definitely not for you.

The truth is, if you have relatively good health and typically do, you will disregard the message. It will not sink in to your cognition enough to invoke fear. You have created good health partially because you presume that your health is good and will remain so. Likewise, if you also deeply believe that health rapidly deteriorates after a certain age, you can be somewhat assured that yours will suffer that fate. You've heard of the power of suggestion or the placebo effect. These two effects operate on the same principle – the body manifests what the mind believes.

The analogy between health and the deep-rooted beliefs that a person holds is the easiest of the three sectors to comprehend, but the essence is the same for relationships and wealth as well.

In a ghetto, the overwhelming majority of children raised in that environment *will* repeat the torturous lifestyle in their adulthood. The reason is that they simple do not know any better. They have layers upon layers masking their inner joy, the compass to a better direction. Should the natural spirit in a person shine through the layers, perhaps there will be a way out. Those who do escape the pattern ultimately always knew that they would have a better life. They didn't just wish it as a vague and undoable notion, they *knew* it. Considering the rareness of exiting dire circumstances that were thrust upon a person since birth, it is easy to see the difference between a wish and a possibility. A possibility is that there is a way and the rising spirit, the light of the soul, will constantly flicker seeking the answer. The answer exists; the soul knows this for certain. The search begins and continues steadfastly until the answer is found and the door out is opened. The stage setting is reset and recast and the door is shut behind him or her.

This same truth exists for those born into wealth or "privilege." Yes, the assumption that such a person will simply inherit the lifestyle is an easy one to make, yet there are many who lose their fortunes and begin again. Inheriting the birth wealth that one is born into is not guaranteed. It is likely, however, that the privilege will continue for the primary reason that the person born into this position believes that the circumstances will always continue. Perhaps they grow up believing that they must be educated in the same profession that brought their parents wealth and pursue such a path. Perhaps they will learn at a young age that hard work and perseverance brought wealth to their entrepreneurial guardians. Whatever they witness, they are likely to expect in their own lives.

Where do you go from here? Your list shows that you do not believe completely that one or more sectors of your life is definitively going to be happy, or it would not appear on the list.

July 8, 2006   (Book Session 66)

The recorded items on your list indicate that you did not expect them in your life, because obviously you have not attained them.

Realistically, every person has some happy situations that they desire yet don't expect. Yes, every person … even the Dalai Lama wants world peace wholeheartedly and believes that it will one day happen, but he doesn't *expect* it to happen during his lifetime. If he *expected* it, would it then happen? Tricky question and worth thinking through, since there may be external factors that affect *your* ability to bring in the list items you desire. It's better to know what parameters exist outside your influence lest you set yourself up for an endless struggle.

The last and final limitation on your list items must be addressed. What is within your realm of influence and what is not?

The answer is that you influence the setting, players, and script on your direct stage. In other words, you cannot declare today that Robert

Redford will appear at your next birthday party, because Robert Redford is not on your personal stage. You may state that your next birthday party will be especially happy, but you will not be able to influence the attendance of those you don't know. As a matter of fact, you will not be able to completely influence the attendance of those you DO know, which brings me to another limitation. You can ask for certain patterns of behavior from those you know, but every individual has their own path and free will. Depending on the strength of their personal pursuits in their soul's quest, their path may not be readily influenced by you.

Therefore, review your list and remove or rewrite those items that specifically require a particular person to act in accordance with your specific desire. Certainly, write, "I want to marry a woman I love who loves me," and the goal is completely doable, but do not write, "I want to marry Jessica Alba." Do not even assume that you can influence a woman you are presently dating. You may, but you may not.

People are off limits on your list.

Next. You hopefully recognize that as one soul you cannot control the weather. Do not write on your list that you want gorgeous sunshine next Sunday. You can't influence the weather as an individual.

You cannot control the length of time that an item takes to be fulfilled. Therefore, remove dates altogether.

You may certainly be altruistic, but set your goal as one that is reachable according to the above limitations. For example, you can want "an end to terrorism," but the effective method of attaining a doable goal would be to recognize your sphere of influence, such as, "I wish to enlighten people about the most effective ways toward eliminating terrorism, by teaching tolerance and the power of emitting positive energy." Now this goal is doable and the wider your circle of influence, the greater impact you can have.

What does that leave within your influence? Plenty. You need not know how some items will be fulfilled, just let the world figure that out. Perhaps you want season tickets to your favorite baseball team. Maybe you will find the money; maybe a friend will give you some or sell you some to start you on your way towards total fulfillment. You don't know how, but the goal is reachable.

Is it reasonable to want to become an astronaut if you have no training and you are seventy years old? No, not really. You must use some common sense to realize that this goal is not within your sphere of influence.

This brings me to one more caveat about your list. I am assuming that if you read this far, you are a fairly level-headed individual. Please use common sense on your list! Certainly, "I want to live to be ninety," is doable but too specific and time-oriented to be reasonable. You can state, "I want to maximize my life span through good health and happiness."

As a fifty-year old woman, will you write, "I want to become a professional football player with the NFL?" No, I don't think so. However, if you honestly rated such a listing as a "six" or above, meaning that it is a possibility, then more power to you – go for it! Just don't come back to me for an explanation as to why you did not succeed.

Everything else is fair game. You can desire "outrageous" items and they can come true if you honestly rated them as "possibilities" and not just wishes.

Next ... I will teach you how to convert your possibilities into reality.

July 12, 2006   (Book Session 67)

If you come to a crossroads where you don't know which path to choose, how do you decide? You think, you determine, you weigh alternatives, you guess, you ask opinions, or perhaps you consult a map. What is fascinating about this process is that you will, nine out of ten times, choose the path that you were initially drawn to regardless of all the analysis you engaged in. The reason for this phenomenon is that everyone has a tunnel to universal truth. Everyone has the ability to tap into "known information" or what is commonly thought of as "truth."

241

Truth enables you to "guess" at the best path ... bearing in mind that the "best path" may not be the simplest one.

Let me further explain. If you choose Path A and your instincts told you to choose Path A, that path may be the right one for you at the moment, but may not, by any means, be the easiest. That path may be the one that brings you to your own personal awareness of what it is you quest to know at that moment in your life. For example, your friend is leaving a party and wants to drive you home. You can choose to leave or stay, obviously. You choose to stay and continue drinking far more than your conscious mind would say was reasonable. You do stupid things, embarrass yourself, and regret your "decision" the next day.

Did you choose the wrong path? It seems like you did. However, your choice was the one that led you to learn what you needed to know at the moment. These choices are virtually made in an unknowing state. The alcohol symbolizes that unknowingness in this case, however, most decisions are made in this unknowing state.

You remained at the party. Can you determine what learning you needed? More than likely you were testing unconditional love or self-love. Your actions may have been unforgivable by people that matter to you. What is their reaction? Are you accepted, forgiven, ostracized, rebuked? What is or was the state of your self-esteem? You acted in a way that demoralized yourself. Do you love yourself more or less? What is your relationship with self-love and how has it been tested, strengthened, or weakened? What result would you have experienced if you had gone home? Would your self-love be strengthened because you would assign good-decision making to your actions and commend yourself? Or perhaps your self-love would diminish because you failed to take a risk or be adventurous. Either path has lessons. Largely, and for most people, entirely, these decisions are made in an unconscious state.

You are eager to learn how to use your list of wants to create the life you desire, so why am I taking you on this tangent about decision making and crossroads?

Clearly, I have a point. There is nothing that I do for no reason.

242

If you can comprehend the "unknowingness" of most decisions that you make, you can comprehend how to change your reality. It is that simple. "Knowing" that unconscious decisions are primarily ruling your life makes you understand the power of the unconscious mind. The reality that you live now is most likely created with your unconscious mind. Just as in the example, you were not at all aware of the reasons the decision was made the way it was; the same is true for the reality you create. You are quite truthfully unaware of the reasons for why you create what you create. It is similar to going through life in a state of drunkenness … you exist, but are not clear about the choices you make or why.

Likely, everyone would agree that to be healthy, wealthy, and surrounded by loving relationships is the preferred lifestyle. Wouldn't you agree? So, if your unconscious mind has created a reality less than the ideal … as most people's have, why would you do that to yourself? The answer is that you simply don't know. You don't know why you created the reality you did.

The beauty of changing your reality from this point forward is that you don't have to know why you failed to create your ideal reality until now. You don't have to over analyze the "whys" and "hows;" you can change at this moment and permanently improve your circumstance.

There is one thing you have to do though … and it is difficult. Actually, it is so easy that people forget about it and, therefore, make it incredibly difficult. You have to remain conscious.

Sounds easy, right? Humans operate on autopilot. Did you ever hear about psychological profiling? Law enforcement experts can pretty accurately predict the behavior of criminals based on their profiles. The accuracy with which this is achieved is remarkable, but understandable when you understand that people operate primarily on autopilot. That means that their behaviors begin and soon after become a habit. Like any habit, the patterns are difficult to break, but more so than a tangible habit because the player is unaware that a habit exists. If you see a cigarette in your hand, you can easily see that you have a habit and seek means to break it if you so choose. The same is not true for behavioral habits because they are largely unrecognized.

You created your present reality by being unconscious. You did not know that you had a choice in the direction of the reality, so you bumped through life taking things as they came. You faced each day making little decisions and just moving along. Most people react in life instead of create life.

Now you know that you can control your reality. Now you know that if you remain conscious, you can change your reality to one that fits more into your ideal.

Liberating yourself from past disappointing realities is quite easy. First, accept that it is what it is … today. The past matters not. The past matters not at all. Consciously accept that truth. It doesn't matter what state your reality is in presently. It doesn't matter what foolish steps you took to get there. It doesn't matter what brilliant things you did that did not amass the reality you want. The only thing that matters is: it is what it is. It's done. Tomorrow is not done. You can focus on that reality. Tomorrow is open to change, yesterday is not.

Are you consciously aware that yesterday is over? Are you awake to the fact that tomorrow is unfinished and can be influenced?

Now is a moment when some of you may choose to review how you were victimized into your present reality. Again … it is what it is. Tomorrow is a fresh day.

Are you present to the knowledge that you can only control this moment forward? (Maybe you know a thing or two about quantum physics and understand that you actually can change the past, but for the purpose of this book, we are going to act upon the assumption of generally accepted "law" that you cannot.)

By not looking back, you are also disallowing yourself the unnecessary and un-beneficial act of reviewing the sorry state your life is in. Yes, you are perhaps not where you want to be. You wanted such and such by this age and those by that age … and look what you've got for your troubles. I apologize that you do not have the luxury of self-pity. Part of accepting consciously that the past is over, is accepting that the past is over regardless of your present circumstances.

Step one: KNOW that the past is past.

Step two: Consciously awaken to the creation of your reality.

Step two is critical because, as I previously indicated, human behavior tends to be on autopilot. You may now become aware of your role in the creation of your reality, but if you go "back to sleep" any time soon, then your awareness is for naught. Don't waste today's consciousness by becoming unconscious tomorrow or even in three weeks. You must remain aware.

Look at your list of ten items. Read it. Read it again. Tape it on your refrigerator. Tape it on your bathroom mirror. Memorize it if that helps. Review it in your mind while you drive to work. Say it into a recording and upload it onto your MP3 player. Use whatever method or combination of methods works for you to remain conscious of your desired reality.

As a basis for you to understand what level of awareness works in changing your reality, realize that a minimum of three five-minute sessions a day thinking about what you want is necessary. That's fifteen minutes a day in total. Can you afford to give your ideal life fifteen minutes a day?

I will tell you this fact, and I tell you because I am challenging you to beat the statistics. Nine out of ten people who read this book will not continue to focus on their list for fifteen minutes a day beyond the first month.

I'm sorry to say that that means most readers will not create the reality that they desire. They will look back with melancholy one day at the book Ayn wrote and wistfully recall that it didn't work. Well … it didn't work because they didn't do it. They didn't do the exercises in the book until this point, or they dropped back into an autopilot state of unconsciousness while attempting to actively change their reality – or both.

Let's get back to your fifteen minutes a day. What should you do during that time? What activity or thought pattern is most expedient in creating a new reality? While you focus on your list of possibilities, be happy.

Be happy.

Don't think about the impossibility of achieving these dreams. Don't worry about how it will happen. Don't wonder if you're doing it right. Think about it like a mini-escape. When you watch a movie that you love, do you constantly review each scene to analyze its practical viability? No, you watch and you enjoy and you escape reality for a bit. Use this method for reviewing your list. Just enjoy it. Lighten up. Fantasize ... see it, be it. Allow yourself a mini-vacation. Just be happy. I am asking you to be happy for fifteen minutes a day.

As you practice, allow yourself to be truly excited about the prospects on your list. Feel a sense of contentment when you dream about living your dreams. Let yourself enjoy this pleasure, this escape, this fantasy. Only through your pleasure of the vision can you attract it in.

If you know a successful entrepreneur, you may realize that he or she does exactly this exercise all the time. They do not rest on their achievements; they consistently dream about new heights, new accomplishments. This focus on future endeavors, this creative look beyond the present at the possibilities is the equivalent exercise as the one that I am recommending.

Perhaps they become jaded by bureaucracy or the annoyance of petty customers. It is at the moment that their jaded view surpasses the strength of their future vision that their improving reality begins to stall.

Did Edison return to his lab each day muttering to himself, "This will never work!?" No, he certainly did not. He had his moments of doubt for sure, but, overwhelmingly, he pictured success. He enjoyed the idea of the big moment. He worked tirelessly to achieve what he believed was "possible."

Any student of the Power of Positive Thinking, or other schools of thought out there which teach you the steps towards happiness, has probably come across a similar theme. The reason that so many theories exist that pose similar methods for the route to happiness is that they are based upon truth.

Relax.

That's part of the equation. When you picture the possibilities for your future, just relax about it. It's not life or death. Really, even if you are battling a disease, you never actually die even if you leave your physical body. So relax. You are eternal and what seems so overwhelmingly critical right now is simply not. As a matter of fact, working from a relaxed frame of mind is more apt to bring about the change that you desire – pretty good incentive to ease your mind.

Now you know.

1. The past is past.

2. The future is yours to create by wanting it and knowing it is possible. By telling the universe that you want it, you remind yourself and the world continually, at a minimum of three times a day for five minutes each time.

3. Be happy. Relax. At this stage, it is safe to assume that you will not be happy all the time, yet. If you know you have it within you for fifteen minutes a day to be happy, then use the time well. As your reality begins to slowly, or quickly, improve, you will naturally find yourself happy more often.

4. The last step, which I have not yet discussed, is to review your list regularly. As you visualize or contemplate your wants list, you will notice yourself "fine-tuning" the items that you want. You may realize that some are not that important anymore, or others need to be more specific. You may think of something you forgot, or notice redundancies in your prime desires.

The document is a living, breathing account of your future. It is the play on your life's stage that is slowly being illuminated. Change it when you realize that an improvement is essential. You may be surprised how dramatically this document changes from week to week, or month to month. The purpose for changing the list is that your attention to your wants allows you to better recognize what it is you really want at your deepest level.

It is only when you know what you really, really want that the world can provide it. Be liberal in your fine-tuning. If you say you want a dog, yet the daily visualizing of owning this dog awakens you to the aspects of dog-ownership that you don't like, then remove it from your list.

The act of remaining awake, the act of consciously deciding what you want is the surefire method towards attaining it.

Now to further make you understand this process of changing your reality to meet your desires, I want to use an analogy that illustrates the importance of certain tasks in the process.

You are a world-class runner who qualified for the Olympics. Until now your list, likely an unwritten one, included goals for running times, races for which you wanted to qualify, objectives for your weight and physical conditioning, and an overall feeling of elation upon achievement. In order to succeed to the level that you have, your focus was on succeeding at your "wants." You knew through each stage that the next step was a possibility, not just a wish.

What now will separate you from the competition? You are all qualified. You are all mentally attuned to the "winning frame of mind" necessary for achievement. What is the difference between the gold and bronze medalists? What is the difference between the last place runner and the first?

The difference is the list. You can be damn sure that the ultimate gold medal winner has winning as a possibility and not just a wish. There is not a cell in his or her body, not a thought in his or her head that believes that the win is only wishful thinking.

You are not, perhaps, an Olympic contender, *but* your goals are important to you. Your goals, within your frame of consciousness, are as important as the goals of these athletes. Why then would you settle for less than best preparation for success?

I am teaching you how to meet your goals. I am teaching you how to create the reality of your dreams. As you begin to realize success, piece by piece or all at once, you will naturally reach a state of heightened bliss. As your state of happiness increases, the happiness of others around you increases because: 1. Happy people are nicer and 2. Your vibrational level increases, thus increasing the vibrational level of those close (in distance and depth of relationship) to you.

For those of you who are very lofty in your ideals, let me tell you now that your success in achieving your goals has no limits in the potential impact it has. You will realize your dreams and you are likely to grow increasingly lofty in your quest. As you set new goals and new "limits" are reached, you will impact more and more on earth in a positive way. To illustrate, I have been recently made aware that Bill Gates has foregone the day-to-day operations of his business in order to dedicate his time to his charitable organizations. If this soul can achieve what he did in business, can you imagine what he can achieve in the realm of helping others on earth in a direct and purposeful manner? Not to brag, since entities are by nature extremely humble (not at all), but I believe it was me who previously indicated that Bill Gates was a Great. And if Karen checks her recording sessions, it seems as though I stated this fact about a year ago in your time reference.

Anyway, the more you achieve personally, the greater your happiness, and therefore, the greater the positive consequence to others.

Let me sidetrack for a few moments. You can obtain a state of bliss without reaching any goal on your list. You know that ... somewhere within your consciousness you understand that this fact is true. However, since the fact is that most people are not blissful, allow my instructions towards dream fulfillment to act as a dependable guide map towards bliss. At the present stage of mass enlightenment for humanity, meeting goals, whether ethereal or tangible, is a desire of most humans. Therefore, since the overall increase in the vibrational level of humans is my goal, then please meet *your* goals.

Another side note. If you meet your "wants" yet are still not happy, then what? As you know, this outcome is quite common. If you reach this point, the initial problem is that you didn't know what you wanted. You made the list, you rated the list, you visualized or reflected joyfully, but you were truly unable to determine what you wanted. Fear not. By realizing what you did not want, you are much closer to realizing what you want. Your efforts have not been wasted. As Edison taught us, every un-illuminating light bulb is one light bulb closer to illuminating. Every "failure" is one step closer to success. Every time a method does not light the bulb, there is one less wrong way to do it and one less possibility of not reaching the goal.

You can learn more from discovering what you don't want then perhaps you can from getting want you want. The reason is that when you get what you want, you really don't think about it much. When you don't get what you want, you think about it a lot.

Look at what you achieved and determine why it did not satisfy your desires. In most cases, your desires were centered about tangibles without accounting for the intangibles that have lasting power. For example, it is wonderful to want a movie theater room in your home. Are you happy once you have it? If not, the reason may be that the goal was not in attaining the room, but in attaining the feeling that the room would provide. Think about it. Perhaps the feeling you wanted was to be like all your friends. Perhaps it was to surpass the level of accumulation your friends have to prove your worth or to evoke envy. Maybe you didn't know why you wanted it.

If, deep down, the reason you wanted the room was to enjoy together time in a fun way with those you love and you did not achieve that desire because there is no resultant happy togetherness, then certainly your "want" was not to attain the room, but to attain the close feeling of unity and love.

The first reasons for wanting the home theater are fleeting. Lasting happiness cannot be achieved by making others envious or by accumulating without a meaningful reason for obtaining or possessing material goods.

In the second instance, if it was family closeness that you desired, then you have realized through this exercise what you want. You want closeness. You want loving relationships. You want a happy family who enjoys each others company. Now as you create your improved list, account for what you really want. Add to the list what is important to you – close relationships. Be specific in what you desire; follow the noted instructions for attaining your goals, and then let it happen. Chances are you will find happiness.

Perhaps you are supposing that I am judging the accumulation of material possessions as being an unworthy goal. I am not. I believe that while inhabiting a body, one should stimulate the senses often and powerfully. If material possessions stimulate you in a lasting way, then accumulating them is your personal path to happiness and, by all means, enjoy it!

Only you know what makes you happy. My directive to you is to pursue with vigor that which makes you happy.

To be happy ... that is the purpose of this book ... ultimately, to teach readers how to be happy. Therefore, I will reiterate the important method to obtaining happiness.

- The past is past.

- Create your "want" list. Make certain the items on the list are "possibilities" in your mind and not just wishes.

- Study your list. Post it. Look at it. Perhaps memorize it.

- At least five minutes three times a day, think about living that list.

- Be happy ... at least just while you are visualizing living your dreams.

- Review your list as you refine your "wants" through your daily exercises.

- Stay awake. Be conscious. Fifteen minutes a day is not a long time to remain aware. You can do it.

- Stay alert for the long haul. Two weeks time is not going to allow the universe to present you with all you desire. If you can't stick with it, you cannot succeed. I want to remind you, once again, that you are likely not living your dream existence. You can continue along that path or you can change it. If you want to change it, then change it. Follow these very simple instructions.

Good luck. May you succeed ... Godspeed!

abacus, 31

ADD, 61

ADHD, 61

ALL THAT IS, 50, 89, 140, 194, 195, 197, 207, 225

All you need is love, 25. See Lennon, John

Ambassadors of the Mission, 120, 121, 124

AMs. *See* Ambassadors of the Mission

angel, 115, 122, 196

antennae, 66, 85, 107, 123, 133, 134, 157, 160, 171, 182, 184, 186, 191, 198, 199, 202, 203, 209, 215, 217, 218, 219, 220

authentic self, 15, 17, 33, 37, 39, 53, 54, 71, 102, 106, 221, 225, 228

Autry, Gene, 213

Bach, Richard, 31

balanced diet, 62, 203

Beatles, 25

Beethoven, 126

belief, 13, 14, 15, 17, 19, 20, 21, 37, 38, 39, 40, 41, 45, 47, 53, 58, 61, 64, 65, 66, 69, 71, 81, 82, 83, 85, 93, 94, 105, 111, 112, 115, 116, 117, 118, 119, 120, 122, 123, 125, 129, 130, 131, 132, 136, 137, 138, 139, 141, 142, 143, 144, 145, 146, 147, 148, 149, 150, 152, 154, 155, 156, 157, 159, 160, 161, 162, 165, 168, 169, 171, 172, 174, 175, 180, 181, 182, 183, 185, 186, 187, 191, 192, 193, 196, 199, 205, 209, 212, 222, 225, 226, 227, 233, 234, 235, 238

Bell, Alexander Graham, 38

Bible, The, 60

bliss, 31, 50, 96, 98, 99, 136, 194, 248, 249

brain, 7, 8, 9, 12, 13, 35, 40, 51, 146, 148, 181, 182, 183, 196, 221, 230

Browning, Elizabeth, 49

Caesar, Julius, 60

Cayce, Edgar, 28, 111, 151, 190, 195

childhood, 15, 27, 55, 74, 81, 123, 149, 154, 197, 201, 206

children, 14, 17, 19, 23, 26, 33, 38, 43, 44, 46, 52, 53, 55, 61, 62, 68, 69, 72, 73, 74, 75, 78, 79, 80, 81, 85, 86, 116, 117, 118, 123, 124, 127, 134, 136, 137, 150, 154, 156, 159, 160, 175, 184, 197, 200, 201, 202, 203, 205, 208, 211, 216, 217, 219, 237, 238

church, 22, 66, 121, 139, 197

cloaks, 136, 142, 149, 156, 157, 159, 162, 166, 167, 171, 174, 182, 183, 196, 197, 198, 199, 201, 202, 205, 206, 207, 209, 211, 212, 214, 216, 217, 218, 219, 220, 225, 226, 228

Constitution, The, 176

creativity, 19, 37, 38, 40, 45, 46, 47, 48, 49, 54, 63, 68, 89, 91, 92, 108, 109, 121, 126, 127, 128, 174, 177, 196, 203, 204, 223, 224, 225

crime rate, 41, 169

cult, 40, 61

Darwin's Theory, 36

Day of Kindness, 59

devil, 197, 225

disaster, 41, 42, 43, 44, 169

disease, 67, 69, 82, 142, 144, 238, 247

Disraeli, Benjamin, 49

drugs, 62, 63, 81, 219

earthquake, 41, 42, 169

Edison, Thomas, 38, 246, 249

Einstein, Albert, 25, 38, 49

Elliot, Cass, 47, 49, 114, 149, 150

energy realm, 3, 29, 60, 98, 126, 173, 193, 194, 200, 201, 215

enlightenment, 1, 32, 43, 59, 71, 177, 249

entities, 1, 2, 3, 4, 28, 29, 33, 41, 42, 48, 49, 60, 86, 87, 88, 89, 99, 106, 110, 113, 114, 115, 120, 121, 132, 147, 169, 172, 192, 195, 206, 207, 210, 212, 215, 216, 226, 227, 249

Exorcist, The, 46

flood, 58, 169

Ford, Henry, 38

Founding Fathers, 62, 176

Franklin, Benjamin, 49

freedom, 3, 21, 23, 37, 53, 56, 61, 74, 86, 87, 95, 98, 128, 132, 172, 188

Galileo, 66
Gandhi, Mahatma, 132, 170, 185
Gates, Bill, 63, 107, 249
global, 4, 43, 174, 176
God, 22, 67, 115, 139, 140, 150, 151, 196, 223
gossip, 36, 70, 132, 133, 179
Greats, 25, 38, 48, 49, 54, 59, 60, 62, 64, 89, 90, 91, 92, 126, 132, 170, 185, 209, 215, 249
greed, 63, 108, 152, 153, 155, 156, 174, 213, 225, 234
Guide Board, 226, 227
guides, 1, 70, 138, 207, 208, 210, 226, 227
guilt, 55, 87, 95, 138, 139, 140, 141, 179, 181, 205, 226

heaven, 29, 196
hell, 93, 196, 225
Hitler, Adolph, 134, 135, 136

identity, 39, 45, 47
Illusions, 31
Independent Thinker, 21, 23, 37, 38, 85, 120, 223
independent thinking, 22, 23, 24, 28, 36, 37, 38, 40, 53, 68, 121, 135, 195, 196, 209, 223
intuition, 32, 33, 34, 35, 36, 37, 40, 62, 69, 77, 86, 88, 90, 91, 96, 113, 114, 119, 120, 121, 131, 141, 142, 151, 157, 158, 160, 170, 171, 172, 174, 177, 190, 196, 197, 198, 202, 216, 220, 224

Jesus, 185, 196, 214
Jordan, Michael, 105, 106

Katrina and the Waves, 65
Keller, Helen, 38, 89
King, Martin Luther Jr., 214, 216

layers, 15, 39, 46, 47, 60, 61, 71, 73, 74, 81, 87, 96, 97, 98, 118, 119, 123, 124, 125, 127, 136, 137, 149, 157, 158, 159, 160, 166, 167, 182, 183, 188, 197, 201, 205, 207, 225, 229, 232, 233, 234, 238

Lennon, John, 25, 27, 28, 33, 126, 214, 216
level of awareness, 31, 37, 49, 84, 89, 91, 93, 94, 95, 99, 103, 106, 120, 124, 127, 162, 167, 226, 245
Lincoln, Abraham, 91, 170, 177, 178, 214
literature, 48, 59, 63
Love, Medicine and Miracles, 82

Mama Cass. *See* Elliot, Cass
Mamas and the Papas, The, 47
masks, 15, 17, 22, 61, 71, 87, 96, 102, 119, 123, 125, 148, 154, 155, 157, 205, 229
mass thinking, 23, 41
mathematics, 7, 31, 48
media, 20, 21, 79, 149, 180, 230, 233
medical, 12, 57, 67, 69, 117, 144, 145
Microsoft, 63, 108
Mohammed, 196

near-death experience, 56, 209
Newton, Sir Isaac, 66

obesity, 148
old soul, 173, 202
optimism, 13, 235
Ouija, 113, 114, 198, 207, 226, 227

passion, 25, 46, 53, 54, 55, 59, 60, 63, 67, 102, 105, 109, 127, 128, 134, 135, 174, 177, 188, 189, 193, 214, 216
peace, 1, 27, 215, 228, 239
physical carriers. *See* physical organism
physical organism, 8, 9, 28, 39, 47, 87, 142, 193, 195, 201, 202, 215
physical realm, 29, 33, 39, 60, 193, 194, 201
physical vehicle. *See* physical organism
Picasso, 126
Pocahontas, 222, 224
Poe, Edgar Allen, 49
political leaders, 203
pollution, 41, 178
power of positive thinking, 54, 172, 246
psychic, 2, 4, 33, 114, 198

quantum physics, 244
quantum theory, 31
quest, 38, 39, 40, 51, 59, 89, 152, 224, 240, 242, 249

Rand, Ayn, 2, 3, 4, 5, 23, 24, 32, 89, 191, 192, 231, 237, 245
religious leaders, 93, 203, 223
Righteous Brothers, The, 46
Robbins, Anthony, 91, 103, 104, 105
Romeo and Juliet, 60

Satan. See devil.
science, 7, 8, 66, 67, 138, 190
scientific, 7, 32, 35, 46, 62, 66, 67, 111, 191
scientists, 7, 12, 35, 190, 203
Seth, 7, 28, 110, 114, 195
Shakespeare, William, 25, 59, 60, 126, 177
Siegel, Dr. Bernie S., 82
Socrates, 25
soul song, 25, 26, 27, 55, 61, 62, 70, 71, 72, 73, 74, 75, 76, 78, 79, 80, 83, 84, 88, 89, 91, 93, 94, 96, 97, 99, 103, 105, 109, 118, 119, 123, 124, 125, 127, 131, 136, 149, 150, 157, 159, 161, 165, 167, 168, 170, 188, 191, 198, 199, 203, 208, 210, 211, 212, 213, 217, 223, 224
spirituality, 215, 216
spiritually, 2, 170
spontaneous healing, 12, 57, 144, 145
stage, 9, 10, 11, 12, 15, 42, 110, 181, 237, 239, 247, 248, 249

technology, 43, 56, 68, 69, 137, 138, 170, 177, 190
telepathy, 196
Thoreau, Henry David, 49, 126
tragedy, 102, 209
truth, 23, 28, 32, 36, 37, 50, 60, 61, 67, 69, 70, 74, 77, 82, 89, 105, 114, 115, 120, 121, 122, 132, 140, 143, 145, 147, 151, 160, 165, 190, 193, 197, 206, 209, 217, 218, 219, 220, 223, 224, 225, 226, 231, 232, 233, 238, 239, 241, 244, 246
tsunami, 1, 43, 44

UFOs, 196
Unchained Melody, 46
United States, 4, 20, 69, 92, 175
universal knowledge, 195, 196, 215, 216, 225

vibrational level, 49, 86, 87, 88, 89, 94, 96, 98, 99, 102, 104, 105, 115, 120, 132, 145, 160, 167, 170, 173, 174, 177, 178, 183, 185, 192, 194, 195, 199, 201, 203, 204, 206, 213, 214, 215, 217, 220, 221, 226, 230, 249
villain, 122

Ward, Montgomery, 212, 213
weather, 41, 42, 240
Westside Story, 60
whole-body healing, 69
Winfrey, Oprah, 59
Wright brothers, 38

THE ANSWERS
Additional Information & Products
www.The AnswersUnlimited.com

Product	Price	Qty.	Subtotal
BOOKS:			
The ANSWERS **(includes S&H)**.....................$23.00		____	_____
For Volume Discounts please contact: discounts@TheAnswersUnlimited.com			

AUDIO PROGRAMS - CD Format. **(All items include S&H)**

Ayn Rand and other Entities ANSWER questions on the following topics:			
Love and Relationships....................................... $25.00		____	_____
Wealth & Abundance...................................... $25.00		____	_____
Life After Death... $25.00		____	_____
Overcoming Fear.. $25.00		____	_____
Why We Are Here – Understanding Quests........ $25.00		____	_____
ENTIRE SET (all five above)................................. $99.00		____	_____

MONTHLY "INSIGHTS" - AUDIO SESSIONS with the Entities- CD Format, on a variety of topics mailed once a month directly to YOU! **(All items include S&H)**

6 Months subscription ($20.00/Month) $120.00		____	_____
Full Year (Save $25.00) $215.00		____	_____
TOTAL:		____	_____

For **personal one-on-one** or **telephone sessions** with Karen Garvey, please contact: **sessions@TheAnswersUnlimited.com** or **call 631.265.2982**

(Please Print)

Name:

_____

Address:

_____

City: _____ State: _____ Zip: _____

Phone: _____ Email: _____

Please send this form along with your check or money order Payable to INTENT to:

Intent, LLC, 373 Nesconset Hwy #125, Hauppauge, NY 11788
Fax 432-225-2982

Check out upcoming Seminars based on THE ANSWERS
www.TheAnswersSeminar.com